ART
THERAPY
and Creative Coping
Techniques for Older Adults

by the same author

Art Therapy Techniques and Applications
ISBN 978 1 84905 806 3
eISBN 978 1 84642 961 3

A Practical Art Therapy
ISBN 978 1 84310 769 9
eISBN 978 1 84642 004 7

Mandala Symbolism and Techniques
Innovative Approaches for Professionals
ISBN 978 1 84905 889 6
eISBN 978 0 85700 593 9

of related interest

The Creative Arts in Dementia Care
Practical Person-Centred Approaches and Ideas
Jill Hayes
With Sarah Povey
ISBN 978 1 84905 056 2
eISBN 978 0 85700 251 8

Art Therapy Exercises
Inspirational and Practical Ideas to Stimulate the Imagination
Liesl Silverstone
ISBN 978 1 84310 695 1
eISBN 978 1 84642 693 3

Creativity and Communication in Persons with Dementia
A Practical Guide
John Killick and Claire Craig
ISBN 978 1 84905 113 2
eISBN 978 0 85700 301 0

Group and Individual Work with Older People
A Practical Guide to Running Successful Activity-based Programmes
Swee Hong Chia, Julie Heathcote and Jane Marie Hibberd
ISBN 978 1 84905 128 6
eISBN 978 0 85700 317 1

ART THERAPY

and Creative Coping Techniques for Older Adults

SUSAN I. BUCHALTER

Jessica Kingsley *Publishers*
London and Philadelphia

First published in 2011
by Jessica Kingsley Publishers
116 Pentonville Road
London N1 9JB, UK
and
400 Market Street, Suite 400
Philadelphia, PA 19106, USA

www.jkp.com

Library of Congress Cataloging in Publication Data
Buchalter, Susan I. (Susan Irene), 1955- author.
 Art therapy and creative coping techniques for older adults / Susan I. Buchalter.
   p. ; cm.
 Includes bibliographical references and index.
 ISBN 978-1-84905-830-8 (alk. paper)
 1. Art therapy for older people. I. Title.
 [DNLM: 1. Aged. 2. Art Therapy--methods. 3. Aged--psychology. 4. Mental Disorders--therapy. WM 450.5.A8]
 RC953.8.A76.B83 2011
 616.89'1656--dc22

British Library Cataloguing in Publication Data
A CIP catalogue record for this book is available from the British Library

ISBN 978 1 84905 830 8
eISBN 978 0 85700 309 6

Dedicated to my amazing children, Jennifer, Adam and Alexandra

ACKNOWLEDGMENTS

To my talented father, Martin Buchalter, who designed the book cover. He is an inspiration and role model.

Special thanks to Dr. Alan H. Katz for his usual superb technical support.

CONTENTS

PREFACE

This publication focuses on ways in which art therapy and various creative coping techniques are used in therapy sessions with older adults. The projects are geared toward seniors but many can be easily modified to suit the needs of other populations. Some themes such as reminiscing are most helpful to those who have lived many years and have had varied experiences. Each group of individuals may require directives and supplies that suit their individual needs. As with other clientele, the seniors prefer certain materials, such as markers, and specific projects, such as collage work. When leading a therapy group, the leader needs to take into consideration the age, population, needs, environment and physical and psychological state of the group members.

One should not view this collection simply as a "cookbook" of therapy techniques. Therapy sessions cannot be scripted ahead of time, but a collection of specific approaches can provide the framework for countless therapeutic interventions. Readers should take it as a challenge to add their own personal touches in order to create sessions that are most meaningful for their particular clientele and themselves. The more ideas the therapist has at his fingertips, the easier it will be to lead a successful therapeutic group. The therapist may modify, change and combine ideas at his discretion.

The group leader will need to decide which directives are too difficult and if directives need to be carried out in more than one session. He always needs to take into consideration the clients' abilities, attitude and psychological state. The group format and exercises must adapt accordingly.

Therapists, psychiatrists, psychologists, counselors, social workers, students, teachers and gerontologists would benefit from reviewing this publication. The vignettes provide readers with descriptions of artwork and associated feelings. They help the reader understand the senior experience. The chapters focus on different types of art therapy themes and coping skills such as stress reduction and self-esteem.

I refer to group members interchangeably as clients and patients, although there are some therapists who do not care for these labels. I also refer to the therapist as "he" to avoid the more cumbersome "he/she". I do not mean to discriminate in any manner.

It is important to refer to the reference section when indicated because some of the projects will need modifications that are suggested in this area. An example would be a project that might be considered helpful for one group of clients but harmful for another group. This information may not be included in the immediate project description due to the specified book format.

When reading through the directives, it is essential to understand that they are designed for people who have the same feelings, wants and needs as everyone else. Older adults want to be valued, loved, accepted and respected. The only difference between seniors and other individuals is that they are older, more experienced and often more vulnerable.

INTRODUCTION

Art Therapy and Creative Coping Techniques for Older Adults undoubtedly will be one of the first of many creative publications dealing with the needs of our aging population. Publications of this sort are needed because there is very little written about the senior client who suffers from depression, anxiety, bipolar disorder or other personality disorders. Most of the articles and books in circulation focus on seniors who suffer from Alzheimer's disease and/or dementia, have significant disabilities or reside in nursing homes. This book is full of techniques that are geared toward higher-functioning clients. As baby boomers age, they will need increased care, both psychologically and physically. Publications that are focused on the care of this demographic are in demand and will be increasingly sought after in the future. Many older adults are in need of psychological care due to anxiety and stress, fear of aging, loss, change in status and lifestyle, the economic crisis and concerns about the safety of our unpredictable world.

The senior population has special needs, which therapists must be aware of in their practice. Therapy will be more effective and enjoyable for the client if the distinctive "culture" of the elderly is recognized and appreciated. Seniors, much like everyone else, yearn to be respected and treated like adults. In general, they don't want to be coddled or given extra assistance unless absolutely necessary. The group leader should pay close attention to the body language and facial expressions of his clients. Individuals usually send non-verbal cues that reflect their attitude, mood, desires, strengths and weaknesses. An individual who groans and grunts upon rising from his chair may be communicating "Help me up", but someone who places their cane on the doorknob as soon as he walks into the room may be saying "I am independent. Leave me alone." Defiant clients who choose not to participate are sometimes conveying the message "I am afraid; I don't know if I can do this."

Older adults often endure many losses and physical disabilities. These problems need to be taken into account when leading groups. Seniors must be able to clearly understand instruction and suggestion. Sometimes directions may have to be repeated two or three times; the therapist must be patient. Therapy groups may need to be adjusted for those individuals who cannot write, read or see well. Many seniors are easily hurt; they are sensitive to their perceived deficits.

Many older adults are faced with an array of problems that often come with advancing years. According to a group of clients some of these issues include:

- sadness
- loneliness
- loss or death of loved ones and friends
- change (moving)
- aches and pains
- surgeries
- poor memory
- children not visiting
- difficulty seeing or hearing
- children becoming the adults ("bossy")
- financial problems (fewer sources of income and/or fixed income)
- difficulty making friends and getting into cliques
- negative physical transformation (weight gain or loss, thinning hair, etc.)
- not being able to do "what I was able to do in the past"
- being patronized (e.g. a waitress saying "honey" or "You're so cute" to an older man)
- difficulty coping with retirement
- change in status (e.g. from a doctor to "an old man whom no one notices")
- boredom—"nothing left to do but wait to die"
- illness.

One client stated, "These are not the golden years; they are the tarnished years."

Encouraging the depressed elderly client to express his feelings can be a difficult and frustrating experience. The client often feels helpless and hopeless, sometimes alienated from friends and family alike. Self-esteem is often low and creativity has withered away. A lot of clients have had unfortunate experiences with art teachers in elementary and/or high school, and have vowed never to draw again. Some individuals do not know how to draw. Stick figures are even alien to them and need to be introduced as one possible method of communicating emotions.

Many individuals are not used to sharing in front of groups and have learned not to express problems to others. Their past experiences have proven that sharing disturbing feelings and concerns will result in the loss of friends. One woman stated, "People don't want to hear sad stories; they turn you off." Some people have been taught not to express themselves. Their family trained them to be reserved and not to speak about their sadness, anxiety or anger.

A lot of elderly clients suffer from arthritis or other diseases such as diabetes, or from Parkinson's disease, which may cause them to shake, move slowly, appear emotionless and/or have difficulty with fine motor skills. Sometimes they feel uncomfortable; hands and legs often hurt. Seniors may experience vision and hearing loss. A hearing aid that is not finely tuned can disrupt an hour-long session with its buzzing and high-pitched tone. The seniors need to use the bathroom frequently, and a much-needed drink due to a dry mouth is often a necessity. Some elderly clients feel nervous about the potential reactions they think they will receive from others and refuse to draw or share their artwork with group members. They say they feel like their grandchildren and choose to withdraw instead of trying something new. This attitude is usually representative of the way they address anything unfamiliar in their life. Therapy helps these individuals understand how such negativity and fear keeps them stuck and despondent. Group disruption and refusal to draw is something the therapist may need to contend with on a daily basis.

All of these problems have to be taken into account when leading a group with this population. The individual has to be well understood, and instead of encouraging the clients to conform to traditional group standards, the group standards need to be flexible and specifically oriented to meet the senior clients' needs.

I have found that this population is most focused and involved in art therapy when utilizing brightly colored markers. The colors are bold and help clients observe variations in tint and shade. Markers are not difficult to hold and glide smoothly on the paper with little effort. They do not conjure up images of kindergarten as readily as crayons and they look attractive upon presentation. Crayons can be frustrating and problematic for those suffering from arthritis. Clients often have difficulty obtaining strong solid color because they need to press hard on the crayon in order to create the desired shade. In addition, the introduction of crayons increases the likelihood of non-participation due to the "childish nature" of the medium. Although unpopular, the crayons may still be provided for the few clients who favor them. Oil pastels are another alternative because they incorporate the benefits of both pastels and crayons and are generally easy to blend.

Paint has positive and negative aspects. Depending on the directive, the individual may need much manual dexterity. This is especially true when creating realistic scenes. Abstract painting may require less dexterity, but it is not always a pleasing art form to seniors. They are often concrete and prefer to understand what they see in front of them. Paints are often messy and many people are concerned with dirtying their hands and clothes. Clients often complain even when the paint cleans off easily with soap and water and is non-toxic. Cleaning up is a chore and the therapist is usually left with the mess. When clients paint, there are greater chances of spills and "artistic failure." During one painting session long ago, a client labeled her work "An Unacceptable Piece of Art." If the therapist chooses to introduce paint, watercolors appear to be the least threatening for clients. They are relatively easy to brush onto the paper and not too messy. Unfortunately, it is often difficult to create bright, vivid colors that do not blend into one another. A lot of people end up with olive-brown abstractions.

I have found most types of clay to be problematic with this population. Terracotta clay, for instance, can be regressive and many clients find it very unappealing. It's drying to the hands and can stain them temporarily, and it is extremely messy. A lot of individuals dislike the feel of the clay and its regressive nature. One woman referred to the clay as feces and then giggled. Many types of modeling clay including Sculpey can be frustrating to utilize. Unless the Sculpey clay is very soft and pliable, individuals have difficulty molding and manipulating it. During two different sessions peanut butter playdough was presented to clients; it is soft, simple to work with and also edible. In both instances the clients were outraged and disgusted with this clay. They disliked its odor and its gritty texture. Many clients stated they felt sick from the smell and the clay's appearance. Model Magic seems to be the best clay to use and the only clay clients have really enjoyed. It's soft, non-toxic and odorless and clean. It can be left out to harden and painted afterwards. Unfortunately, purchasing large amounts of it is quite expensive.

Collage materials that allow for cutting, tearing, gluing and pasting of objects are the most successful medium. Collages geared toward seniors are generally structured and the materials are easy to manipulate. Magazine photos, felt, wool, tissue paper, foam, construction paper and small paper squares are usually focused upon.

Designing collages encourages clients to be resourceful, innovative and creative; this work raises their self-esteem. Success is usually guaranteed because "anything goes" when creating a collage. There is no right or wrong way to work on this project. Collage work provides clients with a sense of structure and ease. The client cannot fail; all attempts are considered triumphant. Individuals with arthritis can tear or cut out desired pictures from periodicals; clients who have memory problems often find that searching through the magazines for words and pictures assists them to express what they cannot find the words to say. Choosing and selecting photos builds decision-making and problem-solving skills.

Clients may be asked to search for photos that are self-representative or representative of friends and/or family. They may be asked to create happiness or anger collages, or a collage of memories. Construction or tissue paper collages may be used to represent feelings and emotions. Group collages, where one patient at a time adds to a large sheet of paper, can be thought-provoking and enhance communication among group members. It's best if the paper is spread out on a table since the seniors often have difficulty moving about. Murals are generally non-threatening and help clients communicate ideas and feelings. Socialization and interaction among clients are enhanced. A group mural, where participants decide on the theme and specific method of design, is very valuable to all involved. Each client participates, and the entire group takes responsibility for its creation.

Seniors often enjoy sharing cooking tips, meals and desserts they have baked over the years. A mural focusing on food can enhance self-esteem, remind people of their skills and encourage clients to be more active. An example of this type of mural might be "Design a meal." Each group member would decide which types of food should be served (e.g. steak for a main dish, potatoes for a side dish). Another group mural project is called "Design a pizza." Each individual designs a slice of pizza (plain, pepperoni, sausage, etc.) and when everyone has drawn their slice of pizza, the therapist tapes the slices together on a large sheet of paper to form a full pie. Patients then speak about their slice of pizza and how it is self-representative—for example, "I am simple, ordinary, much like my slice of white, cheese pizza" or "I like to do a lot of things at once; I am peppy, much like my sausage, onion and pepperoni pizza."

A popular mural titled "Senior center" is a favorite among clients. Group members plan the cost, location, number of rooms and design of the center. They think about tennis courts, saunas, art and exercise rooms and other luxuries associated with the building. This project usually takes a few sessions and the clients become very involved. They have designed centers with heliports, auditoriums, libraries, pools, and fancy halls and dining rooms. There have been playful discussions about where the cabanas near the pool should be placed and where the gardens should be located. The camaraderie is often abundant and a lot of laughing takes place, especially when dress codes are discussed. The goals of these groups include making connections, communication, socialization and gaining control over one's environment. Problem solving and strengthening of thinking is focused upon. Patients often support each other, which increases self-esteem.

Another group project requires clients to create a person. Participants decide the age, sex, culture and family history of the individual. They choose his eye and hair color, weight, shoe size and the way he dresses (modern, old fashioned, neat, sloppy, etc.). Clients determine if he is well-adjusted, anxious, depressed, etc. They choose his job, household responsibilities and marital status. After all the decisions are made, clients either take turns or designate one individual to add all the body parts and features until the figure is completed and meets the group members' specifications.

Similar to the "Create a person" mural is the "Create a family" mural. Clients determine the number of family members, their ages, job status, marital status, etc. Then they take turns designing the family and creating an environment for the family members (e.g. walking in the park, sitting at home, frolicking on the beach).

Clients usually prefer a structured approach to art therapy. Seniors seem lost when offered an empty piece of paper and asked to "draw something." They frequently require an outline, even if it is just a circle or square and they are asked to draw something within it. Group members respond better with a specific theme as opposed to spontaneous art. Themes that have proved successful include drawing family members, creating a family tree, drawing memories and drawing a safe place. Clients enjoy creating mandalas and filling in the circular space. Outlines of pre-drawn pictures are usually desirable because they are almost always attractive when completed. These outlines allow clients to relax and focus on their artwork. They experiment with color and shading, and become familiar with various shapes and forms while they draw.

Older adults have a lot of challenges, but they also possess many strengths. Group members have reported that with age comes wisdom, achievements, experience, family legacy, financial stability and more leisure time. Some individuals stated they feel freer to express themselves and say what's on their mind. Many individuals take time to volunteer and travel. Certain people learn new skills such as cooking, technical skills and sports such as golf. They have time to take classes, teach others and guide their families. They are more savvy and understand the importance of friends and family.

Creative coping techniques help seniors in numerous ways. They learn how to think abstractly and become more open-minded. Seniors develop better communication and coping skills such as utilizing guided imagery and meditation. Positive self-talk and self-processing are learned and incorporated into their daily life. They are introduced to mindfulness, stress-reduction techniques, behavioral and cognitive practices such as avoiding erroneous thinking (catastrophizing, magnification, black and white thinking, etc.) and leisure skills. Seniors learn methods to increase self-esteem and decrease guilt. They are introduced to new techniques and skills that assist them to identify goals and examine methods to achieve them. Socialization, strengths and emotional well-being are focused upon.

Art therapy benefits seniors in many ways. Clients are given the opportunity to express and share their inner experiences in a visual way. They acquire healthy creative outlets for intense feelings. They reduce stress and learn creative stress-management techniques. Clients experiment and learn how to use a variety of media. They develop self-awareness and identify areas of concern. Individuals frequently develop talents and acknowledge strengths (some of which have been long forgotten). They become valued as part of a community that fosters non-judgment and acceptance. Art therapy raises self-esteem through successful completion of exercises and projects, mastery of materials and interactions with peers. Additional benefits of art therapy include the following:

- It aids in problem solving and focusing.
- It is enjoyable.
- It adds to leisure skills.
- It helps teach mindfulness.
- It allows for expression of fears and anxieties.
- It helps seniors identify stressors and explore coping skills.
- The creative act is often cathartic.
- Art may be less threatening than verbalizing fears and concerns.
- The art product can be referred to during discussion and/or at another period of time to examine progress and/or regress in therapy.
- It is difficult to deny feelings when the feelings are symbolized on a piece of paper or in sculpture that is in one's possession.

- The art product may be used to help diagnose organic problems and fine motor skills deficits.

- Clients learn new skills, which raises self-esteem and helps memory and thought (assists in producing new brain connections).

- Unconscious feelings may be made conscious through the work (much like dream symbolism).

- Drawing/creating helps clients gain mastery over their anxiety and associated problems (e.g. drawing a nightmare and analyzing it or creating a more pleasant ending to it gives clients better control over it; their fear may lessen or diminish). The fear is placed outside of the client; it is transformed onto the paper or sculpture where the client can explore it and deal with it on his terms.

- Studies show that being engaged in creative endeavors may help older clients heal quicker and better cope with illness, and may aid in longevity.

- Being engaged in art gives seniors a purpose and a reason to strive, learn and grow.

Art therapy and creative coping techniques provide clients with the motivation and skills to share their experiences and move forward. They have the opportunity to share their wisdom and reflect upon their lives. Clients become increasingly responsible for their attitude, actions and behavior. Every time they work in a creative manner they are gaining knowledge, wisdom and releasing feelings. They are in the moment, making decisions and in control of their world.

CHAPTER 1

WARM-UPS

Warm-ups can be considered "mental stretching." They are usually five to ten minutes in length and help clients become familiar with drawing and expressing themselves creatively. The warm-ups are relatively simple and provide an almost guaranteed successful outcome, which increases self-esteem and makes it more likely that the client will continue to create. This practice helps convey the message that in art therapy "it does not matter how one draws." It is the expression of thoughts and feelings that are important. The warm-ups may relate to the theme of the main exercise, but this is not a necessity. It depends on the needs of the clients and the therapist's view of what the goals and theme of the session will be. Another advantage of the technique is that clients are given time to settle down, relax, catch their breath, socialize and greet each other. Latecomers will not be too much of a disruption because, although significant, the warm-up does not carry the same importance as the main exercise. In addition, basic art therapy concepts and norms may be shared at this time. These creative endeavors allow participants to "loosen up" and relate better to one another. They help desensitize apprehensive individuals to the art experience because they are often enjoyable and easy; there are few risks involved. Quick, imaginative exercises often prove helpful in facilitating group interaction and growth.

Warm-ups do not have to be introduced into every therapy session, but they provide an easy and helpful transition into the next stage of the art therapy group. It is a time to experiment with shape, design and color and to ask questions relating to artwork, materials, technique and style.

Safety net

Materials: Drawing paper, markers and pastels.

Procedure: Ask clients to draw their safety net (something that keeps them from falling/from harm).

Discussion/goals: Discuss the uses for a safety net (e.g. a tightrope walker would use one just in case he fell off the rope). Explore the reasons clients might need a net and its uses for them. Examine the type and size of net drawn. Observe if it is large enough and available if needed.

A female patient in her early 70s, who suffers from major clinical depression, drew her cat as her safety net. This woman lives alone, has never married and doesn't have children. She treats her cat like her child; it helps her combat loneliness and sorrow. She included a rainbow and sun to represent the love and joy her cat provides. A small heart is placed on the cat's fur to symbolize "its loving nature." Ms. W. remarked that her cat is her lifeline: "It keeps me from giving up." When other clients take out pictures of their children and grandchildren, she shares snapshots of Cuddles.

One patient drew an empty net to represent her safety net. She stated that her safety net was herself. She remarked that she had no one in her life to help her and she had to rely on her own strength.

Another client, who took the directive literally, drew her cane. She remarked that she would fall head first on the ground without it.

Quite a few clients chose their family, television, food and books as their safety net. One individual named Anne chose "Oprah" because "I look forward to watching the show every day." She remarked that Oprah gives her something to look forward to even when she is lonely and/or depressed.

Cleaning

Materials: Drawing paper, markers and pastels.

Procedure: Ask clients to draw a broom (or provide a sketch of a broom) and next to it ask them to draw one thing in their life that needs cleaning up. Give examples such as a relationship, their thinking patterns, clutter in their lives.

Discussion/goals: Discussion focuses on exploring the "messy" part of their lives and examining methods to organize and take control. Goals include self-awareness and increased and/or maintenance of independence.

Some clients were very literal in their interpretation of this directive. One patient drew three boxes to represent the need to clean a messy garage. Another individual sketched a dirty sidewalk that needed cleaning, and one woman drew a garbage can.

Three other clients drew their representation of anxiety and stated they wanted to sweep their anxiety away. A woman in her 70s drew her car and stated she wants to overcome her fear of driving. She used to drive, but since she became depressed she is afraid she will have an anxiety attack while she's driving and get into a major accident.

A woman named Enid drew dollar bills and a green squiggly design titled "money problems." She shared that she is overwhelmed with bills, especially doctor and hospital bills. She ignores them, which makes her stressed. "I have no money to do the things I want to do. I don't even have enough money for medicine, it's a real stretch." She stated she would like to sweep all those problems and bills under the rug and keep them there.

A man named Walter drew his children (stick figures) and said sometimes he feels like sweeping them away. He remarked that they like to tell him what to do with his life. They want him to sell his home and move to an assisted living community, but he doesn't want to do that. He wants to remain in his home of 45 years and be left alone. Walter remarked that he has friends on his block and likes his house. He tends to the garden and sits on his porch and "watches all the people go by."

Traits

Materials: Drawing paper, markers, oil pastels and crayons.

Procedure: Direct clients to represent their positive traits by using color and shape. Each shape will be considered a positive attribute.

Discussion/goals: Discussion focuses on the shapes and associated symbolism. Goals include increased self-awareness and self-esteem.

Flower sketch

Materials: Drawing paper, markers, oil pastels and crayons.

Procedure: Leader outlines a large daisy with a circular center and at least six substantial petals on a piece of paper (8.5 × 11 inches).[1] The outline is copied and distributed to each group member. Ask clients to fill in the petals with colors that represent various moods they experience at different times of the day. For example, a client may feel bright (red or orange) in the morning so he might color in a few petals red/orange, but as the day progresses, he starts to feel lethargic and sad, so the next few petals might be brown or black.

Discussion/goals: Encourage clients to examine how mood changes are symbolized in their flower drawings. Goals include greater self-awareness and understanding of how mood affects behavior (and vice versa).

Inspiration

Materials: Drawing paper, markers, oil pastels and crayons.

Procedure: Ask clients to illustrate one item, thought, feeling or affirmation that helps get them through the day. Examples might include a morning cup of coffee or tea, a phone call from a family member or reciting an affirmation such as "Taking one day at a time."

Discussion/goals: Discussion focuses on motivation, strengths and attitudes. Goals include expanding clients' repertoire of coping techniques.

One patient drew a series of hearts and wrote, "I share feelings with my children and speak with them on the phone; I love them very much." Another client drew her cat, and another drew a rainbow and wrote, "Memories." Other clients drew a coffee, teacup or oatmeal in a bowl, and one older man drew a smiling face with the words "Going home" near it. This client imagines himself relaxing in his easy chair, and that thought helps him function and participate in the therapy groups.

A woman named Irena drew a portrait of herself; it represents her physically and emotionally. The image is detailed but not filled in. Irena usually dresses very nicely with full make-up and a lovely hairstyle; unfortunately, her self-esteem is low and she feels "lost inside." The tiny

semblance of hands and feet may symbolize her inability to move ahead with her life. Irena is a recent widow who is stuck in the past. She remarked, "Her family and hope is what gets her up in the morning and keeps her going." She mentioned she "is happy to wake up" (happy to be alive).

Strength

Materials: Drawing paper, markers, oil pastels and crayons.

Procedure: Direct clients to rate their strength on a 1–10 scale where 0 is the weakest and 10 is the strongest. Next ask them to draw a shape that represents their degree of strength.

Discussion/goals: Explore the size and color of the shape. Is it congruent with the number they chose on the strength scale? What does it say about their mood and attitude? Goals include exploration of emotional and physical fitness and coping skills.

Memory

Materials: Drawing paper, markers, oil pastels and crayons.

Procedure: Ask clients to draw two images (anything they wish—perhaps animals, fruit, houses, etc.). Next suggest they turn their paper over. Ask each client to try to remember as much as they can about each picture.

Questions include:

1. What did you draw?

2. What colors did you use?

3. What size was it?

4. What was significant about it?

5. What meaning does it have for you?

Discussion/goals: Discussion focuses on the images, their meaning and how well the client remembered what he drew. Goals include focusing, memory practice and creative expression.

Possessions

Materials: Drawing paper, oil pastels, markers and crayons.

Procedure: Ask clients to draw "something they have." Tell them it may be an item, thing or person.

Discussion/goals: Explore the image and the importance of it to the client. Goals include focusing on being positive instead of negative, and acknowledging what clients have instead of what they don't have or have lost.

Shooting star

Materials: Drawing paper, markers, oil pastels, pastels and markers.

Procedure: "Legend has it that if you wish upon a shooting star, your wish will come true." Ask clients to draw one or more shooting stars. Next have them write a wish at the bottom of the paper.

Discussion/goals: Discussion focuses on the size, shape and appearance of the star, and the connection between the star and the wish. Clients are supported to focus on dreams, goals and desires.

Healing energy

Materials: Drawing paper, markers, oil pastels, crayons and pastels.

Procedure: Suggest clients draw "healing energy." Ask: "What might it look like? How do you think it feels? Think about colors shapes and movement."

Discussion/goals: Discussion focuses on the type of energy portrayed and its meaning for the client. Goals include a focus on power, control, healing and thinking positively.

Smile (1)

Materials: Drawing paper, markers, oil pastels and crayons.

Procedure: Suggest that clients fold their paper in half. On one side of the paper have them draw a smiling face and on the other side ask them to draw or write the reason for the smile.

Discussion/goals: Discussion focuses on the positive aspects of one's life. Goals include reinforcement of positive thoughts and feelings and optimism.

Although clients are not asked to directly portray themselves, invariably the face becomes their face. Very few individuals decide to draw an arbitrary face or give a random reason for the smile. Usually, clients who do so are very literal and/or have mild cognitive deficits. One woman named Pearl drew a tiny figure with a frown and remarked, "The person is smiling because she is happy." This individual described her picture with little affect.

A 72-year-old widow named Janet, diagnosed with clinical depression, drew a large smiling face with a wide smile, cheerful eyes and curly brown hair. Janet stated she had been feeling better after a long bout with severe depression. Her support system consists of her children and a scattering of friends. She was able to identify with the smiling face. When asked, she stated the large red mouth symbolized the fact that she "talks a lot, I like people."

The other side of the page consisted of two small dogs named "Dana and Lila." These are Janet's "grandchildren." Her daughter does not have children and sees her pets as her babies; Janet feels the same way as her daughter. Janet stated that she smiles when she walks into her daughter's house because the dogs "bark with glee and jump on her, and are so glad to see her." She remarked she feels loved.

Another client in her 70s symbolized herself as a child. The face she sketched appeared to be that of an infant. She stated the reason for the smile was "Going to a party, playing with her dog, seeing her mommy and daddy and reading a story." When asked about this portrayal, she stated that she had a lovely childhood. "It was a carefree time with two warm, supportive parents." She remarked she wished she could return to that period of her life.

A woman named Ida drew an attractive face, which clearly represented her. Both she and the woman in the portrait have blonde hair, blue eyes and a pleasant smile. The symbols representing the reason for her smile included her grandchildren and daughter (drawn as stick figures). Ida spoke about her husband's recent death and the support she received from her family. She spoke about the close relationship she has with her grandchildren and the special bond between them.

A single woman in her 70s drew a bright smiling face outlined in purple marker. She stated the face (she) was joyful because she was able to focus and read 72 pages of a new book. This individual stated this was the first time she was able to read in more than a year. She wrote, "Happiness is reading."

Rona, a woman in her 80s, focused on her grandson whom she adores. She drew his smiling face on one side of the paper, and on the other side she drew him again, but this time as a full figure. She stated he is smiling because he is attending the college he wanted to attend. Rona remarked, "When my grandson is happy, I am happy."

Celebration (1)

Materials: Drawing paper, markers, oil pastels, crayons and pastels.

Procedure: Provide an outline of a simple cake (or have clients draw their own cake) and ask clients to decorate it. Next have them inscribe the reason for the celebration on top of the cake (similar to the way the cake decorator would do so in the bakery).

Discussion/goals: Discussion focuses on the type of cake designed and its significance. Goals include sharing joyful events and achievements.

A client named Jonathan drew a bright pink cake with colored sprinkles and wrote "Happy Birthday, Jack" on top of it. He stated the cake was for his brother who lives in Indiana. Jonathan remarked that he and his brother are very close but they rarely see each other. It is very difficult for both of them to travel due to various physical disabilities. Jonathan remarked that his brother deserves all the best, and he would like his brother to have the cake so he knows how much he is loved and admired.

A woman named Lena drew a chocolate cake with decorative red roses for her granddaughter, Wendy, who just graduated from college. She remarked that they are very close. She emphasized how proud she is of her granddaughter and how much she loves her. Lena "played" with the idea of symbolically baking a cake. She stated the cake is Bavarian cream and the icing is butter cream. She mentioned that it was decorated with tiny gold edible beads, especially for "my princess." She remarked that it will feed 20 people and invited everyone in the group to a party. Group members chuckled and pretended they would be there.

A widow named Mara drew a "Victory Cake" to represent the lifting of her depression. Mara decorated it with vivid swirls and colorful stars. She filled it "with chocolate mousse" and remarked that she " worked hard and earned the cake."

Celebration (2)

Materials: Drawing paper, markers, oil pastels and crayons.[2]

Procedure: Suggest that clients draw a celebration of their life. Have them include symbols of their life, people/pets who might be included, awards, where it would take place and what would be happening during the festivities.

Discussion/goals: Discussion focuses on joyful times and achievements. Have clients explore who is at the celebration, what type of celebration it is, and what is taking place. Goals include increased self-esteem and acknowledgement of positive aspects of one's life.

Life (1)

Materials: Drawing paper, markers, oil pastels and crayons.

Procedure: Ask clients to randomly draw symbols representing various parts of their life and then to label them (e.g. a wedding gown, a new baby, diploma, first apartment, boyfriend). Have them draw whatever "pops into their head."

Discussion/goals: Discussion focuses on memories and significant events. Goals include memory stimulation, life review and sharing with others/socialization.

Vibrations

Materials: Drawing paper, markers, oil pastels, crayons and pastels.

Procedure: Discuss the meaning of vibration (a tremor, shake, quiver and/or emotional feeling one person can get from another). Then ask clients to draw their vibration/s. Ask them if they are sending out positive, negative or neutral vibrations, and have them represent what those vibrations might look like (wavy, straight, chaotic or zigzag lines, etc.).

Discussion/goals: Clients explore the way they come across to others and the "vibes" they are sending out. Goals include self-awareness and exploration of mood.

Recharge

Materials: Drawing paper, markers, oil pastels, pastels and crayons.

Procedure: Ask clients to draw the way they "recharge" (the way they gain energy and improve their attitude). For example, do they walk, exercise, meditate, get a good night's sleep, swim?

Discussion/goals: Discussion focuses on the drawings and symbols drawn that represent renewal. Goals include exploring methods to energize and inspire.

The flower

Materials: Drawing paper, markers, pastels, oil pastels and crayons.

Procedure: Ask group members to draw a flower in any stage of growth. Have them determine if it is a bud, in the process of growing, blooming or wilting, or has it been picked? Suggest that clients will be asked if they could relate to the flower they draw.

Discussion/goals: Discussion focuses on the significance of the flower and how it may represent the client's thoughts about his mood, attitude, recovery and feelings about his life.

Cerebral health

Materials: Drawing paper, markers, oil pastels, pastels and crayons.

Procedure: Discuss the importance of keeping one's mind active and stimulated. Next ask clients to draw their answer to the question "How do you feed your brain?" Examples may include reading books, puzzles, working on the computer, lectures, attending plays, drawing, problem solving, exercising. Suggest that clients may, in addition to following the directive, create a puzzle or write brainteasers or riddles for others to guess.

Discussion/goals: Discussion focuses on reviewing methods to keep one's mind healthy and strong. Goals include focusing and problem solving.

Clouds

Materials: Drawing paper, markers, oil pastels, pastels and crayons.

Procedure: Have clients draw a large cloud or offer a pre-drawn cloud taking up a large portion of a piece of paper (9 × 12 inches). Ask participants to draw a figure above, below, inside or on the side of the cloud. The leader may choose whether or not to suggest to clients that the figure will be self-representative.

Discussion/goals: Discussion focuses on the significance of the figure and its placement. Goals include self-awareness and exploration of independence and safety issues.

Group members appeared to enjoy this exercise and focused on it for a long time. If the therapy group is motivated, this directive could be the main focus of the session. It is of interest to note that many clients place their figures inside the cloud to symbolize safety and comfort.

A widow in her 70s, who is clinically depressed and often lonely, drew herself with a slight smile, standing inside the cloud. She stated that she feels warm and comfortable in the cloud: "It is like standing on a large ball of cotton." She mentioned she likes the security the cloud provides.

A female client in her early 80s drew herself standing under the cloud and stated the cloud is "on top of me." She remarked that she "feels the weight of the cloud and it feels uncomfortable." The cloud was huge compared to her tiny self-representative stick figure. She admitted she is not in control of her feelings and her depression as of yet.

A male client in his 80s drew himself holding up the cloud. Although very depressed, he still saw himself as physically strong. He mentioned that he lifted weights when he was younger and won wrestling competitions. He believed that although the cloud—"his depression"—was strong, he would eventually be able to "lift it."

Hearts

Materials: Drawing paper, markers, oil pastels and crayons.

Procedure: Ask clients to draw three large hearts (or provide outlines). Next suggest they fill in each heart with someone in their life (past or present) that they like and/or love.

Discussion/goals: Encourage clients to share thoughts and feelings about the people they have chosen. Explore ways in which they have affected the client's life. Goals include exploration of support systems, relationships and positive thoughts.

Drawing upside down

Materials: Drawing paper, markers, colored pencils, oil pastels, pastels, crayons, objects such as fruit or a simple sculpture and/or pictures from magazines such as a bird, dog, cat or house.

Procedure: Suggest that clients choose a photo or object to draw, and then instruct them to draw it upside down.

Discussion/goals: When drawing an object upside down, the client is looking at it as an abstraction and is less likely to worry about the outcome. It is a problem-solving technique that inspires creativity, focusing and abstract thinking.

Most clients find this creative exercise non-threatening and enjoyable. One individual discovered that he drew much better upside down. He felt that by studying the lines and shapes, and not worrying about the figure as a whole, his "drawing anxiety" lessened and he was better able to capture the image.

The box

Materials: Drawing paper, markers, oil pastels and crayons.

Procedure: Ask clients to draw a box, or provide an outline of one. Suggest they draw someone, something or a shape (representing a person) trying to get out of the box.

Discussion/goals: Discussion focuses on the size of the box, the type of figure in it and the way the figure is trying to escape. Examine ways in which the client might relate to the figure drawn. Encourage the participant to examine whether the figure is comfortable in the box, trying to escape, has already escaped or is hanging on to the top of the box (in tenuous control), etc. Relate the box to possibly feeling "boxed in" by depression or being in a rut. Goals include awareness of attitude, strength, goals and stage of recovery.

The following picture was drawn by a widow in her late 70s named Margaret. She suffers from depression and anxiety. She drew herself in the middle of the box. Her eyes are closed and she is smiling. She has broad shoulders and is standing on the grass. The grass appears to have sharp points, which Margaret calls "spikes." Margaret also designs her suns

and flowers with spikes. The spikes represent " the sharpness of life." This individual stated she is smiling because she "has improved, but is still feeling depressed and not ready to leave the box." She likes the outpatient facility and feels comfortable and safe there. Her eyes are closed because she "is very tired; sleep is a problem." Margaret stated she is not ready to think about leaving the box but feels that in a few weeks she might consider "thinking about an escape plan."

A client named Lily drew a dog in the middle of the box. When asked, she stated she wished she were a dog because then she'd be living in a safe environment in "some nice person's home." This woman was a widow and loneliness was an issue for her. She remarked that dogs are loved and cared for and don't need to make major life decisions.

A woman named Sharon drew a stick figure holding on to the edge of the box. The figure's legs are dangling and its arms are outstretched. Sharon remarked that she is "hanging on for dear life." She stated she is trying to get out of the box (her depression) but it is very difficult for her. She mentioned that she feels better one day and poorly the next. She was not sure if her arms were strong enough to accommodate the weight of her body so she could pull herself up and out of the box. Sharon remarked that she would continue trying.

Out of sight

Materials: Drawing paper, markers, oil pastels and crayons.

Procedure: Ask clients to draw something they can imagine but can't presently see. Examples include wet sand, waves at the beach, a rose garden. Suggest they try to represent through color, shape and line the essence of the scene, person or object.

Discussion/goals: Explore the feelings and associations elicited from the imagery. Focus on the senses and mindfulness. Goals include abstract thinking and increased awareness of the richness and beauty of one's surroundings.

Line dialogue

Materials: Drawing paper, markers, crayons and colored pencils.

Procedure: Suggest clients create a dialogue (connection/relationship) between two or more lines.

Discussion/goals: Discussion focuses on the interplay of the lines. Suggest clients relate the lines to the way they connect with others. Goals include exploration of communication skills and relationships.

Funny

Materials: Drawing paper, markers, oil pastels and crayons.

Procedure: Ask clients to fold their paper in half and write the word "Funny" on one side of the page and draw something to symbolize humor and/or an amusing incident on the other side of the page.

Discussion/goals: Discussion focuses on the importance of humor in one's life.

Explore how having a good sense of humor helps people:

- stay young at heart
- cope with illness

- cope with stress
- enjoy life
- become more spontaneous
- relax and recharge
- gain/change perspective.

It also:

- lowers blood pressure
- endears people to you
- lightens burdens in difficult moments
- releases endorphins
- boosts immunity
- decreases pain
- relaxes muscles
- helps prevent heart disease
- eases anxiety and fear
- improves mood
- strengthens relationships
- diffuses conflicts
- enhances resilience.

Many clients drew clowns to symbolize humor. One woman drew a "jester" and wrote "Funny, Ha Ha" next to her picture. She stated that her deceased husband was a jester and "a lot of fun to be around." She remarked that he was very smart and always joking. She stated his sense of humor is what attracted her to him: "He really was not too good-looking, but he was so very funny."

A woman named Jan drew a figure of herself laughing. She remarked that she used to be "the funny one" in the group: "I was the life of the party. You'd never know to look at me now." Jan stated her sense of humor disappeared when she became depressed. She expressed hope that it would come back some day.

Positive moment

Materials: Drawing paper, markers, oil pastels and crayons.

Procedure: Suggest that clients draw a positive moment in their lives—for example, the day their child was born, the day they were married, their daughter's first smile, graduation from college.

Discussion/goals: Explore the achievements and joyful events. Goals include focusing on the positive and increasing self-esteem and self-awareness.

Ida, a woman in her 80s represented her graduation from high school. In the drawing she is looking up toward the left and throwing her diploma in the air with joy. She stated it was one of the proudest days of her life. Ida remarked that it was very difficult to get through school because her family was very poor; her father died when she was ten years old. She had to do a lot of housework, watch her younger siblings and work long hours in a pharmacy. "There were times when I was up until two or three in the morning

studying and doing homework." Her mother was not supportive and often told her it was useless to complete school. She did not acknowledge Ida's good grades and she took no interest in her school activities. Ida worked through all of these obstacles and became a graduate, something she is still very proud of and sees as a great achievement. A reminder of her past success helped her think about her strengths and view herself as more than just her illness.

Marvin, a man in his 80s, symbolized his grandson's graduation. He drew his grandson in his cap and gown, smiling and standing under a bright yellow sun. A large tree with green foliage and a thick brown trunk is situated next to the young man (possibly symbolizing Marvin). Marvin remarked that he loves his children, "but there is something indescribable about having a grandson." He stated he's his pride and joy. Marvin's eyes lit up and he sat straighter in his chair when he shared his feelings about this young man.

Pamela, a woman in her 70s who has never been married, drew her first boyfriend. She portrayed him as a large purple figure. He is smiling and his arms are spread outward, appearing as if he is about to hug someone. She shared his many positive qualities and her "great misfortune that he left her and moved to another state." Pamela stated she wished she had fought harder to keep the relationship intact. Sharing her feelings with group members seemed to give her comfort. Every day Pamela would listen to group members speak about cherished family members and now she had the turn to share her own love story.

Chloe, a woman with very low self-esteem, drew herself on graduation day. She drew a petite stick figure (looking much like the client), smiling and holding a diploma. This was the first time Chloe drew a smiling face; she rarely smiles and looks solemn most of the time. Her mouth is usually held tightly shut in a very rigid manner. She appears stiff and controlled. Chloe remarked that she graduated at the top of her class and worked very hard in high school and college. She snapped at the writer when asked if she was studious. She remarked, "Of course. I had very difficult courses and was head of the debate team!" Unfortunately, she wouldn't acknowledge her strengths even though she shared this special achievement. She stated, "That was in the past and now I am worthless." This drawing will be kept in her folder for future reference as she learns how to appreciate her strengths and wisdom. It will be referred to as a representation of past successes.

Waves of emotion

Materials: Drawing paper, markers, oil pastels and crayons.

Procedure: Each individual receives a piece of paper with three pre-drawn waves on it. Ask clients to fill in the waves with colors that represent emotions they are presently experiencing.

Discussion/goals: Discussion focuses on the colors used to convey the emotions. Explore the reasons clients feel joyful, sad, angry, etc. Goals include identification and expression of feelings.

A 75-year-old woman draw three black waves and stated her life is "just filled with emptiness." She was not able to see anything beyond the black in her life, but she was able to admit that she chooses to be a victim because she is afraid. She also shared that she wears a frown on her face because she wants others to see that she is angry and depressed. This woman never smiles. It was suggested that she share her feelings in a healthier manner so that she won't keep others at a distance. This individual wants people to like her but she is in a quandary because she's afraid of rejection.

An 80-year-old man named Ben drew each wave in varying shades of yellow, orange, purple and red. He approached the directive differently from the other clients. He stated that he associated the waves with the beach and spoke about enjoying summer vacations with his family at the Jersey shore. Ben remarked that he used to swim "far out," and his wife would yell for him to come back to shore. He smiled poignantly as he recalled enjoyable days in the sun and surf. Ben mentioned that he is no longer able to swim due to painful legs and a hip replacement. He did say that he is still able to watch his grandchildren swim, and that gives him much pleasure. The bright colors of the waves represented the "the sun and fun."

Ben wrote a brief poem related to his picture:

I used to swim and laugh all day,
With my children I would play.
I'd roll with the waves and never fall,
I wasn't fearful, not at all.
But now it is not the same,
There is no one to blame.
I am not quite so bold.
It is no fun getting old.

Many clients used yellow to represent hope and black to represent depression. Most stated that they were feeling like the black wave but had hope for the future. One individual who was feeling better drew her wave in various shades of blue, stating she is more at peace with herself.

Pets

Materials: Drawing paper, markers, oil pastels and crayons.

Procedure: Ask group members to draw all the pets they and other family members own and/or have owned in the past.

Discussion/goals: Clients share information about the pets and explore the significance of the pet/owner relationship. Goals include reminiscing and examining the impact that pets have on one's life and well-being.

Clients often have strong feelings about their dogs and cats. Some individuals view them as their children. Loss can be very difficult; therefore, talking about beloved pets helps to ease the loss and bring back fond memories. Communication and sharing is enhanced because most people can relate to having had a pet at some time in their life.

Exit sign

Materials: Drawing paper, markers, oil pastels and crayons.

Procedure: Ask clients to draw an exit sign and something or someone under or near it.

Discussion/goals: Discussion focuses on the significance of who or what is placed near the sign. Clients explore what needs to be "exited" from their life. They may examine who may be leaving them or whom they may be leaving. Goals include exploring change and loss.

Lucky charm

Materials: Drawing paper, oil pastels, markers and crayons.

Procedure: Ask clients to draw their lucky charm. Examples might include a four-leaf clover, horseshoe necklace, rabbit's foot, child or grandchild, special number, religious symbol, ring.

Discussion/goals: Clients share positive thoughts and the good fortune they have had in the past. Goals include thinking optimistically, exploring gratitude and affection, and hope for the future.

A divorced woman drew her four grandchildren as her lucky charms. She stated that they have helped her through her depression and give her a purpose in life.

Mr G., a highly anxious man whose main problem is worrying, drew a large red heart. He stated that his lucky charm is his heart and thinking of his wife on Valentine's Day. Mr G. explained that although his wife can be a nuisance at times, he loves her very much and couldn't live without her. He remarked, "When it is 'our time' I hope we hold hands, lay down next to each other, close our eyes and fall into our deep slumber."

A woman in her early 70s, who sees herself "as a nothing," drew a large, bright-green four-leaf clover. She remarked that her birthday is on St Patrick's Day, and family members had given her many clover pins, earrings and accessories over the years. She stated she carries one of the pins with her every day, as a reminder of her loved ones "who are long gone." She stated she has some faith that it might help her in some small way. This woman is very despondent, but progress in therapy is demonstrated by her ability to symbolize luck and faith in the drawing of the four-leaf clover and in her willingness to share a bit of hope verbally.

Wish, feel, love

Materials: Drawing paper, oil pastels, markers and crayons.

Procedure: Have clients write "wish", "feel" and "love" on their paper and then draw their representation of the words in any manner they please. They might choose to be abstract and use color and shape, or draw tangible items such as wishing for money or loving a daughter.

Discussion/goals: Discussion focuses on emotions, thoughts and relationships. Goals include self-awareness and expression of feelings.

Hairdos

Materials: Drawing paper, markers, oil pastels and crayons.

Procedure: Ask clients to draw various hairdos they wore during different stages of their life (e.g. a ponytail as a youngster, page boy as a teenager, beehive as a young woman).

Discussion/goals: Discussion focuses on connecting the hairdos to events that occurred during different stages of life. For example, the flip hairdo might remind a client of the prom, braids might elicit childhood memories. Goals include reminiscing and self-reflection.

Rainbow tree

Materials: Drawing paper, markers, oil pastels and crayons.

Procedure: Direct clients to create their own unique "rainbow tree." Encourage them to think about what they would find at the end of the rainbow or at the top of the tree.

Discussion/goals: Clients share the type of tree depicted and the way it might represent their hope for the future and their present mood and attitude. Goals include exploration of mood and feeling, and a focus on optimism and positive thinking.

A woman named Lois drew her own unique version of a rainbow tree. It is surrounded by swirls of red, blue, pink and yellow, and a variety of flowers. Lois remarked that it is whirlwind of color. The top of the tree has the initials LPC, which stands for "Love, peace and clarity."

A woman named Patricia drew a tree with colorful hanging bells. Daisies and birds surround the tree. It is firmly planted as indicated by the strong root structure. Patricia remarked that her tree is special because it looks beautiful and also sounds beautiful. "When the wind blows the bells ring and everyone is happy." A butterfly is placed on top of the tree to represent "freedom."

A widow named Harriet drew a very large and bold tree. The trunk is purple and the foliage contains the colors of the spectrum. The sky and ground are pink. Harriet remarked, "It is an amazing tree; it looks like it is ready to jump off the page." She stated it represents her optimism for the future and her highly improved mood. Harriet spoke about the difference in her attitude and behavior, citing how depressed she had been only eight weeks earlier. When asked, she stated the top of the tree is filled with prayers and blessings so that "everyone, including myself, will get well and stay well."

This woman drew a rainbow tree that reminded her of a brightly colored bush she used to admire in her backyard when she was a child. She stated she used to pretend that it was a magic bush and it could speak; she shared her secrets with it. When asked what she might find on top of the rainbow tree (instead of at the end of the rainbow), she stated "love and hope."

Self-esteem doodle

Materials: Drawing paper and markers.

Procedure: Suggest that clients draw doodles for a few minutes. Ask them to observe their drawings and relate the sketches to themselves in a positive way. For example, strong lines equal a strong personality or wavy lines equal a fun loving person.

Discussion/goals: Clients analyze the doodles and share strengths. Goals include increased self-esteem, abstract thinking and identification of positive characteristics.

Age (1)

Materials: Drawing paper, markers, oil pastels and crayons.

Procedure: Ask clients, "How old would you be if you didn't know how old you were?" Next suggest they draw themselves or aspects of themselves at that specific age. Representations may include sketches of hobbies, friends, hairstyles, clothes, foods they liked, etc.

Discussion/goals: Clients reminisce and share enjoyable experiences. Discussion may focus on how age affects mood, behavior and attitude. Goals include thinking in a positive manner and reviewing life experiences.

Power thinking

Materials: Drawing paper, markers, crayons and oil pastels.

Procedure: Suggest that clients use lines and shapes to represent positive thoughts and healthy thinking (e.g. being flexible, accepting change, being patient, taking one day at a time, accepting oneself, not filtering or catastrophizing).

Discussion/goals: Clients share their shapes and their "thinking strength." Explore the importance of strengthening thinking in order to increase self-esteem, vigor, motivation and hope.

Colors

Materials: Drawing paper, markers and oil pastels.

Procedure: Introduce the concept that colors elicit a wide range of feelings and have various meanings in different cultures. For instance, in China, red symbolizes both fire and prosperity, yellow represents supreme power and black represents water. In Spain, orange represents energy, vitality and health. Next ask group members to select a color they feel represents strength, health or wellness and have them create a design of their choice using that color.

Discussion/goals: Clients share ways in which the design and color selected represents energy and vitality. Goals include a focus on control, power and thinking in a positive manner.

Notes

1. This type of construction can be made using the basic tools on Microsoft Word or a flower may be used; the petals act as the projections.
2. This project would also work well using mixed media.

CHAPTER 2
DRAWING

Drawing allows the client the opportunity to communicate thoughts, feelings, concerns, problems, wishes, hopes, dreams and desires in a relatively non-threatening manner. It serves as a vehicle to express unconscious as well as conscious issues and beliefs. Creative expression provides the individual with the freedom to represent his inner and outer world in any way he chooses. It also gives him the chance to reconcile the two worlds with an artistic dialogue. There are no judgments and the client is told that any way he chooses to draw is perfectly acceptable. The individual is informed he may use stick figures, line, color, shape, abstractions or realism to portray his thoughts. Markers, oil pastels and sometimes crayons and colored pencils are presented to older adults; markers appear to be their favorite drawing tool. I usually provide two different sizes of paper (11 × 14 inches and 9 × 12 inches). In this way, clients can make decisions as to the materials they want to use. Decision making is very important; it helps enhance thinking skills and increases independence and self-esteem.

Groups with older adults are more productive when they are structured and clear directions are provided. The participant is always free to follow or modify the guidelines and artistic themes. Clients are usually more willing to begin creating with this type of approach. Seniors who are reluctant to draw will usually participate if they have some sort of organization to the paper, such as a pre-drawn circle. The exception to this is the individual who has an art background; he may prefer to create his own designs.

Taking time during the session to discuss the artwork allows clients to observe, analyze and relate to representations and figures illustrated. It allows for group interaction and feedback from others. Group members are able to reflect on the symbols drawn, and thoughts may be conveyed that would otherwise not be shared verbally. The drawings benefit the client in a variety of ways: they are concrete so the client is not able to deny representing a certain concept because it is right in front of him; they may be saved and referred back to during the course of therapy; and they serve as a compilation of feelings, problems, concerns and solutions that are exclusively the client's own. Images serve as vehicles which facilitate communication, growth and insight.

Kitchen table

Materials: Drawing paper, markers, oil pastels and crayons.

Procedure: Provide an outline of a simple table or have clients draw their own table. Suggest that group members draw individuals who would typically be sitting around their kitchen table on a Sunday afternoon (now or in the past).

Discussion/goals: The kitchen is often a place of warmth, comfort and of family gatherings. A lot of discussion, support and interaction take place in the kitchen. It is often considered the most important room of the house. Discussion focuses on who is seated around the table (friends, children, husband/wife, etc.) and what might be taking place (a Sunday dinner, friendly chat, family squabble, etc.). Goals include expressing feelings about significant people in one's life, reflections of past relationships and thoughts about present circumstances.

A depressed and sometimes confused 70-year-old client named Beatrice drew her table as it was in the past. She included her daughter, son, son-in-law, daughter-in-law and her husband. She remarked, "Those were the best days when my husband was alive. I would cook big dinners and everyone would be so happy. My husband would laugh and tease me, and say he would eat all the food." Beatrice stated that her family was closer then; she saw her daughter and son-in-law more often. She mentioned that she "wasn't depressed in those days." When asked if she would cook for her family now, she replied, "No, it isn't the same anymore; I have no interest." She was supported to try to find new ways to enjoy her family, perhaps celebrate in ways that are different from the past. Beatrice agreed that it might be fun to eat out more often or allow her daughter do the cooking now.

A vibrant 89-year-old woman named Muriel, who had been in much denial, drew the March Hare, Alice and the Mad Hatter seated around her dining-room table. She stated she often had eccentric and very interesting guests to dinner. Muriel remarked her dinner parties were a lot of fun and always filled with surprises. Everyone in the group laughed when she shared the picture, and Muriel had a wide grin on her face. She was pleased with the positive response and pleased that her superficial picture allowed her to keep her barriers up. Although she was extremely friendly and personable, with lots of insight into others' issues, she rarely shared her own issues and almost never spoke about her family. It seemed too painful for her to share thoughts and feelings about deceased loved ones and the death of her husband. Muriel did explore coping skills and thought she might volunteer to help others in need, as she had done in the past, when she left the program.

Smile (2)

Materials: Drawing paper, markers and pastels.

Procedure: Ask clients to fold their paper in half and draw a person smiling on one side of the paper and the reason the person is smiling on the other side of the paper.

Discussion/goals: Discussion focuses on happiness and positive thinking. Clients are encouraged to look at their gifts and achievements. Goals include increasing self-awareness and self-esteem.

Feelings

Materials: Drawing paper, pastels and markers.

Procedure: On one side of the paper have clients draw feelings that they rarely express or that they hide from others, and on the other side of the paper ask them to draw feelings they frequently and openly express.

Discussion/goals: Discussion focuses on the positive and negative consequences of expressing and/or hiding feelings and emotions. Goals include self-awareness and sharing of emotions previously hidden from others in order to gain greater insight.

Leisure skills

Materials: Drawing paper, pencil, markers and pastels.

Procedure: Have group members take turns reading the list of things people do to have fun in their leisure time. Ask clients to choose one or more of the activities on the list and sketch it in any way they please. Tell them to include themselves in the picture in a realistic or symbolic manner.

- taking a walk
- going to a movie/play
- reading
- journaling
- writing stories or poetry
- meditating
- exercising/yoga/water aerobics
- drawing/painting/crafts
- woodworking
- beading
- sewing
- arranging photos
- visiting a friend
- going to a museum
- cooking
- playing with grandchildren, nieces and nephews
- volunteering.

Discussion/goals: Discussion focuses on the activity depicted and the positive feelings that result when engaging in the pursuit. Goals include exploring leisure activities that are meaningful and enjoyable, give clients a purpose and raise self-esteem.

Signals

Materials: Drawing paper, pastels and crayons.

Procedure: Discuss various signals that most people encounter frequently (e.g. signaling to go right or left when driving or a police officer holding up his hand to let us know we should stop). Ask clients to fold their paper in half and draw one signal they present when they want to be close to someone and one signal they present when they want someone to stay away.

Discussion/goals: Discussion focuses on the way clients communicated their thoughts and feelings to others. Goals include self-awareness and exploration of relationships.

The wound

Materials: Drawing paper, markers, pastels and crayons.

Procedure: Ask clients to fold their paper in half. On one side of the paper ask them to draw a time in their life they were wounded (physical and/or emotional wound), and on the other side of the paper ask them to draw the actual wound using line, shape and color.

Discussion/goals: Discussion focuses on the size and type of wound. Questions to ponder include:

1. When did the wound occur?
2. Did it hurt?
3. Did it heal or is it still in the process of healing?
4. Did anyone in particular inflict the wound?
5. What did/do you need to do to heal it?
6. Is there a scar?
7. Did you learn anything from receiving the wound?

Discussion/goals: Discussion focuses on expression of past painful experiences and lessons learned. Goals include greater awareness of strengths and coping mechanisms.

Roles in life

Materials: Drawing paper, markers, crayons and pastels.

Procedure: Distribute pre-drawn pages filled with outlines of a variety of hats (e.g. chef's hat, Easter bonnet, chauffeur's cap). Ask clients to color in the hats that represent different roles they play in life. Suggest they may add more hats if desired.

Discussion/goals: Discussion focuses on the various roles clients play in relation to their families, communities and environment. Goals include self-awareness and increase of self-esteem. Clients are encouraged to acknowledge that they are remarkable people with many interests and functions, and they are not their illnesses.

Lethargy

Materials: Drawing paper, pastels, markers and crayons.

Procedure: Explore the meaning of lethargy (weariness, tiredness, laziness) and ask clients to draw their interpretation of it. Ask them to symbolize the essence of the word.

Discussion/goals: Discussion focuses on the way lethargy is represented artistically (is it colorful, dark, dull, large, or small?) and the significance of the drawing to the client. Questions such as "What is the impact lethargy has on your life?" and "How can you overcome and/or lessen the lethargy?" may be examined.

Aging (1)

Materials: Drawing paper, pastels, markers and crayons.

Procedure: Ask clients to draw what they see in the mirror when they look at themselves in the morning. They may draw in a realistic or abstract manner.

Discussion/goals: Discussion focuses on the artwork and associated references. The idea that "beauty is only skin deep" may be examined. Goals include accepting aging as a natural part of life and adjusting to change.

One 84-year-old man named Martin, who actually suggested this theme, stated, "When I look at myself in the mirror I shout, 'Holy Shit!'"

A 79-year-old woman exclaimed that she looks at herself with "one eye closed."

Another woman complained that she used to smile when she looked in the mirror, but now she only frowns. She did say that she'd rather see herself and frown than "be dead."

Time gone by

Materials: Drawing paper, pastels, markers and crayons.

Procedure: Ask clients to discuss the expression "Where has the time gone?" Then ask them to draw significant people and events in their life in order of importance.

Discussion/goals: Discussion focuses on life experiences and people that have had an effect on clients' present circumstances. Accepting and coping with changing roles and lifestyles are explored. Goals include self-acceptance and self-awareness.

My hands

Materials: Drawing paper, markers, pastels and crayons.

Procedure: Ask group members to outline their hands and fill them in as realistically as possible (include moles, veins, wrinkles, marks, rings, etc.). Have clients draw straight lines from various parts of their hands to the outer white part of the paper and list what their hands have done during their lifetime. For example, perhaps they baked and cooked, took care of their children, built their own home, knitted, took care of relatives.

Discussion/goals: Discussion focuses on the physical importance of one's hands (and other parts of the body) as opposed to their appearance. Goals include acceptance and examining strengths.

Choices

Materials: Drawing paper, markers, oil pastels and crayons.

Procedure: Read the story below and then ask clients to fold their paper in half and draw the outline of a heart on each side of the page. Suggest they fill in one of the hearts with shapes, colors and/or figures that represent their loving, forgiving side, and then ask them to fill in the other heart with shapes, colors and/or figures that symbolize their stubborn, angry and/or unforgiving side.

"Two Wolves: A Native Cherokee Tale"
A native grandfather was talking to his grandson about how he felt.
He said, "I feel as if I have two wolves fighting in my heart. One wolf is the vengeful, angry, violent one. The other wolf is the loving, compassionate one."
The grandson, with his head bowed, thought about it for a while. Finally, lifting his head and looking deep into his grandfather's eyes with concern, he slowly asked, "Which wolf will win the fight in your heart, grandfather?"
The grandfather answered, "The one I feed."

Discussions/goals: Clients explore various aspects of their personality and choices they make in their relationships and lifestyle. They are encouraged to observe the differences between the two hearts, studying size, shape and color. Have them examine which heart they tend to utilize more often. Goals include self-awareness and emphasis on choice in dealing with our actions and feelings.

CHAPTER 3
SELF-AWARENESS

With our busy schedules, it might be difficult to find time to think about who we are, our strengths and weaknesses, our drives and personalities, our habits and values. Many people just aren't inclined to spend too much time on self-reflection. Even when personal feedback is presented to us, we're not always open to it.

Self-awareness is important for many reasons. It can improve one's judgment and help identify opportunities for personal growth and professional development. Self-awareness builds self-esteem and confidence. It helps individuals decide which direction their life should be following and what their needs and desires are.

Being self-aware includes acknowledging and understanding:

- wishes and desires
- strengths
- weaknesses
- motivation for health and happiness
- challenges
- relationships with others
- barriers to achieving wishes
- beliefs and values
- self-esteem.

If an individual wants to change his life in any way, he needs to know and understand himself before he can take action. He must be aware of his desires, fears, dreams, goals and motivations. If he is unhappy or indecisive, he must have a plan and know what has to be completed in order to head in the right direction. Until an individual recognizes his purpose, thinking patterns and life path, he will have difficulty forging ahead and overcoming obstacles.

Self-awareness (1)

Materials: Drawing paper, markers, crayons and pastels.

Procedure: Writer and group members will read the summary below about self-awareness. Then have clients fold their paper into six boxes and ask them to draw figures and/or symbols representing what they know about themselves. For example, one box may contain a smile (the person is friendly), one box may contain a rock (the person is stubborn), one box may contain children (the person loves his family), etc. The boxes may be pre-drawn and copied for clients.

Self-awareness is the ability to understand one's emotions, actions, motives, behavior, moods, attitudes, personality and behavioral patterns. It allows us to appreciate what makes us unique.

Self-awareness gives us the opportunity to be mindful, alert and cognizant of our actions and interactions with others. It includes understanding why we behave as we do, and what motivates our behavior.

We acknowledge our dreams, hopes, challenges, values, beliefs and drives. We become familiar with our strengths, weaknesses and habits.

Self-awareness permits us to better understand others and how others perceive us.

Discussion/goals: Discussion focuses on the symbols represented in the clients' artwork. Reflections of clients' personality and roles in life are shared. Goals include increased understanding of thoughts, feelings, wants, needs and insights.

Identification

Materials: Drawing paper, markers, crayons and pastels.

Procedure: Ask clients to fold their paper in fourths, and in each fourth of the paper ask them to draw their answer to the following statements:

I am . . . .

I am not . . . .

I wish . . . .

I used to be . . . .

Discussion/goals: Discussion focuses on the symbols presented and the clients' reactions to the sketches. Goals include self-awareness and identification of needs, hopes and goals.

Holding on (1)

Materials: Drawing paper, markers, crayons and pastels.

Procedure: Suggest that group members draw themselves holding on to something they love.

Discussion/goals: Discussion focuses on who or what the client is holding on to, its importance in his life and the degree of strength needed to hold on. Goals include exploring reality and fantasy, loss and change.

Mood totem pole

Materials: Drawing paper, markers, crayons and pastels.

Procedure: Provide clients with a simple rectangle 4–6 inches wide divided vertically by 4–5 lines as separations. This will serve as the totem pole. Have clients fill in the squares that make up the totem pole with expressions that symbolize their various moods. Ask clients to place their most prevalent mood first and other moods in order of prevalence.

Discussion/goals: Discussion focuses on the design of the totem pole and associated references. Goals include self-awareness and exploration of the way one's mood affects behavior, attitude, communication skills and relationships.

Blocks of feeling

Materials: Distribute cardboard templates of various size squares. Suggest that clients use the templates to outline a series of squares (about five or so) and then cut them out. Once the squares are cut out, ask group members to work together to create a color graph that connects color to feeling (e.g. red = happiness; blue = peace; brown = depression). Once clients have decided which emotion each color will represent, ask them to build a tower by taking the squares, coloring them in, placing one on top of the other and gluing them on a sheet of paper in order from their most common feeling (at the top of the tower) to their least common feeling (at the bottom).

An example might be:

red on top (happiness)

green next (peace)

purple next (feeling powerful)

blue next (sadness)

black on bottom (depression).

Discussion/goals: Discussion focuses on the design of the tower, the order of colors and the clients' associated emotions. Clients will explore the way in which they express or contain their emotions and conflicts that may arise as a result of their individual coping techniques. Goals include examination of healthy coping mechanisms and self-awareness.

Family members

Materials: Drawing paper, markers, oil pastels and crayons.

Procedure: Ask clients to draw a symbol to represent each family member; they may choose as few or as many family members as they please. If a client doesn't have family members, he may use friends or significant others. Symbols may include whatever the client wishes. Examples include a cake for a baker, paints for a person who is creative, tools for the handyman, a smiling face for a cheerful individual, a frown for a stubborn person.

Discussion/goals: Discussion focuses on the various symbols depicted and their meaning to the client. Goals include exploration of significant relationships.

King/queen

Materials: Drawing paper, markers, oil pastels and crayons.

Procedure: Ask group members to draw themselves as king or queen of their home. Suggest they include a symbol of a king or queen (e.g. a crown, staff or jeweled gown) and a symbol of their home (e.g. their favorite easy chair, a beloved sculpture or an antique clock, dresser).

Discussion/goals: Discussion focuses on the client's role at home and his feelings about his home environment. Goals include exploration of the way in which one's home life affects one's mood and attitude.

Many older individuals are forced to move from a home they lived in for many years to a smaller home in a different neighborhood or to an independent or assisted living facility. They move away from familiar surroundings and long-time friends and neighbors. This can be a very difficult transition and often devastating to many individuals. Moves such as this usually occur because of disability, problems with finances or death of a spouse. It is often tremendously difficult for seniors to move into a smaller space (usually a much smaller apartment) after living in a three- or four-bedroom home for 40 or 50 years. A directive such as this one is a relatively non-threatening way for clients to express their feelings about their present home, a recent move and/or a recent loss. Many clients will say they used to be king or queen of their castle (home) but now they are alone, uncomfortable and lonely.

Keys (1)

Materials: Provide outlines of keys of various sizes and shapes (the leader might draw the outlines on one or two sheets of 8.5 × 11 inch paper and make copies for clients); construction paper, glue markers, oil pastels and crayons.

Procedure: Have clients color in and then cut out at least three or more keys and glue them on a piece of construction paper.

Discussion/goals: Clients share the significance of the keys and explore what they might open now or what they opened in the past (e.g. the key to one's heart, the key to a car, one's home, safety deposit box). Goals include introspection, reminiscing and creative thinking.

Feeling associations

Materials: Drawing paper, markers, crayons and oil pastels.

Procedure: Suggest that clients draw a quick sketch to represent at least five of the following feelings:

- happiness
- anger
- anxiety
- boredom
- sadness
- fear
- loneliness
- frustration

- depression
- shame
- confusion
- feeling overwhelmed.

Discussion/goals: Examine the drawings in terms of intensity, color and symbolism. Use the artwork to explore the ways in which clients express or hold in their feelings and how emotions impact behavior and attitude. Goals include identification of feelings and learning healthy methods to share them.

Treasure chest

Materials: Drawing paper, markers, oil pastels, crayons, outline of a treasure chest for group members if they seem reluctant to draw.

Procedure: Ask clients to draw a treasure chest and place their most valuable possessions in it.

Discussion/goals: Discussion focuses on the valued possessions and the way in which they reflect the client's personality, needs and desires. Goals include examination of values and satisfaction with one's life.

The escalator

Materials: Drawing paper, markers, crayons and oil pastels.

Procedure: Ask clients to draw two escalators or staircases, one going up and one coming down. (The therapist may provide a sketch of an escalator and distribute one to each participant or the clients may draw it themselves.) Direct participants to place themselves on the escalator by using a figure or shape. Ask them to think about whether they are going up the escalator (towards recovery), down it (still in depression), or somewhere in-between (on the road toward recovery, but not quite there yet, or possibly stagnating).

Discussion/goals: Discussion focuses on the client's strengths and attitude toward recovery as represented by where he placed himself on the steps. For example, if a client draws himself at the bottom of the steps (depression), does he see a future where he will eventually be standing on a higher step (closer to good mental health)? Does he need assistance to accomplish this task, and, if so, who would be the helper? Goals include gaining a greater understanding of where the client is in his recovery and exploration of progress and/or regress in therapy.

Cocoon[1]

Materials: Drawing paper, markers, crayons and oil pastels.

Procedure: Describe what a cocoon is and how a butterfly eventually emerges from it. Focus on the fact that the cocoon keeps the butterfly safe until it is ready to leave and fly away. Next ask clients to draw their own personal cocoons.

Discussions/goals: Discussion centers on the symbolism of the cocoons. Are they large or small, comfortable or uncomfortable, safe or threatening? Ask clients how long they have been in their cocoons and what benefits the cocoons provide for them. Do they want to stay in their cocoons or break away? How can they escape? Goals include exploration of safety concerns and dependence versus independence.

Motivation (1)

Materials: Drawing paper, markers, oil pastels and crayons.

Procedure: Ask clients: "What motivates you to get up in the morning?" Have them draw their motivation—for example, a cup of fresh-brewed coffee, a pancake breakfast, hot oatmeal, sipping green tea, going to a social club, going shopping, visiting with friends.

Discussion/goals: Discussion focuses on motivation and individual coping skills. Goals include helping clients to find enjoyment in life and to identify things that may give them incentive to learn, explore and challenge themselves.

One client who lived alone forced herself to get up early every morning. Her incentive was going to the local supermarket, getting a cup of coffee and buying the newspaper. She remarked that she knew the people who worked at the supermarket and they always asked her how she was feeling and welcomed her every morning. She stated this ritual was what she needed to motivate her and it started her day off "on the right foot."

Another client, Mr Miller, 75 years old, drew a picture of a tall, thin woman wearing glasses. He said that his motivation was his wife, who would almost literally push him out of bed so he would be showered and dressed early enough to eat a healthy breakfast and drive her to the supermarket or to her daughter's house to visit with her and her grandchildren before they went to school. Mr Miller's wife would say that sleeping late was not an option because it was for "the very young or the very old." She didn't see her husband or herself in either category. Mr Miller remarked his wife "kept him young and on the run."

Jane, an 82-year-old widow, stated that her incentive is to feed the birds and her cat, Patti. She remarked that they are waiting for her very early in the morning. She drew a picture of a very large bird and cat (almost an abstraction) sitting on her bed waiting for her to wake up. She remarked that they are so grateful for their breakfast that she feels guilty if she oversleeps.

Safe/unsafe

Materials: Drawing paper, markers, oil pastels and crayons.

Procedure: On one side of the page ask clients to draw a place where they feel safe, comfortable and secure, and on the other side of the page ask them to draw what they perceive to be an unsafe and/or dangerous place.

Discussion/goals: Discussion focuses on clients' associations to the drawings. Their issues and concerns often become clearer as they share unsafe aspects of their life. Goals include exploration of methods to better cope with frightening and uncomfortable feelings by using the positive thoughts and feelings associated with the safe and comfortable places. Coping skills are examined.

Drawing backwards

Materials: Drawing paper, markers, crayons and oil pastels.

Procedure: Ask clients to draw a picture backwards, as if it is a tape being rewound. For example, suggest that if they were drawing a figure and would normally begin by drawing the head, then body, arms and legs, they reverse and draw the legs first, then the arms, body and head last.

Discussion/goals: Discussion focuses on the ease or difficulty of the directive and the person, scene or symbol depicted. Goals include abstract thinking and problem solving. A directive like this one helps the therapist assess which clients are able to focus and which clients are perhaps somewhat confused and/or are having difficulty following directions.

Questions for clients to ponder may include:

1. Would you like to rewind any part of your life?
2. Do you feel that you are moving forward or backward in your life?
3. What would it be like if your thinking was rewound so that you approached life's "ups and downs" the way you did when you were in your 20s? How would your attitude be different?

Happy/sad

Happy/sad refers to two conflicting feelings being expressed at the same time. For instance, watching your child grow up and become independent is happy because this is natural, and this is what is best for your child, but it is also sad because your relationship with him is changing and he is leaving you (e.g. going to college, renting his own apartment).

Materials: Drawing paper, markers, oil pastels and crayons.

Procedure: Ask clients to draw a happy/sad time in their life and/or anything they are feeling happy/sad about now.

Discussion/goals: Group members will be supported to explore thoughts, feelings, concerns and coping mechanisms. Individuals will gain greater awareness as they learn that they are allowed to express more than one feeling at a time. Many clients think in "black and white." They believe that if one area of their life is unpleasant, then their whole life is awful. If they are sad about a specific event, then they do not give themselves permission to take delight in anything; everything is depressing. This directive gives clients the opportunity to understand that people may experience a variety of feelings at one time and can view life from many different perspectives.

Personality design

Materials: Drawing paper, markers, crayons and oil pastels.

Procedure: Ask clients to create a design that represents their personality. Suggest they use line, shape and color. For example, someone who uses bright colors might be lively and gregarious; straight lines might symbolize a more conservative or rigid individual.

Discussion/goals: Discussion focuses on the design and how it characterizes the individual's personality. Goals include self-awareness and exploration of how others see us versus how we see ourselves.

A woman named Colette drew a colorful lined pattern. She took much care making sure the lines were straight and "made sense." She stated that she "is a little obsessive-compulsive and likes things just so." Colette mentioned that she spends much time cleaning her house and won't hire anyone to help because they "are sloppy and put things in the wrong places." She admitted that being a perfectionist could be problematic: "It holds me back from doing things that are different." She also stated that she doesn't always enjoy company "because of the mess."

Anxiety sketch

Materials: Drawing paper, crayons, oil pastels and markers.

Procedure: Ask clients to draw (realistic or abstract) two or more of the people, places and/or things in their life that cause anxiety.

Discussion/goals: Discussion focuses on the symbolism and intensity of the sketches. Goals include examination of anxiety, identification of issues and resulting symptoms and exploration of coping mechanisms

Adoration

Materials: Drawing paper, markers, oil pastels and crayons.

Procedure: Suggest that clients draw one or more people they love. Ask them to draw their feelings about these individuals by using various shapes and colors to surround them. For example, someone who adores his mother might draw a female figure with red hearts or wavy pink lines surrounding her, or yellow projections near her and a bright sun overhead.

Discussion/goals: Clients explore how significant connections in their life may help with personal struggles such as depression, loss and anxiety. Goals include exploration of relationships and support systems.

The path

Materials: Drawing paper, markers, oil pastels and crayons.

Procedure: Direct clients to fold their paper in half. Have them design a pathway on one side of the paper and draw it leading to a destination, which will be sketched on the other side of the paper.

Discussion/goals: Discussion focuses on plans and goals and methods to achieve them. Obstacles to recovery and feelings of control/lack of control over one's life and future may be explored.

My house

Materials: Drawing paper, markers, oil pastels and crayons.

Procedure: Ask clients to draw the type of house that represents their style and personality. Examples of houses include a mansion, ranch, apartment, condominium, modern/old-fashioned home, colonial, townhouse, tent, row home, townhouse, log cabin, villa.

Discussion/goals: Clients might discuss the ways in which they relate to the house. For example, are they modest like a small apartment, old-fashioned like a colonial, showy like a mansion, down-to-earth and "outdoorsy" like a log cabin or tent? Personality characteristics are shared and explored. Goals include self-awareness and identification of individual traits.

Broken entity

Materials: Drawing paper, markers, oil pastels and crayons.

Procedure: Ask clients to draw an item, idea, feeling and/or special possession that has been broken in the past. Examples may include personal belongings, dreams, goals and relationships.

Discussion/goals: Discussion focuses on the object/thought symbolized and its importance. Explore how it was broken, when it was broken and if the client ever tried to fix it. Goals include dealing with hurt, loss and disappointment. Personal resilience may be explored.

Picnic basket

Materials: Drawing paper, markers, crayons, oil pastels, scissors, glue and magazines.

Procedure: Have clients draw the outline of a picnic basket or provide an outline to each group member. Ask participants to place the items they would need in the basket in order to have a successful outing. They may draw the items or cut out relevant pictures from the magazines.

Discussion/goals: Discussion focuses on the size, shape and number of items in the basket. Clients may be informed that the basket, in this exercise, will be used as a metaphor for one's life. Ask group members to relate their life to the basket and inquire:

1. Is your life rich and full, moderately full or empty?
2. Are the contents of the basket for one, two or more people?
3. Who would be sharing the contents of the basket with you at the picnic?
4. When was the last time you felt your life was like "a picnic" (or was "no picnic")?

Goals include exploration of relationships, needs and life satisfaction assessment.

Anxiety dialogue

Materials: Drawing paper, markers, oil pastels, crayons, pens and pencils.

Procedure: Ask clients to draw their anxiety (what it looks like using line, shape and color). Next ask them to write to it. Allow them to say anything to their anxiety that they please.

Discussion/goals: Discussion focuses on the size, shape, strength and significance of the anxiety as well as the written response. Goals include identifying stress and exploring methods to gain control over it. Writing to the stress automatically gives the client some measure of control. It is now transformed from "inner to outer" so that the client can talk to, write to and observe it; he can change it in any way he pleases (e.g. crossing it out, drawing over it). When an individual symbolically controls his stress, whether it is through drawing, painting, movement or writing, it is the first step to controlling it. He doesn't own it so much. It is outside, instead of inside where it simmers and causes uncomfortable and sometimes life-threatening symptoms.

Mandala: My world[2]

Materials: Drawing paper, paper plate, markers, crayons and oil pastels.

Procedure: Ask clients to outline a circle using the paper plate as a template. Next ask them to draw the world they have created for themselves within the mandala. Explain that their world may contain whatever they like—for example, favorite items, pets, people, places they have visited, their home, and feelings represented by colors and/or shapes.

Discussion/goals: Discussion focuses on each person's world and the client's thoughts about it. Goals include identification of positive and negative aspects of one's life. Desired changes may be examined.

A female client in her 70s drew her world as a beautiful place with birds, flowers, trees and love. She stated she enjoys gardening in the spring and adores looking at the stunning assortment of flowers she lovingly grows. She has come a long way in her therapy. A few months ago when given this creative exercise, she shared an almost empty circle, which was filled in with a few tiny stick figures outlined in black to represent her children.

Some clients will draw a beautiful scene or still life to represent the way they would like their world to be. This probably was partially true for this client. Even though she was indeed feeling better, she still had a long way to go before she was well enough to leave the program and become fully involved in her previous activities.

A female client in her 70s, who was recovering from clinical depression, drew a series of small pictures to compose her world. She included her cat, a bird, her home, a flock of geese, bananas, an apple, a fern, an anchor (to represent "possibly going on a cruise in the future") and flowers. This woman was pleased with her mandala and stated she derived pleasure from looking at it. It is noteworthy that people were not included in the mandala; loneliness has been a major issue for this woman. One of her desired goals was to become more social. In contrast to the previous client, this client depicted a very realistic portrayal of her world. Analyzing it has helped her become aware of her need to focus on making friends and developing new relationships.

Ann, a woman in her late 70s, drew her world as a maze of shapes drawn in a haphazard manner. She stated, when asked, that her world is chaotic and she doesn't know "what the future will bring." The shapes are outlined in a light purple color and most of them are not connected to one another. The starkness of the mandala combined with the disparate shapes represents her isolation and loneliness as well as the confusion she is presently experiencing.

Elsa, a client in her mid 70s, included her children, grandchildren, a microwave oven, flowers, a pizza pie, and most importantly, handbags in her world. She stated she adores handbags and has been collecting them for years. There is one black bag that is prominent in her mandala. It overshadows everything else including her family. When this was observed, Elsa remarked that the bag represents independence. She stated that when she takes her handbag with her, she carries her keys, her medicine, her identification and her money. It allows her to shop, drive, go to restaurants and enjoy herself. She remarked that she can't afford vacations or luxury items, but she can afford to collect a variety of handbags, "one for every occasion."

Retirement

Materials: Drawing paper, markers, oil pastels and crayons.

Procedure: Ask clients to draw a symbol, sketch or feeling (using color and shape) related to their retirement. Examples may include an image showing the type of work they did, a picture representing how they spend their time now, a sketch of their retirement party, a design portraying "the colors of retirement" (bright and colorful or dull and dreary).

Discussion/goals: Discussion focuses on feelings and thoughts associated with retirement, and how retirement has affected clients' lives. Goals include dealing with change and exploration of coping skills.

Family conflict

Materials: Drawing paper, markers, oil pastels and crayons.

Procedure: Direct clients to draw (represent) family members or close friends (who are like family) disagreeing about something. Ask them to write down what the disagreement is about on the back of the paper. Tell group members the disagreement may be real or imaginary (less threatening).

Discussion/goals: Older adults may become depressed when their family doesn't turn out the way they always imagined. Perhaps their children or grandchildren divorce or are not as respectful as they would like them to be. Maybe their children's values are different from their own. This can lead to unhappiness and friction. Sharing these issues helps clients to explore methods to be flexible, allows them to vent and to cope with situations that arouse anxiety.

Health

Materials: Drawing paper, markers, crayons and oil pastels.

Procedure: Suggest that group members draw health concerns and/or events—for instance, a recent fall, a broken hip, heart surgery, knee surgery, cataract surgery, cancer, loss of hearing, eyesight, arthritis. They may represent their issues in any way they please (realistic or abstract).

Discussion/goals: Health problems pose a major problem for older adults. Depression might ensue after surgery or when diagnosed with a health condition. Drawing and then sharing the problem affords clients a way to analyze it, explore their feelings about it and examine ways to cope. Clients often feel better when everyone shares their health concerns; they see they are not the only ones experiencing discomfort, anxiety and the annoyance of doctor and hospital visits.

Figures

Materials: Drawing paper, markers, oil pastels and crayons.

Procedure: Provide a sheet of paper with the outline of a figure to each group member; the figure should take up most of the page. Have clients divide into pairs. Next ask group members to write their name at the bottom of their paper, exchange papers and fill in their partner's figure in any way they please. When they have finished, have them return the drawing to their partner.

Discussion/goals: Discussion focuses on the interaction between the clients and their associations to both the figure they drew and the figure drawn by their partner. Encourage group members to observe the figure and look for similarities to themselves or to their partner. Examine how it felt to draw for someone else and how it felt to receive a drawing. Goals include socialization and identification of physical and psychological characteristics.

Variations of this project include:

- Drawing a person who appears similar to one's partner (the previous exercise doesn't specify if the form should look like anyone special).

- After the client signs his name to the page, the figures may be mixed up and given to group members in an arbitrary manner. They are filled in and then returned to the original owner.

- Each group member may receive two outlines and fill one in so that it resembles himself and the other to represent someone close to him. Role play may include the figures speaking with one another (e.g. a mother and her son).

The road

Materials: Drawing paper, markers, oil pastels, pastel and crayons.

Procedure: Ask clients: "What do you need on the road to creating a new life?" Have them draw their response. Suggest they may, if they like, draw a road and place their needs on it.

Discussion/goals: Clients explore necessities and desires, goals and hopes. Realistic expectations are examined. Goals include planning, looking toward the future and exploring methods to attain objectives. This is a beneficial directive to do when the theme of loss is a focus. It helps clients to cope better and think about moving ahead with their life.

Houses through the years

Materials: Drawing paper, pencils, markers, oil pastels, pastels and crayons.

Procedure: Ask clients to fold their paper in half. On one side of the paper have them list and/or describe all or most of the houses they have lived in over the years. Next suggest they choose their favorite or most meaningful home and draw it on the other side of the paper.

Discussion/goals: Discussion focuses on the description of the house chosen and the clients' analysis of it. Have clients share what life was like when they lived there. Goals include reminiscing and life review.

Most clients drew the house they lived in as they were raising their children. Many of the houses were colorfully outlined, but not colored within. Trees, flowers and a sun were placed near many of the houses. Many of them were small and inconsequential-looking. Some of them had quite a bit of smoke coming from the chimney. One client only drew half of the outline of a house. When asked about this presentation, she stated it was too difficult to think about the house because it was such a happy time and she missed her husband so much. He had died three years earlier of a sudden heart attack. The house outlines seem to represent the fact that there is a missing component in these individuals' lives. Many of the clients really do feel like "a shell" of their former selves.

Draw a stream

Materials: Drawing paper, markers, oil pastels, pastels and crayons.

Procedure: Suggest that group members draw a stream (as small as a brook or as large as a river).

Discussion/goals: Ask clients questions such as:

1. How does the stream represent your "life flow?"
2. Where is it going?
3. Is it shallow or deep?
4. Is the current strong or calm?
5. Is there anything in the stream?
6. Where does it begin and end?

Goals include exploration of the recovery process and assessment of goals and life direction.

As I introduced this directive to clients, I was not sure how they would react or if they would understand the concept. It took most group members a few minutes to ponder the problem, but all of them were able to follow directions successfully and process their artwork. The senior clients appeared to enjoy this project and participated more than usual during the group discussion.

A depressed woman in her mid 80s named Rhoda created a light blue stream, which flowed "into a waterfall." She stated that if she didn't get well she might fall over the waterfall and drown. She did see some hope because "the water was shallow and choppy; not impossible to survive a fall out of a boat."

A woman named Joan drew her river flowing upstream. She stated that she is feeling better and "is hoping to defeat the odds." Joan saw the river as a positive sign because she placed fish and a frog in it, which "represented new life." This woman remarked that this is the first time in a year that she saw the possibility of "not being depressed."

Elena drew a navy-blue river that was completely horizontal, stretching from one side of the paper to the other. She stated that she felt stable, "not happy, and not sad." She remarked this was an improvement because she had been feeling depressed for a very long time. It is of note to mention that this woman's affect was very much like her river; she appeared solemn. Her mouth was small and straight; she showed little emotion.

Passion

Materials: Drawing paper, markers, oil pastels and crayons.

Procedure: Suggest that clients draw things they are passionate about. Examples may include children/grandchildren, pets, hobbies, work, art, volunteer positions, sports (e.g. golf).

Discussion/goals: Discussion focuses on the importance of having a passion and/or a purpose in life. Explain the benefits:

- Individuals are generally more positive.
- They often have higher self-esteem and less depression.
- They have more energy.
- They are more likely to fight off disease and illness.
- They live longer.
- They stay younger and think younger.
- They are more exciting and enjoyable to be with.

- Boredom is rarely an issue.

- Having a passion makes it easier to start the day; there is a reason to get up in the morning.

Goals include exploring and developing new hobbies and interests and resuming activities that clients once found fulfilling.

Family chain

Materials: Drawing paper, markers, oil pastels and crayons.

Procedure: Direct clients to draw a chain that will represent the strength of their family. For instance, if the family is close, the chain might be thick and the links might be larger; if the family is dysfunctional or alienated, it might be small, fragile and not well connected. Suggest that charms (family members) may be added to the chain if desired.

Discussion/goals: Discussion focuses on the size, length and strength of the chain and the significance of the charms. Goals include exploration of family dynamics, roles and connections.

A client named Frances drew a colorful chain, which comprises most of her family members. She stated it included her children, grandchildren, great-grandchildren, nieces and nephews. She is represented as the large yellow heart, the fifth charm from the left. Frances remarked that her family chain

is strong. "My family is very close and supportive and helps me through difficult times." She focused on the red charm placed next to her, which symbolizes her daughter. Frances remarked that her daughter gives her strength and unconditional love. "I am very lucky to have her and her husband in my life." When asked, she stated that the chain gives her a positive feeling. She declared that the chain is unbreakable.

A client named Mildred drew a vibrant chain that looks like a caterpillar. The chain is comprised of colorful circles and lines extending out of the circles like arms with small colorful balls protruding from them. Mildred remarked that each circle represents a family member and each arm with the connected ball symbolizes more distant relatives and her great-grandchildren. The chain begins at the bottom of the page, climbs to the top and then goes back down again on a relatively sharp angle. When asked about this presentation, Mildred replied that her family grew over the years and was very close in the 1970s and early 80s. As the years passed and her children and grandchildren grew up, went to college and entered the work force, they moved to different states and became more interested in their own pursuits than in keeping the family together. Mildred stated the family is still close, but not as close as in the past. She remarked that the chain is less solid and unfortunately on a downward trend. Mildred expressed hope that it would not break in the future.

Holding on (2)

Materials: Paper, markers and pastels.

Procedure: Ask clients to draw what they are holding on to. This question may be clarified by asking what types of people/things are difficult to "let go of"—for example, stubbornness, independence, youth, memories, a home lived in for many years, a child who is moving away.

Discussion/goals: Discussion focuses on what needs to be released and how to let go of certain feelings, concerns and obsessive thoughts. Goals include acknowledging and accepting change. If clients aren't ready or willing to "let go," they may be encouraged to "loosen their grasp" on their unproductive beliefs, ideas and desires.

A widow in her 70s named Emma depicted her mother. She stated her 92-year-old mother is in a nursing home suffering from Alzheimer's disease and heart problems. "She doesn't have much longer to live," Emma whispered. She stated she has to loosen her hold on their relationship, but as of yet it has been something she has been hiding from and unable to

do. Emma portrayed her mother as a young vibrant, beautiful woman. She stated her mother, even now, makes sure her hair is perfect and her nails are polished.

Emma expressed conflicting feelings. On the one hand, she remarked that she likes to view her mother as she used to be years ago, full of life and energy, and, on the other hand, she acknowledged that her mother is very sick, old and fragile, and will leave her soon. Emma became teary as she described her illustration. She also shared a photo of her mother when she was about 30 years younger and passed it from group member to group member. She smiled as her peers stated how lovely her mother was and how much Emma looked like mother.

Emma examined her drawing and noticed she represented her mother with strong, wide shoulders. She studied the illustration and stated it symbolized her mother's bright spirit. During discussion she was able to acknowledge her own strength and determination. This seemed to help dry some of her tears. Emma admitted she had to accept the fact that her mother will die soon. She remarked that she's glad she has the people in the senior program to help her get through this extremely difficult time in her life.

A very scholarly woman in her late 80s drew a figure playing a guitar in a cloud. The illustration was full of movement as the lines were wavy and the figure appeared to be dancing with joy. This woman remarked that she used to love to play the guitar, but because of arthritis she isn't able to play the guitar or any other instrument anymore. During discussion she stated she listens to guitar music as a substitute, but she still misses the fun of actually playing herself.

A client in her late 70s drew a set of boxes to illustrate that she must get rid of much of her furniture and many of her household items. She was moving to a smaller apartment to be close to other family members. She remarked she was having a difficult time sorting out items that were a part of her home for over 40 years. She believed everything to be a treasure; she didn't want to part with anything. The theme of moving to a smaller house or apartment is common with seniors and so she received much support and empathy from her peers.

Myrna drew a figure (herself) next to "her brain." She stated her teenage years were horrific and she wanted to forget them. The brain was large, colorful and full of movement. It was quite a contrast compared to the pale, lightly drawn figure. Myrna remarked that the brain is so large because it is full of unwanted memories. Myrna had been in a detention camp in Poland with her family when she was very young, and when they were freed, they lived a very poor life. Her mother was bitter and berated her often. Her sister followed in her mother's footsteps. Her siblings were treated much better than she was; she considered herself the "Cinderella of the family."

A very attractive woman in her late 70s copied a poster of "The Scream" by Edvard Munch. She stated it represented her intense anxiety. She remarked she could relate to the illustration because she always feels as if she is jumping out of her skin. She stated she related to the figure in the painting "holding his hands to his ears, seeming to try to shut out the world, and close his ears so he does not hear his auditory hallucinations." She went on to say she feels "ghost-like at times." She lives alone and feels she is disappearing and "no one notices." She hoped to work on coping skills to lessen the stress and anxiety she constantly feels.

A widow named Lucille in her early 80s drew the home she lived in with her family for 45 years. She stated her husband added a pond and other beautiful features to it. Lucille remarked she hadn't lived there for seven years, but still couldn't drive by the house because the memories and sadness overwhelmed her. She stated she wished she could think about the wonderful times she experienced while living in the house and not feel so sad. She wanted to try to stop obsessing about that period of time so she could better function and enjoy the present. Another client named Marge, who had experienced a similar problem, encouraged her to visualize the house "on fire and then gone." Marge remarked, "The house has changed; it is not the same anymore, and you have moved on, forget it." Some of the clients liked this idea, but Lucille did not. It was suggested, instead, that Lucille work on loosening her grip of the memory, but not erase it entirely. She was more accepting of this idea.

Culture

Materials: Drawing paper, markers, oil pastels and crayons.

Procedure: Ask clients to think about various aspects of their culture. Suggest they draw symbols representing their culture/religion, traditions, spirituality, etc. Examples include a menorah, Christmas tree, Buddha, cross, rosary beads, Seder dinners.

Discussion/goals: Explore the impact that culture has on attitudes, relationships, identity and self-worth. Goals include sharing, socialization and self-awareness. Speaking about one's customs and background often increases self-esteem and discussion among seniors. It frequently elicits memories of joyful family events and gatherings. Many seniors find prayer and religion to be a major coping skill.

Animal association

Procedure: "The following animals appear in a variety of cultures and represent a variety of things. In one case an animal might symbolize something good, while another culture might consider it representative of evil. Each animal below is followed by symbols from different cultures and religions."[3]

Read this introduction to clients and provide the following list of animals for them to review. Ask group members to share the animal they relate to the most and illustrate it. A background may be added if desired. Encourage clients to write a brief summary of why they are similar to the chosen animal.

- *alligator*—aggression, survival, adaptability, cunning, deceptive

- *ant*—group-minded, perseverance, self-discipline, group effort, teamwork, industriousness, orderliness, virtue, strength, stamina, honor

- *antelope*—lunar animal, associated with the mother, grace, beauty

- *ape/monkey*—mischief, mimicry, cunning, benevolence, humanity, nurture

- *bee*—immortality, rebirth, industry, order, purity, soul, chastity, messengers between worlds, secret wisdom, mother and priestesses, community

- *birds*—the soul, transcendence, spirits of air, ascent, communication, freedom, sight

- *bear*—primal power, mother, cunning, healer, gentle strength, dreaming, sovereignty, intuition married with instinct, nurturing, protective

- *buffalo*—sacredness, life builder; the buffalo provides all good things for living and bestows great curing powers

- *bull*—wealth, potency, beneficence, generative force, male procreative strength, kingship, taming of the masculine and animal nature, destructive force

- *butterfly*—metamorphosis, carefree, transformer, immortality, rebirth, resurrection, grace, light, soul

- *cat*—guardianship, detachment, sensuality, stealth, desire, liberty, pleasure, magic, lust, pride, vanity

- *cougar*—leadership, courage, power, swiftness and balance

- *cow*—nourishment, motherhood, power of Earth, plenty, procreation, gentleness, nurturing

- *deer*—love, gentleness, kindness, gracefulness, sensitivity, purity of purpose, walking in the light, swift, nimble, meek, gentle, meditation, love, longevity, wealth

- *dog*—guidance, protection, loyalty, fidelity, faithfulness, watchfulness, the hunt

- *dolphin*—kindness, play, savior, guide, sea power, swift, intelligence, communication, breath control, awareness of tone

- *donkey*—humility, patience, peace, stupidity, stubbornness, lewdness

- *dragon*—power of Earth, combining bird and serpent as matter and spirit, breath of life, supernatural power, magic, strength, wisdom, knowledge, guardian
- *eagle*—divine spirit, air, the sun, power in battle, protection from evil, clear vision, success, prosperity, wealth, intelligence, renewal, courage
- *elephant*—strength, fidelity, memory, patience, wisdom, intelligence, power
- *fox*—cunning, provider, intelligence, feminine magic, diplomacy, wildness
- *frog*—power of water, sensitivity, medicine, hidden beauty, power
- *goat*—vitality, fertility, creativity, virility, abundance, lust
- *goose*—guardian, watchful, wind, the sun, war, inspiration, swift, happiness, providence
- *grizzly bear*—mother, nature's pharmacist
- *horse*—stamina, mobility, strength and power, coping under difficult circumstances, love, devotion, loyalty, the land, travel, life and death symbol, intellect, wisdom, power, nobility, energy, freedom, wildness, divination, prophecy, fertility
- *hummingbird*—messenger, stopper of time, optimism, sweetness
- *lion*—solar, splendor, power, majesty, strength, courage, nobility
- *lizard*—conservation, agility, promotes dreaming
- *moose*—headstrong, unstoppable, longevity, value, integrity
- *octopus*—the spiral, water, unconscious
- *otter*—laughter, curiosity, mischievous, feminine power, grace, empathy, joy, play, helpfulness
- *owl*—wisdom, truth, patience, darkness, a death messenger, divination, solitude, detachment, wisdom, change, totem of clairvoyants and mystics
- *python*—darkness, feminine, power of Earth, wisdom
- *rabbit*—alertness, nurturing
- *seahorse*—confidence, grace
- *shark*—hunter, survival, adaptability

- *snake*—shrewdness, transformation, life, death and rebirth, rain, fertility
- *spider*—creative, pattern of life, connects the past with the future, creating possibilities
- *swan*—grace, balance, innocence, faithfulness, solitude, retreat, poetry, sincerity
- *tiger*—creator, destroyer, strength, ferocity, power, anger, power of Earth
- *turtle*—self-contained, creative source, Earth, informed decisions, planning, adaptability
- *unicorn*—chastity, purity, dreams, virtue, strength, integrity, magic, healing, freedom
- *whale*—power of water, regeneration, death, rebirth
- *wolf*—loyalty, success, perseverance, stability, thought, pathfinder, teacher, intuition, learning, the shadow.

Discussion/goals: Discussion focuses on the illustration (animal selected, size, color, position on the page, environment surrounding it). Clients become more aware as they relate to the animals drawn and examine their own positive and negative characteristics.

Time capsule

Materials: Drawing paper, markers, oil pastels and crayons.

Procedure: Have clients design a time capsule and draw what they would want to include in it for posterity.

Discussion/goals: Discussion focuses on valuables, sentimental possessions, achievements such as trophies and awards, and objects of importance. Goals include analysis of what is significant to clients, their legacy and their history.

Family portrait[4]

Materials: Cardboard frames, markers, oil pastels, glue, sequins, collage materials, construction paper, scissors, magazines and tissue paper.

Procedure: Provide a cardboard picture frame (8 × 10 or 9 × 12 inches) to each group member. Have clients decorate it using the materials of their choice. Next ask them to glue the frame on top of a sheet of construction paper and fill in the frame (the construction paper) with family members. Clients may draw family members, use a family photograph and/or use magazine pictures to represent family members.

Discussion/goals: Explore whether the design of the frame reflects the client's feelings about his family. For instance, would a plain frame indicate that the family connection is strained? Would a colorful frame symbolize a healthier, brighter relationship? Goals include exploration of family relationships and the family's impact on one's emotional well-being.

Famous artist puzzle

Materials: Outlined copy of a famous work of art,[5] scissors, glue, markers, oil pastels, crayons and drawing paper.

Procedure: Make copies of a famous painting such as "Starry Night" by Vincent Van Gogh. Cut each page into about eight puzzle-like pieces. Distribute these to clients and ask them to put the pieces together to form a completed puzzle. The final step is to fill it the puzzle with color.

Discussion/goals: Discussion focuses on famous artists, especially artists who began working later in life such as Anna Mary Robertson (Grandma Moses) in her 70s, Alfred Wallis, age 70, and Bill Traylor, age 83. Suggest that it is never too late to begin drawing, painting, enjoying crafts or engaging in other hobbies. Ask clients what leisure activities they may try in the future or have enjoyed in the past. Goals include problem solving, focusing and exploring new interests.

"The Scream"

Materials: Drawing paper, watercolor paper, watercolors, brushes, markers, oil pastels, pastels and crayons.

Procedure: Introduce clients to the painting "The Scream" by Edvard Munch. Explore clients' reactions to the painting and examine the symbolism. Ask group members to share what they think the ghost-like figure in the painting is upset about and why he might be screaming. Have clients try to create their own interpretation of the painting in any way they please. Encourage them to list on the back of the picture reasons they also might want to scream. Examples might include anxiety, fear, old age, disabilities, illness, loss.

Discussion/goals: Discussion focuses on the paintings and the clients' unique interpretations. Goals include expression of issues, fears and anxiety.

Abstract photograph

Materials: Magazines, scissors, glue, markers, oil pastels and crayons.

Procedure: Direct clients to find a photograph in one of the magazines that takes up much of a 9 × 12 inch sheet of drawing paper. Next have them cut the photo into strips about one inch wide. Ask clients to glue the strips onto the drawing paper in order to recreate the original photograph, but ask them to leave out every other strip (piece of photograph) so that there are spaces between the strips. The clients will fill in the missing strips (white areas of the paper) in any way they please.

Discussion/goals: Discussion focuses on the photo chosen, its meaning for the client and the way it was completed. Goals include problem solving, creativity and focusing.

Memories on tile

Materials: Pre-drawn sketches of floor tile designs on standard sheets of 8.5 × 11 inch computer paper (or, if desired, clients may create their own tile designs);[6] markers, crayons, oil pastels, pens and pencils.

Procedure: Provide clients with three possible tile designs for a kitchen floor. (Leader makes up these designs, outlines them with black marker, copies them and distributes. The tiles should be large enough to contain small pictures.) Ask clients to fill the "kitchen tiles" with small pictures that reflect things that have occurred in their kitchens over the years. For example, a cake may be drawn in one tile to represent birthday parties, another tile may contain a turkey to represent Thanksgiving celebrations, and another might include family members.

Discussion/goals: Discussion focuses on memories and experiences. Goals include sharing experiences, increased pleasure and increased self-esteem.

A brief summary of the decades of my life

Materials: Drawing paper, pastels, crayons, markers and booklet (see below).

Procedure: Clients are given a stapled booklet (made from 9 × 12 inch paper) that has the decades between 1920 and 2010 printed on top of each individual page. The number of decades included depends on the average ages of the clients. Group members are directed to draw symbols, people, places and things that are representative of their life during each decade.

Discussion/goals: Discussion focuses on important events in one's life. Explorations of experiences, both positive and negative, are examined. Conversation may focus on how to use past strengths and experiences to deal better with present and future challenges. Goals include reinforcement of one's identity, enhancement of self-esteem and realistic assessment of accomplishments.

Emotions mandalas

Materials: Manilla folders, markers, oil pastels, crayons and a coffee can.

Procedure: Instruct clients to outline a circle, using the bottom of the coffee can as a template, on the outside and inside of the folder. Ask group members to fill the outside circle with colors, shapes, figures and/or a design that would represent a specific emotion. Have them represent the opposite emotion on the inside circle.

Examples of opposites:

- happy/sad
- anxious/calm
- irritable/easy-going
- fear/confidence
- brave/cowardly
- hostile/peaceful
- loving/hateful

Discussion/goals: Discussion focuses on the expression of feelings and concerns. Goals include examining methods to effectively communicate emotions and reconcile conflicts.

A variation of these mini mandalas might include "life mandalas." Here clients would fill in the first mandala with colors and shapes that represent their "present life—life as it is now" and the inside mandala would represent "past life—life as it used to be." Here you might discuss differences between past and present lifestyle and environment. Goals would include exploration of the past and present, acceptance and attitude toward change.

Internal/external

Materials: Drawing paper, markers, oil pastels and crayons.

Procedure: Ask clients to fold their paper in half and on the first half of the page draw something internal (e.g. loneliness, boredom, pain) that affects mood and behavior, and on the other side of the page draw something external (e.g. visiting with friends, under- or over-eating, losses, physical disability) that affects mood and behavior.

Discussion/goals: Discussion focuses on identifying and sharing physical, environmental and psychological pleasures, triggers and "red lights." Goals include awareness and examination of the self.

Love (1)

Materials: Drawing paper, markers, oil pastels and crayons.

Procedure: Fill a sheet of paper with 6–8 hearts, make copies and distribute to group members. Ask clients to fill in the hearts with people, places and things they love or have loved in the past. They may use symbols as representations. For instance, a cake may stand for a beloved grandmother who enjoyed baking; a bone or leash might represent a treasured pet.

Discussion/goals: Discussion focuses on significant others, adored family members, pets and friends. Goals include increase of self-esteem, positive mood and awareness of the impact of past and present relationships.

The storm

Materials: Drawing paper, markers, crayons and oil pastels.

Procedure: Have group members close their eyes and imagine they are at a picnic in the forest:

All is well; it is a bright sunny day and you are enjoying the woodsy smell and delicious aroma of hot dogs, hamburgers and steak on the grill. Your stomach is grumbling a little too loudly, so you decide to take a nature walk before lunch. You enjoy observing the exquisite flowers and sniffing in their unique fragrances. The wind picks up a little, but you are too entranced by the daisies and wild flowers to take notice. When your cap falls off because of a strong gust, your heart skips a beat and you decide to turn back towards the picnic grounds. After a few steps the wind blows madly, the rain begins coming down in torrents, lightning and thunder make their presence known, and you think you might see a funnel in the distance. There is no obvious shelter nearby and your friends are half a mile away. What do you do?

Have clients draw what they would do next.

Discussion/goals: Discussion focuses on the clients' choices and reactions to the emergency. Goals include problem solving and examining each individual's resourcefulness. Particular attention may be paid to the client who might give up and wait for help and the client who immediately acts (e.g. quickly finding a low lying area to burrow into until the storm/possible tornado passes).

Wise owl

Materials: Drawing paper, markers, oil pastels and crayons.

Procedure: Provide a photo of an owl to each group member (may be found on Google Images) and instruct them to glue it on their paper. Direct clients to draw a time in their life when they made a wise decision and/or gave clever advice.

Discussion/goals: Discussion focuses on wisdom as a benefit of aging, past successes and achievements. Goals include increased self-esteem and positive thinking.

Tipping tree[7]

Materials: Drawing paper, oil pastels, markers and crayons.

Procedure: Have clients draw a tree that is beginning to tip over. Ask them to add a background.

Discussion/goals: Discussion focuses on the drawing of the tree, its surroundings and the degree to which it is tipped. Goals include exploration of identity, strength and perseverance.

Questions to consider:

1. Does the client relate in any way to the tree?
2. Describe its size, width and height.
3. Are there any distinguishing characteristics?
4. Is the tree alone or grouped with other trees?
5. Is there any type of animal living on or in it?
6. Is the tree stable or in a precarious position?
7. How did the tree get into this position?
8. Is there anything that can be done about its angle?

Age (2)

Materials: Drawing paper, markers, oil pastels and crayons.

Procedure: Discuss the saying "You are only as young as you feel." Next ask clients, "What age do you feel at the moment?" Have them draw something about that age. For example, if they feel 80 years old, they might draw a pair of glasses or a hearing aid; if they feel 17 years old, they might draw a bicycle or ice-skates.

Discussion/goals: Discuss the symbolism and reasons for representing a specific age. Explore how thinking young helps keep seniors young at heart, healthier and more content. Goals include emphasis on the importance of attitude and choice when trying to create a happier and more fulfilling life.

Inheritance

Materials: Drawing paper, markers, oil pastels and crayons.

Procedure: Draw something you'd like to hand down to your children and/or grandchildren. It can be an item, such as a treasured antique or money, or an attribute, such as a good sense of humor, creativity or a lovely singing voice.

Discussion/goals: Explore family relationships, treasures, possessions and gifts. Goals include reflecting on one's legacy, strengths and wisdom.

Dreams and goals

Materials: Drawing paper, markers, oil pastels and crayons.

Procedure: Ask group members to draw their childhood dreams and goals.

Discussion/goals: Have clients share their artwork and discuss the following:

1. Did you accomplish your goals?
2. Were they realistic?
3. What did it take to accomplish them?
4. Is your thinking regarding your dreams and objectives similar or different from your thinking in the past?
5. Have your accomplishments affected your self-esteem?
6. If applicable, has your inability to achieve your goals affected your self-esteem?

Goals include comparing the past and present, self-assessment and self-awareness.

Luck

Materials: Drawing paper, markers, oil pastels and crayons.

Procedure: Have clients draw the break they received and the break they were never given in life. Examples include receiving an inheritance to help start a business, affording college, marrying a healthy, wealthy person; on the other hand, not having the money to attend college, becoming pregnant at an early age and having to quit school.

Discussion/goals: Discussion focuses on the role of luck, hard work and perseverance when assessing one's accomplishments. Discuss how getting the break or not getting it has affected mood, attitude and relationships. Goals include self-assessment and self-awareness.

Danger

Materials: Drawing paper, markers, oil pastels and crayons.

Procedure: Ask clients to draw ways in which they protect themselves from danger. The danger can be concrete, such as fire or theft, or psychological, such as depression or anxiety.

Discussion/goals: Discussion focuses on fears, anxiety and safety concerns. Goals include identification and significance of danger sources and exploration of realistic methods to combat perceived threats.

Barriers

Materials: Drawing paper, markers, oil pastels, crayons, pens and pencils.

Procedure: Ask clients to draw a landscape/scene that includes a series of holes in the ground. Group members will be told the holes are representative of problems, obstacles and setbacks in life.

Discussion/goals: Explore the landscapes and examine the number, diameter and depth of the holes. Have group members relate the holes to the pitfalls they have had to surmount and/or are in the process of working through in their life. Goals include identifying and examining problems and searching for ways to patch or fill in the holes for safety. Coping skills will be explored.

Draw yourself in the future

Materials: Drawing paper, markers, oil pastels and crayons.

Procedure: Ask group members to draw how they think life will be for them in three to five years from now.

Discussion/goals: Discussion focuses on how clients look, feel, who they are with, and what they are doing. Will they be the same or different in the future? Will they be living in the same house or some place else? Will they be satisfied with their life? Goals include self-awareness and exploration of skills needed to accomplish objectives and desires.

Patricia, a single woman in her 70s, suffering from depression and a severe personality disorder, drew herself grinning. She is situated in-between a heart (love to give) and a house (her family home from years gone by). She stated she wants to become "unstuck, to learn to smile and to enjoy life."

She remarked that she hopes to leave the past behind, to have friends and be closer with her family in the future. Her goal is to be able to demonstrate love and adoration for her nieces and nephews. At the moment she has virtually no affect. Her face appears stiff, her mouth looks like a pencil line, and smiling is a burden for her. She says she is unable to move, to feel much of anything. She knows she needs to let go of the past and move on to the future, but this is an insurmountable task for her. Patricia has agreed to take tiny baby steps to try to reach her goals.

A woman named Maria, who had a history of physical and verbal abuse, sketched a series of small symbols to represent her hope for the future. She included figures walking, vacuuming, cooking, shopping, dusting and washing the kitchen floor; she also drew a bucket and a mop. Maria added words and phrases to her design. They included "Be well, enjoying my new surroundings, exercising, having friends and family, learning the computer." This individual was working on increasing her self-esteem and giving herself permission to accept her family's love. Her goal was to be more assertive and fill her own needs as well as the needs of others.

Life (2)[8]

Materials: Drawing paper, markers, oil pastels and crayons.

Procedure: Have clients randomly draw symbols representing various parts of their life—for example, a wedding dress, a diploma, a new baby; whatever comes into their mind. The symbols may be labeled if desired.

Discussion/goals: Discussion focuses on examining both positive and negative aspects of one's life. Goals include stimulating memories, self-exploration and sharing with others.

Feeling shapes

Materials: Drawing paper, markers, oil pastels and crayons.

Procedure: Have clients work in pairs. One person will draw a shape representing a feeling and then his partner will have the option of either drawing a response next to it or writing down the way the "feeling shape" makes him feel. Alternate roles until six feelings (three from each participant) have been expressed. Provide a list, which may include angry, surprised, depressed, joyful, anxious.

Discussion/goals: Discussion focuses on the various ways clients represent their emotions and the reactions to the artwork by both partners. Goals include communication, socialization and self-awareness.

Tiny victories

Materials: Drawing paper, markers, oil pastels and crayons.

Procedure: Have clients fold their paper in fourths and ask them to fill in the squares with small achievements. Examples may include learning how to cook or sew, getting a driver's license or learning new coping techniques to help to reduce anxiety.

Discussion/goals: Encourage clients to share their victories and associated feelings. Discuss the importance of acknowledging good work; emphasize that small successes are significant. Goals include increased self-esteem and a focus on strengths.

Cookie cutter design

Materials: A variety of cookie cutters (plastic is best), markers, pens, pencils and drawing paper.

Procedure: Provide cookie cutters and suggest that group members use them as stencils to create a design that has significance for them. For example, they may use flower cutters to represent a love of nature and gardening, holiday cutters to represent celebrations and customs, or abstract shapes to symbolize certain memories, feelings and/or thoughts.

Discussion/goals: Discussion focuses on the design completed. Encourage "cookie cutter discussions." Explore whose life is "cookie cutter-like" (much like everyone else's, doing what is expected) and who has taken risks in their life. Goals include focusing, structure, introspection and creative expression.

Children (1)

Materials: Drawing paper, markers, oil pastels and markers.

Procedure: Ask clients to fold their paper in half and draw their children, nieces or nephews when they were young on one side of the paper and the way they are now on the other side of the page.

Discussion/goals: Explore past and present relationships. Goals include examination of change, acceptance and coping skills.

Past and present (1)

Materials: Drawing paper, markers and oil pastels.

Procedure: Have clients fold their paper in half. On the furthest left side ask them to draw a symbol of their past, and on the furthest right side ask them to draw a symbol of the present. Examples might include young children to represent the past and a small apartment or solitary figure to represent the present. Next have group members connect the symbols with a line. Encourage them to give thought to the connecting line; this line will represent their life road. Will it be smooth, bumpy or zigzag, for instance? Will it have barriers, rocks, bumps, holes or hills?

Discussion/goals: Discuss the past and present symbols as well as the connecting path. Goals include linking the past with the present and life review.

Love (2)

Materials: Drawing paper, markers, oil pastels and crayons.

Procedure: Ask clients to draw a picture that is filled with things they love—for example, family members, coffee, chocolate, food, books, a summer day.

Discussion/goals: Discussion focuses on the items depicted, their size and significance. Goals include assessing what is important and meaningful in one's life and positive thinking.

Depression

Materials: Drawing paper, markers, crayons and oil pastels.

Procedure: Explore the saying "Depression can be fed." Next ask clients to draw how they "feed" their depression. Examples may include staying isolated, sleeping too much, over- or under-eating, being a victim, not bathing, maintaining a negative attitude, dwelling on the past, not exercising or paying attention to one's physical health.

Discussion/goals: Have clients share the symbols drawn and their associations to them. Goals include self-awareness, taking responsibility for one's health and exploration of coping skills.

Hourglass

Materials: Drawing paper, markers, oil pastels, crayons and magazines.

Procedure: Have clients design an hourglass by drawing one triangle and placing an upside-down triangle on top of it and rounding the center point. Suggest that group members fill the top of the hourglass with words and pictures of things they want to do in the future. Have them fill the bottom of the glass with things they have accomplished/experienced in the past. Photos from magazines may also be used if desired.

Discussion/goals: Discuss experiences, hopes and goals. Explore possible timetables for future events if clients are nearing completion of therapy. Goals include assessment of satisfaction with one's life and sharing of desires and goals.

Age (3)

Materials: Drawing paper, markers, oil pastels and crayons.

Procedure: Ask clients to write one of the numbers representing their age on the paper (the number should be large). For example, if they are 70 years old, they may write a 7 or 0. Next have them create a self-representative design from that number. Ask clients to place the second number that compromises their age somewhere else in the design.

Discussion/goals: Clients share associations to their artwork and will usually relate the design to thoughts about their age. The second number is incorporated into the design so clients aren't threatened. They do not have to reveal their age if they don't want to do so, although they are usually more than willing to share and compare notes. Goals include creative thinking and examination of the effect that age has on one's mood, health, experiences and attitude.

A woman named Hannah created a large figure 8 as the focus of her design. It was bright red, surrounded by yellow fiery lines. She added many colorful swirls and a variety of designs to the picture. The other figure, a 3, was well hidden. Hannah enjoyed this directive and took a leadership role in the group. She showed her peers the picture and had them guess where the

3 was hidden. To her delight, it took quite a while until an elderly man pointed out the number. She was pleased when group members told her they couldn't believe she was 83 years old. Hannah had a positive attitude toward aging, saying she is lucky she has lived so long and thanks God every morning: "When I wake up I say a prayer of thanks." She mentioned that her parents died at a much younger age and she thought she would follow in their footsteps. She had conquered breast cancer, a heart attack and severe arthritis. After Hannah had her turn, most group members chose to play the guessing game and allowed participants to find the missing number. They shared positive and negative aspects associated with aging.

Symptoms (1)

Materials: Drawing paper, markers, oil pastels and crayons.

Procedure: Ask clients to draw their relationship with their symptoms or illness. Suggest they draw a stick figure to represent themselves and an abstract design to represent their illness or symptoms.

Discussion/goals: Support participants to explore:

- the size of the self-representative figure versus the size of the symptom/s
- similarities or differences in color and shape
- distance from the symptoms
- which figure appears stronger—is one overpowering the other?
- is there a love relationship or a hate relationship?
- are the figures touching or overlapping?
- is one figure above or below the other figure?

Goals include exploring clients' connection with their symptoms/illness, how much they have invested in the symptoms/illness and the effect their symptoms/illness have on their life.

Acceptance

Materials: Drawing paper, markers, oil pastels and crayons.

Procedure: Ask group members to draw things they have accepted in their life (e.g. less stamina, moving to a smaller home, certain health conditions, loss of friends and/or family members, perhaps divorce or never marrying).

Discussion/goals: Clients share their losses (an important move toward reconciliation and healing). They share experiences, both good and bad, and examine how they endured when life was difficult. Goals include exploration of acceptance, change and examination of methods to attain health, recovery and future goals.

Going with the flow

Materials: Drawing paper, writing paper, markers, oil pastels, crayons, pens and pencils.

Procedure: Discuss the meaning of the phrase "going with The flow." Generally, it means not to resist what happens naturally, to conform, to move along in a specified manner, to act in accordance or harmony, to travel along.

Next, read this Taoist story:

A Taoist story tells of an old man who accidentally fell into the river rapids leading to a high and dangerous waterfall. Onlookers feared for his life. Miraculously, he came out alive and unharmed downstream at the bottom of the falls. People asked him how he managed to survive. "I accommodated myself to the water, not the water to me. Without thinking, I allowed myself to be shaped by it. Plunging into the swirl, I came out of the swirl. This is how I survived."

Ask clients about their reactions to the story and then have them draw themselves in a swirl of emotion or in a swirl of problems. They may represent themselves and the swirl in any way they please.

Discussion/goals: Clients share their swirl and their connection to it. Questions to ponder include:

1. How enmeshed are they in their emotions/problems?

2. Do they try to fight their feelings and circumstances or do they work through them and accept life's changes?

3. Are they able to view life as a process?

Goals include self-awareness and exploration of coping skills.

An 84-year-old man drew "a mathematical design." Howard stated that he is "working hard to learn how to go with the flow." He remarked that "the artwork began on the left side of the page; the swirly shapes and messy lines are the chaos." Howard stated that gradually the swirls—"the mess"—become smaller and neater, more in control; they become tiny until they form a complete circle—"control." The angled lines, according to Howard, "eventually become smoother, straighter, they dip, even out, get smaller and then exact. Eventually they equal one large straight line—health and wellness." Howard stated this was his ultimate goal. There are two equal signs to show that "chaos will eventually equal stability."

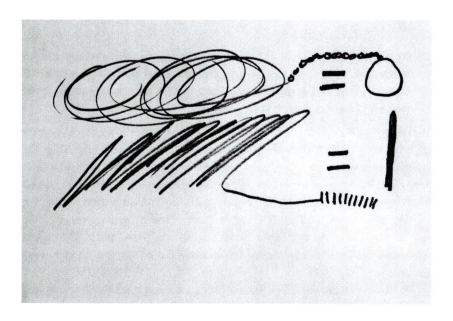

Grief exploration

Materials: Drawing paper, markers, oil pastels and crayons.

Procedure: Ask clients to draw a symbol of grief, a time they felt grief and/or what grief means to them.

Discussion/goals: Discussion focuses on clients' experience/experiences of grief and the way they handle/handled the grieving process. Goals include expression of sorrow, release of distressing feelings and working through unresolved losses.

The golden egg

Materials: Drawing paper, markers, oil pastels and crayons.

Procedure: Discuss the meaning of the golden egg. In yoga practices, it often means being enlightened, the supreme highest self. One's inner voice that is always calm and perfect, and connected to" the true self."

Next ask clients to draw a golden egg or an enlightened figure/symbol of themselves.

Discussion/goals: Clients discuss their associations with the egg and/or figure. Ask them to share the type, size and color of the egg or symbol. Goals include self-awareness and exploration of ways to attain inner peace and knowledge.

This directive was going to be introduced as a brief warm-up, but it became an hour-long project because clients enjoyed drawing and exploring the images and their meanings. Group members became focused and relaxed as they filled in the eggs with color. When the eggs were completed, there was much bantering back and forth. Group members playfully teased each other, making statements such as "My egg is more colorful than your egg", "My egg is brighter", "My egg looks more like an egg than yours." One client told another client her egg looked like a kitsch hat or perhaps an over-done Easter egg.

A woman in her early 70s named Norma drew a bright yellow egg and a stick figure (herself) situated over it. They were approximately the same size. She stated the figure was on top of the egg trying to get warmth and guidance from it. The head of the figure was filled in with black marker—"a sign that the depression is still with me." Norma stated she hoped the egg would eventually help her see the light. She remarked that the figure was as large as the egg because she had been trying to practice her coping skills and was hoping to feel better. Norma remarked that the egg was a bright yellow to represent hope.

A heavyset man in his 80s drew a light brown, misshapen egg. It was very large, taking up most of the paper. He stated, "This is a tarnished egg like me; I used to be gold but now I am brown." He related the egg to his age and his varied disabilities, such as having difficulty walking and needing to use a cane.

A woman in her late 70s drew a large colorful egg filled with wavy lines in the center of two smaller light orange eggs. On first glance, the picture looks like a womb with two ovaries on either side of it. When asked about the drawing, this individual stated she hoped the brighter egg would help

her through her depression. It is noteworthy that her focus is usually on her children and being a mother and grandmother.

A woman named Theresa drew a large golden egg-shaped sun and a small figure situated next to it (upper right-hand side). The sun is clearly pointed at the figure, almost overwhelming it with its size and rays. The artist stated that "the sun is spreading its rays on me, and I am also emitting rays." She remarked that the rays represented health and support. Theresa stated that she felt insignificant compared to the sun because she has such a long way to go in order to get well. She admitted that her self-esteem was very low.

Family

Materials: Figure outlines (see below), markers, oil pastels and crayons.

Procedure: Go to Google Images and search "outlines of people." Find an outline that can be manipulated to about 3–4 inches in height. There is a figure available that looks like a gingerbread man; this outline is well suited to the directive. Copy and paste four of these figure outlines on a page, duplicate the sheets and distribute to clients. Suggest clients fill them in so that they represent family members; ask them to label each figure. They may try to make the figures look more realistic by adding features and clothes or design them as abstractions using colors and shapes. For instance, a jolly family member may be orange and a solemn individual may be filled in with black, brown and other dark colors.

Discussion/goals: Clients introduce family members through their artwork and share notable personality characteristics. They discuss their thoughts and feelings about them. Goals include exploration of close relationships, communication and identification of the impact the relationships have on life, mood and attitude.

Seniors are often reluctant to explore their family relationships. They enjoy bragging about children and grandchildren, but they usually don't want to share much more than this. They have been taught over the years that family matters are private. Having the figures outlined and ready to fill in appears to decrease their guardedness and increase the likelihood that they will engage fully in this exercise and share details of their personal relationships.

Escape

Materials: Drawing paper, markers, oil pastels and crayons.

Procedure: Direct group members to draw themselves escaping from something, someone or someplace.

Discussion/goals: Clients explore fears, denial and barriers to action and recovery. Discussion may focus on ways to accept reality and not allow oneself to become paralyzed by discomfort or fear of the past, present or future. Goals include identification of anxiety and exploration of ways to cope with it. Clients are encouraged to take action by making small transitions so that the prospect of change is not quite so overwhelming. They are supported to develop healthier self-talk and a more positive attitude.

Path to recovery

Materials: Drawing paper, markers, oil pastels and crayons.

Procedure: Have clients draw a representation of what their path to recovery might look like. Suggest they use objects such as mountains, trees, flowers, houses, cars, signs, crossroads, people, bumps, stones and detours.

Discussion/goals: Discussion focuses on the length of the path and what is placed on it. For instance, is the path bumpy, smooth and/or winding? Are there obstacles on the road? Is the path full of flowers and trees or potholes and swamps? Clients explore goals, methods to attain them, assessment of the amount of therapeutic work ahead and attitude toward recovery.

Building blocks of happiness

Materials: Drawing paper, markers, oil pastels and crayons.

Procedure: Direct group members to draw at least four squares, one on top of each other, and fill them in with things they need to achieve happiness in their life. For example, one block may contain a heart and another may contain figures representing children.[9]

Discussion/goals: Clients share their wishes and needs. They identify what they want and explore ways to attain what is required for a full, satisfying life. Goals include positive thinking and a focus on goals.

Notes

1. Modified from a suggestion by Maggie Russian, LPN.
2. Mandala is Sanskrit for circle. At Princeton House it is used in art therapy as a way to focus and heal. Clients fill in the circle in various ways, usually starting from the inside out.
3. Information from Wikipedia.
4. Modified from a suggestion by Tracylynn Navarro, MA, ATR-BC.
5. Adult coloring books with works of famous artists can be found in Barnes and Noble and other bookstores.
6. Other sites also have tile patterns to copy.
7. Modified from *The House-Tree-Person Techniques* by J.N. Buck (1978), Los Angeles, CA: Western Psychological Services.
8. Modified from a suggestion by Lois Smith.
9. Another variation of this exercise might be to provide blocks, which group members cut out, glue on the paper and fill in with the positive symbols.

CHAPTER 4

SELF-ESTEEM

Self-esteem affects all areas of life. It has a huge impact on confidence, motivation, attitude, personality and overall happiness. Self-esteem determines our goals, self-worth, behavior and satisfaction with friends and family. Positive self-esteem promotes openness, honesty, cooperation, independence, creativity and flexibility. Negative self-esteem can cause physical and psychological illness, apathy, narrow-mindedness and a negative attitude. It can keep a client powerless and in a victim role.

While learning how to increase self-worth, individuals come to understand the significance of accepting themselves unconditionally and appreciating their strengths and achievements. They discover how to focus on their skills and positive characteristics. Individuals realize that helping others and choosing how they view themselves is vital. They examine positive affirmations and statements. Eleanor Roosevelt once said, "No one can make you feel inferior without your consent," and "Life has got to be lived—that's all there is to it. At 70 I would say the advantage is that you take life more calmly. You know that this, too, shall pass!"

Clients begin to understand the role self-talk plays in their self-esteem. For instance, they can label themselves smart and creative or slow and ignorant; it is up to them. People can focus on mistakes and guilt or forgive themselves and move forward. Clients come to realize that they are not their illnesses; depression or bipolar disorder, for instance, is just one part of their persona. They are individuals with many aspects to them. For example, someone may be a teacher, wife, mother, grandmother, volunteer, cook and seamstress. Clients become aware that, as children, they might have felt powerless, but, as adults, they have control. Individuals discover that they are in charge of their self-esteem. They have the power to increase or decrease it, and live happier, more fulfilling lives.

Strengths

Materials: Writing paper, drawing paper, markers, oil pastels and crayons.

Procedure: Ask clients to list at least three strengths. Next have them choose one of the strengths and draw a symbol, design or picture representing that attribute. For example, if the client is intelligent, he might draw a brain or diploma to represent intelligence. If he is loving, he might draw a heart or a cupid.

Discussion/goals: Discussion focuses on the clients' strengths and associations with them. Goals include increase of self-esteem and identification of positive qualities.

Shared attributes

Materials: Pens, pencils, markers, writing paper, glue, scissors, index cards and construction paper.

Procedure: The leader will give each client an index card with the name of one of the group members. Clients will be asked to write a positive quality about that person on the card. Next, clients will give the card back to the person whose name is on it. Clients will now glue their card on a sheet of construction paper and then draw and/or find a magazine picture to represent their special quality.

Discussion/goals: Discussion focuses on the attributes chosen for each individual, the client's reaction to his attribute and the picture/drawing that depicts it. Goals include connecting with others and identifying positive characteristics.

Memorable moment

Materials: Drawing paper, markers, oil pastels, crayons and pencils.

Procedure: Ask clients to draw one of their most memorable moments. Suggest they write a title and/or caption for their picture.

Discussion/goals: Discussion focuses on the significance of the sketch and the client's associations with it. Goals include sharing momentous life events as a way to focus on joyful and positive aspects of one's life.

Penelope, a woman in her 60s who never married, drew a large, bright-pink boat. She described the wonderful time she had many years ago on a Bermuda cruise. She shared her most joyful experience, which was when she met the man of her dreams on the cruise. Penelope stated they dated for 12 days. Unfortunately, they lived far away from each other and eventually they stopped writing letters and "he faded away." Penelope stated, with a sigh, that that was the closest she ever came to getting married. She wondered aloud if she should have been more aggressive and continued writing or calling. Penelope remarked that she has always been passive and that may be why "I am lonely now."

A man in his 70s drew a representation of his college graduation. He included a stage filled with students and many people sitting in chairs on the grass watching the graduation. He placed a heavy outline around his wife and himself. This individual mentioned that he went to college at night for six years while he worked full-time during the day and also took care of his wife and children. He remarked that it was a grueling schedule but well worth it when he attained his goal and graduated. He stated he felt a huge sense of achievement.

A widow named Margaret drew the house she and her husband spent much time fixing up many years ago. It was drawn with much detail and included a wrap-around porch, brightly colored shutters and yellow shades decorating the windows. A light circle of smoke is seen floating out of the chimney. There are two detailed doors and a variety of colorful flowers surrounding the house. A swing set and two children playing on it are situated in the front yard. A personalized doghouse and three trees are included. Margaret stated the house was originally an old barn that they completely renovated. She described the process of tearing parts of it down and putting up a new roof, walls, a staircase, etc. She stated she loved that house and felt safe and comfortable there for over 40 years.

Positive word design

Materials: Drawing paper, markers, crayons, pencils and pens.

Procedure: Ask clients to create a free-form design using positive words such as bright, cheerful, smart, relaxed, optimistic, winner. Next ask them either to circle the words that best describe their qualities or to write a list of them next to the design.

Discussion/goals: Discussion focuses on the uniqueness of the design created and the words utilized. Goals include identification of positive traits and broadening awareness of skills and attributes.

Remembrance

Materials: Drawing paper, markers, oil pastels and crayons.

Procedure: Ask clients to draw one or more images representing the answer to the question "What do you want to be remembered for?"

Discussion/goals: Discussion focuses on achievements and positive characteristics. Goals include increasing self-esteem and self-assessment.

Inner beauty

Materials: Drawing paper, markers and oil pastels.

Procedure: Suggest that clients draw their "inner beauty." Ask them: "What would it look like? What colors, shapes, lines would compose it?" Next ask them to write a few words to describe the images.

Discussion/goals: As individuals age, their outer beauty often fades but their inner beauty remains. It is important for clients to acknowledge their inner beauty in order to raise self-esteem and to help them focus on their special qualities and what is really important in life.

Hugs

Materials: Writing paper, pens and pencils.

Procedure: Ask clients to give imaginary hugs to each other by saying, "I hug you because..." and completing the statement. Have each individual share until everyone receives a hug. After all group members are hugged, have clients write down or draw their reactions to being hugged or to giving a hug.

Discussion/goals: Discussion focuses on giving and receiving support. Goals include increasing self-esteem and gaining a greater awareness of strengths and positive characteristics.

This project works particularly well when a group member is very upset. In such a case, each client supports the one individual as he receives all of the group's love and comfort. In a recent therapy session, a male patient felt unloved, undeserving and "less than a man." He was tearful and extremely depressed. The support from his fellow group members helped him feel less isolated and he felt needed; he felt part of the community. Although he wasn't at the stage in his recovery where he actually believed all of the compliments he received, he was able to find some comfort in the warmth and friendship bestowed upon him. It helped him open up and share some of his issues, which include being abused as a child and discounted by his mother; "You are worthless," she had said as she spat on him. This was an example of the verbal abuse he shared with the group members. At the end of the session, he walked out of the room with his peers surrounding him and guiding him. They were able symbolically to replace the affection he didn't receive from his own parents. Although temporary, the support probably helped him avoid an inpatient hospital stay.

Strength/affirmation tree

Materials: Distribute an outline of a bare tree (with a variety of branches and large leaves on it) to each group member, together with oil pastels, crayons, markers and colored pencils.

Procedure: Have clients decorate the tree and fill in the leaves with positive thoughts and statements.

Discussion/goals: Explore the range of decorative effects and strengths written on the leaves. Goals include awareness of coping skills, positive self-talk, increased self-esteem and acknowledgement of achievements.

A woman named Maureen designed a very large old oak tree, which she related to herself. She stated that, "it has been around for a very long time and has been able to remain intact through many storms over the years." She added a fair number of leaves to represent her attributes, some of which included "strength, perseverance, helpful, good mother, good cook and healthy eater." Maureen felt that the tree was stronger when her husband was alive, but her children and grandchildren keep it "from toppling over."

Wanda, a petite woman in her early 80s, created a small, fragile-looking tree with very few leaves. She remarked that the tree appears weak and can fall at any time. When asked, she related the tree to herself, saying she is very depressed and doesn't think she'll be able to feel well again. She had a very difficult time thinking of attributes; group members had to assist her. Wanda welcomed their help although she was reluctant to acknowledge the supportive statements, which included "helpful, sweet, kind, and thoughtful." Group members gave Wanda suggestions about her tree (herself) and how to make it stronger. They were able to connect the importance of watering and nurturing the tree to the importance of nurturing oneself in order to thrive.

A client named Marc designed a large flowing tree with many colorful leaves. He stated the tree is flourishing and growing upwards. He related the tree to his progress in therapy and to his positive attitude. Marc stated he was particularly proud because he is structuring his time, especially on the weekends, and socializing as much as he did before his depression.

A client named Myrtle drew a bright, colorful tree filled with affirmations. The leaves are plentiful and pointing upwards. Myrtle includes grass and flowers next to the tree. A light-blue sky fills the background. She stated that she feels encouraged when she looks at the tree. She added many affirmations on the leaves, which include "I accept me, one day at a time, I am strong, and I will try to live in the moment." Myrtle remarked that she plans to tape it to her refrigerator so she can remember to be positive.

Music and cheer

Materials: A variety of cheerful songs on CD, CD player, pens, pencils, writing and drawing paper, markers, crayons and oil pastels.

Procedure: Play a number of upbeat songs for clients and have them list all the positive words and phrases they hear as they listen. Then ask them to illustrate at least two of the words or phrases.

Discussion/goals: Discussion focuses on the melodies, lyrics and associated drawings. Goals include increased self-esteem and a focus on being positive and optimistic. Examples of songs include: "What a wonderful world" (Louis Armstrong), "Don't worry, be happy" (Bobby McFerrin), "Here comes the sun" (The Beatles), "Top of the world" (The Carpenters), "I got rhythm" (Gershwin and Gershwin) and "Happy days are here again" (Milton Ager and Jack Yellen).

Word list pass and mandala

Materials: Pencils, pens, drawing paper, paper plates, markers, oil pastels, crayons and colored pencils.

Procedure: Ask clients to sign their name at the bottom of their sheet of paper. In this way they know which paper they began working on first. Instruct them to write a positive word or brief phrase on the paper and then ask them to pass their paper to the person sitting to their right (wait a few minutes before asking them to pass their paper so they have time to reflect). Now everyone has a second sheet of paper and they write another positive word on this sheet of paper, and then again they pass the paper to the person on their right. This keeps happening until everyone has written a positive word on everyone else's paper and the clients receive their original sheet back (they will know it is theirs because they will see their name written on the bottom of the page). Each client should now have a sheet filled with positive words and statements. Next have them outline a circle from a paper plate on a sheet of drawing paper in order to create a mandala. Suggest they create a design within the mandala that reflects feelings associated with the positive words. For example, a mandala that focuses on words such as "cheerful," "friendly" and "fun" might be filled with colorful shapes, movement, wavy designs or smiling faces, suns and flowers.

Discussion/goals: Discussion focuses on the word lists and the composition of the mandala. Goals include being positive and exploration of attitude, mood and perspectives on life.

This project may need two sessions if there is a time constraint or if clients/leaders feel there are too many steps to follow.

Recipe for self-care

Materials: Recipe card outline, pencils, markers, oil pastels and crayons.

Procedure: Provide a recipe card "Self-care" to be filled in by group members (type the outline on a sheet of computer paper, make copies for each group member, and distribute). Example:

A Recipe for Self-care

3 tbs. of ....

2 tsps. of ....

½ cup of ....

3 pinches of ....

1 dash of ....

1 oz. of ....

Mix all of the ingredients and apply as needed. Take one day at a time.

Discussion/goals: Discuss the recipes and "the ingredients." Explore the ease or difficulty of the instructions and whether or not clients are following their recipes. Goals include exploration of coping techniques and objectives.

Attributes

Materials: Envelopes, pens, pencils, writing paper, markers, oil pastels and colored pencils.

Procedure: Provide each client with an envelope and several small slips of paper. Each group member writes his name on the envelope, decorates it and then writes an attribute about the person sitting next to him. The attribute is then placed in the envelope. The process is repeated as the envelopes are passed around the room from one individual to another. The exercise is over when everyone has written a comment for everyone else in the group. When the envelopes are full, they are given to the leader who selects one of the envelopes and chooses a comment to read. The person about whom the comment was written will try to guess the name of the person who wrote it. At the end of the exercise each person may keep his envelope as a reminder of his positive qualities.

Discussion/goals: Goals include increased self-esteem and confidence. Questions to ponder include:

1. How do you feel after hearing the supportive statements?
2. When was the last time you received a compliment (before today)?
3. What is the benefit of hearing and giving support?
4. Were you able to accept the support?
5. What will you do with your envelope?

Being positive

Materials: Writing paper, drawing paper, pencils, colored pencils, markers, oil pastels and crayons.

Procedure: Help clients to create a list of positive images such as flowers, rainbows, a sun, sunsets, babies, smiling people, families, vacation spots, nature. Next suggest clients choose one or more of the images and illustrate them.

Discussion/goals: Explore the positive imagery and the feelings elicited. Goals focus on the benefits of having an optimistic attitude. Benefits of being positive include:

- increased life span (some studies show an increase of approximately seven years)
- lower rates of depression

- better mood and outlook
- lower stress levels
- greater resistance to certain illnesses (especially colds)
- reduced risk of death from cardiovascular disease
- better coping skills
- better performance at work and play
- more successful relationships
- broader perspective on life.

Affirmation magnets

Materials: Drawing paper, colored pencils, pencils, markers or permanent markers if available, magnet backing, magnetic write-on/wipe-off strips or magnetic circles.[1]

Procedure: Review various affirmations and distribute a list to clients. Suggest they choose an affirmation that appeals to them. Have clients write the affirmation on the drawing paper and create a design next to or surrounding it. Ask them to repeat the same sketch on the magnet. It is helpful to experiment first on the drawing paper since it is difficult to change words/illustrations once a marker is used on the magnetic surface. Suggest that the magnet be placed on their refrigerator or other surface that can be viewed daily.

Sample affirmations:

- Loving myself heals my life. I nourish my mind, body and soul.
- My body heals quickly and easily.
- I know that I deserve love and accept it now.
- I attract only healthy relationships.
- I am my own unique self—special, creative and wonderful.
- I am at peace.
- I pay attention to everything around me and I am careful and deliberate with each of my movements. I am graceful and mindful.
- All things happen for a purpose. My past experiences also had purpose. I have learned from my past and am now free from it. I choose to release the past and live in the now.

- I accept and love myself.
- This too shall pass.

Discussion/goals: Discuss the affirmation list and the chosen affirmations. Review the positive impact that the words and phrases can have on one's mood and attitude. Goals include increased self-esteem and awareness of the power of self-processing and self-talk.

Support in a box

Materials: Tissue or cigar box, or white cigar-shaped box,[2] glue, scissors, construction paper, magazines, tissue paper, a variety of collage materials such as buttons and sequins, small strips of paper, pens and pencils.

Procedure: Clients decorate the box using magazines photos, positive words, colorful shapes and other collage materials. Next they cut out 5–10 small strips of white paper (or leader distributes the strips already cut out). Have clients write positive statements and affirmations on each slip of paper and place the slips in their boxes. Suggest they keep their boxes at home and read the affirmations when they feel anxious and/or depressed.

Discussion/goals: Discussion focuses on the box designs and the positive statements placed in them. Goals include self-acceptance and exploration of coping techniques to self-soothe.

Self-esteem maze

Materials: Give a maze to each client.[3] Clients may design their own maze if they prefer. Provide markers, pens and pencils.

Procedure: Ask clients to write affirmations, positive words and statements in their maze. Next suggest they draw a line demonstrating the way out of the maze. Have them place a small figure or shape somewhere in or out of the maze to represent where they are in terms of their self-esteem. For example, are they about to leave the maze (higher self-esteem), in the middle of it (moderate self-esteem) or just entering the maze or lost in it (low self-esteem)?

Discussion/goals: Discussion focuses on the design of the maze, the words and affirmations that comprise it and the placement of the figure (the client) in the maze. Goals include exploration of self-esteem and positive thinking.

The apex

Materials: Drawing paper, markers, oil pastels, crayons, pens and pencils.

Procedure: Ask clients to draw a mountain and place themselves on top of it. Then ask them to write about a time they reached a goal and/or "felt on top of the world."

Discussion/goals: Discussion focuses on achievements and high points in one's life. Goals include increased self-esteem and review of strengths and accomplishments.

Self-esteem warm-up

Materials: Writing paper, pens and pencils.

Procedure: Ask clients to write as many positive things about themselves as they can in five minutes.

Discussion/goals: Discussion focuses on sharing positive attributes. Goals include increased self-awareness and acknowledgement of strengths.

Self-esteem circle

Materials: Pre-drawn circle with 6–12 petal-like projections emanating from it (shapes should be large enough to include one sentence), markers, pens and pencils.

Procedure: Direct clients to write something positive about themselves in the center of the design. In the other areas, have them list accomplishments (even minor ones).

Discussion/goals: Clients share accomplishments, awards and achievements. Goals include increased self-esteem and acknowledgement of positive work and experiences.

Awareness

Materials: Writing paper, pens and pencils.

Procedure: Direct clients to fill in answers to the following statements and then share with group members.

- I remember . . . .
- I realized . . . .

- I have learned . . . .
- I am pleased to think of . . . .
- I was surprised when . . . .
- I would like to remember that . . . .
- I understand that . . . .
- The thing I treasure most is . . . .
- I am good at . . . .
- I am special because . . . .
- I would like to share . . . .
- I need to remember that . . . .
- A lesson I learned was . . . .
- My wishes came true when . . . .
- As I grow older I feel . . . .
- When I was younger I felt . . . .
- The best time in my life was . . . .
- I was embarrassed when . . . .
- I felt proud when . . . .

Discussion/goals: Discussion focuses on the sharing of wisdom and experiences. Goals include increased self-esteem, socialization and recollection of specific events and strengths.

Self-esteem exploration

Materials: Writing paper, pens and pencils, drawing paper and markers.

Procedure: Have clients read the statements below and rate their response to each statement on a scale of 1–10 (10 is the highest and 1 is the lowest). Next ask them to draw a symbol of their self-esteem using shape and color. For example, someone with positive self-esteem might draw a large bright shape, while someone with poor self-esteem might draw a small dark form.

- I like myself. . . . .
- People seem to like me. . . . .
- I have talents. . . . .

- I am a good and worthwhile person. . . . .
- I will do well in the future. . . . .
- I feel well today. . . . .
- I feel comfortable at social events. . . . .
- I like to be with friends. . . . .
- I am good to myself. . . . .
- I have hobbies. . . . .
- I find time for fun in my life. . . . .
- I laugh at least once a day. . . . .
- I compliment myself. . . . .
- I forgive myself when I make a mistake. . . . .
- I eat in a healthy manner. . . . .
- I visit the doctor and dentist regularly. . . . .
- I exercise. . . . .
- I treat myself as I treat others. . . . .
- I seek help when I need it. . . . .
- I don't have to be validated by others. . . . .
- I am allowing myself to learn new things and have new experiences. . . . .
- I try to accept change. . . . .
- I can accept support from others. . . . .
- I can acknowledge my accomplishments. . . . .
- I can say no. . . . .
- It is OK if I am not perfect. . . . .
- I love myself "just because I am me." . . . .

Discussion/goals: Discussion focuses on the questionnaire and the significance of the self-esteem drawings. Goals include self-awareness, identification of areas that need to be worked on and exploration of methods to increase self-esteem.

Communication skills (1)

Materials: Writing paper, drawing paper, pens, pencils, markers, oil pastels and crayons.

Procedure: Suggest to group members: "Share a time that your words healed someone else. What did you say? How did it feel to be supportive?" Next ask clients to list at least five words that may be used to encourage others and then draw a picture, write a poem or write a description symbolizing the feeling/s gained from helping another person to feel better.

Discussion/goals: Clients share their positive experiences and strengths. They discuss what it feels like to be the helper in a relationship. The importance of one's words, actions and attitude is explored. Goals include increased self-worth, assessing positive qualities and exploring new goals and volunteer opportunities. Clients are often awakened to the possibilities of helping others; they begin to see how they can be a powerful force in others' lives.

A woman named Josephine wrote, "When I try to help another, it encourages more openness and a feeling of bonding over the event being shared. I recently helped a neighbor who had trouble reading a letter from a relative in California. Her English is not strong, so I translated. She was so pleased and thankful. She baked me a pie and brought it to my house. I felt so good and the pie was delicious."

A 71-year-old woman named Noreen shared, "My friend was sick and needed to go to the hospital, so I took her. It felt so good to be able to help her. I told her not to worry, that I would be there for her." Noreen drew a large smiling face to represent her feelings about the experience. She titled the picture "Happy."

Rose, a 74-year-old woman, described what she says to her grandson: "You are my pride and joy. I support whatever courses you decide to take in college. I know you will do well. I am always here for you if you need me."

A woman named Doris decided to create a cinquain[4] instead of writing a description:

Healing
Feel happiness,
Good thoughts,
Pleasant, joyful, lovely,
Spectacular, amazing,
Helper.

Courage

Materials: Magazines, drawing paper, markers, pens, glue and scissors.

Procedure: Direct clients to find pictures of people they think appear courageous. Have them write down the reason/s they appear brave. Next ask clients to list ways in which they are or have been courageous in the past.

Discussion/goals: Group members share positive traits and strengths. Goals include acknowledgement of power and increased self-esteem.

Cartooning for self-esteem

Materials: Drawing paper, pens, pencils and markers.

Procedure: Provide a sheet of paper (8.5 × 11 inch) and draw a frame around it (freehand or using a computer program). Ask clients to draw a cartoon of someone (or themselves) doing something very brave. Have them describe the cartoon and then share instances in which they were courageous.

Discussion/goals: Clients share the cartoons and then describe instances in which they behaved in a heroic manner. Emphasize that bravery comes in all forms (making life changes, dealing with illness, going to the hospital, asking for help, assisting another person, etc.). Explore ways in which being brave relates to self-esteem. Goals include increased self-worth and focus on strengths and achievements.

Honor

Materials: Drawing paper, markers, oil pastels, paper plates, pen and pencils.

Procedure: Have clients complete the following sentence: "I honor myself because..." Next ask them to draw a symbol that would demonstrate how they might show admiration for themselves and/or why they deserve a tribute (e.g. being a good parent, a good friend, intelligent, a college graduate, good cook). A circle might be used to help clients structure their work if desired. They can trace it from a paper plate and place their symbol inside it. Examples of possible symbols: an award, a trophy, star, jewelry, heart, smiling face, flowers, a banner, a medal, applause (hands clapping).

Discussion/goals: Clients share their representations and achievements. Goals include increased self-esteem and identification of strengths.

Happiness (1)[5]

Materials: Writing paper, drawing paper, pens, pencils and markers.

Procedure: Ask clients to write a list of things that make them happy. Compare the lists among group members; look for similarities and differences. Next ask clients to draw a time (recently or in the past) they felt joyful. Discuss the drawing, focusing on specific people, circumstances and/or environment. Discuss methods of attaining the happiness that was represented in the drawings. Examine each group member's present level of happiness. Ask clients to score their happiness on a 1–10 scale where 10 is feeling the most happy and 1 is the least happy. Suggest the group members compose a list of ways to increase joy. Some examples are:

- finding fulfilling hobbies
- volunteering
- joining a group or club (to make friends)
- accepting yourself for who you are
- being kind to yourself
- *carpe diem* (living for the day, being mindful, taking time to smell the roses).

Discussion/goals: Discussion will focus on what happiness means to each individual and various methods to attain contentment in life will be explored.

Tower of strengths (1)

Materials: Drawing paper, markers, oil pastel, pens, pencils and crayons.

Procedure: Suggest that clients create a tower to represent their strengths, achievements and attributes. Encourage them to think about the size, width, color and strength of the tower. When it is completed, ask them to list their strengths and achievements next to it.

Discussion/goals: Clients examine the relationship between the tower and their feelings of self-worth. Goals include identifying attitudes, self-talk and positive attributes.

Examples of strengths include: friendly, smart, loyal, polite, funny, good-natured, good parent, good grandparent, wonderful cook, sincere, organized, artistic, creative, energetic, relaxed, patient, curious, persistent, willing to take healthy risks, honest, trustworthy.

Tower of strengths (2): Self-esteem

Materials: Drawing paper (12 × 18 inch), glue, scissors, pens, pencils, markers, magazines, pre-drawn squares (2 × 2 inch) printed on 8 × 10 inch paper (ready to cut out).

Procedure: Clients cut out a minimum of four of the boxes and glue them on the large sheet of paper in order to create a tower. They may place one box on top of the other or create their own unique design (one client chose a zigzag pattern). Next ask them to fill in the squares with symbols, colors, shapes, magazine photos, positive words and affirmations that help increase self-esteem.

Discussion/goals: Participants share their attributes (e.g. good cook, good wife, peacemaker), specific items/people (e.g. money, nice house, children, family) and feelings (e.g. love, joy, purpose) needed to achieve happiness. Goals include self-awareness and a focus on positive aspects of one's life.

Clients enjoy this directive because it is clear and structured. It allows them to "build" their self-esteem by identifying what they need to feel better about themselves and their life. Individuals gain insight by exploring the size, strength and number of items needed to complete the tower.

A woman named Annette included words and symbols representing love, family, children and pets in her tower. Another client added flowers, the sun, her grandchildren and music notes. Other symbols included books, a sewing kit, an oven, trees, butterflies, birds, a happy face with "smile" written next to it, hearts, a cross, an artist's palette and phrases such as "Today is the most important day of your life" and "Love yourself first, then love others." A client named Erwin included a symbol for each of his family members in the squares. Those symbols included hearts, small animals, an angel and an apple. He discussed how his family's love and support increase his self-esteem and always bring a smile to his face.

Self-esteem bucket

Materials: Markers, oil pastels, pens, pencils and an outline of a bucket that fills a sheet of paper (8.5 × 11 inch).

Procedure: The leader provides each client with an outline of a bucket. The bucket may be hand-drawn or downloaded from Google Images. Clients are asked to decorate the bucket and fill it in with color. Inform group members that the amount of color they use to fill it will represent their degree of self-esteem.

Discussion/goals: Clients will observe if their bucket is full, half full, moderately full or empty. They will relate this presentation to their feelings of self-worth. Questions to ask include:

1. Are there holes in the bucket? If so, how many? What could the holes mean in terms of self-esteem?

2. Were there fewer holes in the past?

3. Is there a way to patch the holes?

The holes will relate to loss of self-esteem. Goals include identifying reasons for poor self-esteem and exploration of ways to increase it.

A 70-year-old client named Irving filled his bucket with abstract shapes and bright colors. He remarked his bucket is full and "has no holes, but not so long ago it was almost empty." Irving remarked that he had suffered a severe depression and thought it would be impossible to get well. All he wanted to do was sleep, and that was what he did for two weeks. His wife finally convinced him to get help. With therapy and the proper antidepressants, he is now joking and "feeling like my old self."

A client named Ron filled his bucket with layers of color. He titled the bucket drawing "Layers of Feelings." Richard included seven layers ranging from dark to light, black representing the bottom layer and yellow the top layer. He labeled the individual layers:

Depressed with very low self-esteem.

Sad and lonely, unsure.

A bit calmer, self-esteem better.

Occasional happiness.

Brighter days, better self-esteem.

Feeling better more often and more confident.

Much more confident.

Ron remarked that his work in therapy has been difficult; he still has holes in his bucket, but far fewer holes than in the past. He stated he knows he could revert back to the lowest black layer if he doesn't watch himself carefully and keep busy.

A 74-year-old woman named Sandra drew a very colorful bucket with a variety of attractive patterns and a large pink focal point. She stated, when asked, that she is the pink focal point. She remarked she is feeling much happier, brighter and more alert. She stated that she feels she has more control of her moods, feelings and life. Sandra declared she is once again enjoying reading, art, doing crossword puzzles and crocheting. "When I see my grandchildren, I can feel the happiness I missed feeling while I was depressed." She titled the bucket "My Bucket of Joy."

Positive traits

Materials: Drawing paper, markers and colored pencils.

Procedure: Instruct group members to write a positive characteristic about themselves using each letter of the alphabet (they have the option of skipping a few difficult letters such as X and Z). The letters may be pre-written so clients will find the directive easier to follow. When this is completed, ask clients to create an illustration using the letter that represents their most outstanding quality. They may decorate the letter and in addition represent the quality they described. For example, if the letter C stood for creativity, a design might include a colorfully decorated C and a palette drawn next to it. If the letter H stood for humorous, the person may draw the letter H using lots of colors and add a picture of a smiling face next to it.

Discussion/goals: Clients share strengths and talents. They identify abilities and focus on positive attributes.

Support (1)

Materials: Drawing and writing paper, pens, pencils, markers.

Procedure: Have clients share ways in which they gain support from their family members and other people in their environment. Suggest they divide into pairs and discuss their support systems with each other. Next have each client draw someone or something they believe would provide support for their partner.

Discussion/goals: Discussion focuses on methods of asking for help, attaining needs, and awareness of people and places that may provide assistance when needed.

Notes

1. Magnets can be purchased from www.MagnetValley.com.
2. Boxes may be purchased from S&S Worldwide at www.ssww.com.
3. Draw one maze and distribute, or make copies from Google Images or elsewhere on the internet.
4. Cinquain (created by Doris) is a type of poetry:
   One word or two syllables—subject name
   two words or four syllables—description
   three words or six syllables—action
   four words or eight syllables—description
   one word or two syllables—summation.
5. This directive may be broken up into two or three sessions.

CHAPTER 5
STRESS REDUCTION

Stress-reduction techniques help clients to relax, reduce anxiety, lessen the degree and frequency of anxiety attacks and learn how to be mindful. Clients learn skills to cope with illness, fear, frustration and relationship problems. They discover the importance of positive thinking, self-processing and self-talk. Clients become skilled in identifying and changing erroneous thinking such as catastrophizing, over-generalizing and labeling. They learn methods to stop worrying such as thought stopping, positive self-talk and identifying realistic and unrealistic fears. They practice meditation techniques such as deep breathing and guided imagery. Meditation helps individuals find a sense of calm, inner peace and balance. Some research shows that meditation techniques may improve immune system functioning, allergies, asthma, cancer, depression, fatigue, heart disease, sleep problems and high blood pressure. Clients are taught the importance of being mindful. Mindfulness increases self-esteem, self-awareness and self-acceptance. It improves concentration and creativity. When clients are in the "here and now," they have more physical stamina; they are more confident and their moods are more even; they have better ability to concentrate and memory improves.

Clients become increasingly aware of harmful roles they may take on, such as being a victim or scapegoat in the family. They identify negative relationships and life patterns, and try to change and/or improve them. Individuals learn coping techniques such as choosing one's battles and focusing on the positive aspects of their life instead of the negative. They discover how to be patient by taking one day at time, taking tiny steps forward and not allowing themselves to be overwhelmed by adversity. Clients learn how to identify and avoid anxiety triggers. They focus on support systems and asking for help when needed. Individuals come to understand the importance that attitude and motivation play in reducing stress, and they learn self-soothing techniques such as taking long walks, celebrating achievements and exercising. Clients learn to take care of themselves physically and psychologically and to focus on their strengths and attributes.

Relax and express

Materials: The CD *A Moment's Peace* by Tracy Carreon[1] and a CD player; drawing paper, markers and pastels.

Procedure: Tell patients to close their eyes (if they are comfortable doing so), relax and listen mindfully to track 7 on *A Moment's Peace*, "Garden of the Soul." Encourage clients to focus on all aspects of the music while they listen. Then ask them to draw what they felt and/or imagined while they listened to the CD.

Discussion/goals: Discussion focuses on the connection between the artwork created and the music. Goals include increased relaxation, exploration of stress-reduction techniques and feelings associated with being tranquil.

Attitudes

Materials: Drawing paper, writing paper, pencils, pens, markers, crayons and oil pastels.

Procedure: Explore what "attitude" is (approach, outlook, feelings) and examine various attitudes with group members—for example, being positive or negative, feeling guilty or refusing to feel at fault, staying angry or forgiving, being supportive of oneself or self-deprecating. Next suggest that clients fold a piece of drawing paper in half. On one side of the paper ask them to use line, shape and color to symbolize a positive outlook, and on the other side of the page have them represent a negative outlook. Next suggest they write a line or two about the design that best describes their current view regarding their recovery.

Discussion/goals: Discussion focuses on how the artwork and descriptions represent the clients' attitudes toward getting well. Goals include becoming aware of self-defeating as well as healthy thought patterns and learning to transform negative beliefs into positive ones. Encourage clients to notice that a brighter attitude will decrease stress and better enable them to feel stronger, more adaptable to various situations and more content with life.

Support (2)

Materials: Writing paper, pencils and pens.

Procedure: Have clients share occasions when they supported various people in their life. Ask them how they felt and how they think the other person/s felt at the time. Discuss the fact that roles may change as we age; we are allowed to ask for help. We do not always have to be the caregivers. Suggest clients speak about ways in which they need support now (e.g. help doing laundry, lifting heavy items, car rides, assistance with grocery shopping, cooking). Next ask participants to divide their paper in half and write ways they could gain support from others on one side of the paper and ways they could feel positive about taking the support on the other side of the paper.

Examples might include:

- *Support*—arranging not to be alone, asking children to visit more often

- *To feel positive*—bake them a cake, tell them how much you admire them

- *Support*—going to a support group or senior center

- *To feel positive*—give support and feedback to others, bring cookies or other treats

- *Support*—moving to an independent living community where life is made simpler

- *To feel positive*—create new friendships, share interests with others, take up a new hobby

- *Support*—asking friends and/or neighbors to drive you to the supermarket or help carry your bags into your house

- *To feel positive*—make them a cup of tea, help them if possible when they are in need, be there to listen to them when they need advice or desire to vent feelings.

Discussion/goals: Discussion focuses on the conflict between being the *helper* and *helpee*. Goals include acceptance, increasing self-esteem and focusing on ways to get needs met in a healthy manner.

Stress in a box

Materials: Small index cards, pens, pencils, markers, coffee can or shoe box.

Procedure: Group members are asked to write and/or draw one aspect of their life that is causing them anxiety and to place it in the box. The box is passed around the room and each client reads and/or describes one of the comments/questions written/drawn on the index card. If it is a sketch, it is shown to group members. Clients work together to think of solutions to each issue.

Discussion/goals: Discussion focuses on the problems and possible solutions. Goals include problem solving, stress reduction and increase of coping skills.

Drumming for good health and inspiration[2]

Materials: Frame drum and hand or drumstick. If possible, each group member would receive a drum or drumstick, or the group leader alone may do the drumming.

Procedure: Clients and/or leader begin to drum with a solid beat, mimicking a heartbeat while the leader shares the following inspirational meditation.

Begin by entering into a private space, which you can define as "sacred space." Try to be near a window facing nature or be outdoors, weather permitting. Allow yourself to feel your feet fully immersed in the earth; barefoot is best, but, even with shoes on, imagine your feet rooted in the earth. Spread your toes. Feel the roots in the soles of your feet reaching deep down into the earth, confirming your belonging. Say to yourself, "I am here," affirming your physicality in this world. Imagine yourself, like a tree, with a firm trunk, rooted with stability and security.

Bring your breath and your awareness up into your belly. Practice deep abdominal breathing while you listen to the simple beat of the drum, allowing the drumbeat to carry you further away. Try to have your inhale equal the same number of beats as you exhale—for example, if you are breathing in to the count of three, then breathe out to the count of three. You may find yourself feeling slightly dizzy or lightheaded. If so, try to move through the impasse, allowing yourself to experience something different. Simply notice your busy thoughts—as the Yoga tradition calls it, "the Monkey Mind." Your mind initially will be very active and perhaps distracting. Simply notice this busyness of mind, bringing your focus back to the drum. The drumbeat will always bring you back to your quiet space inside.

Your body may want to spin slightly with an ease of movement, expressing a sort of "untwirling." This movement allows your body to "unravel," releasing any excess stressors, unwanted obsessive thoughts or unnecessary anxieties and fears. Imagine releasing these undesirable emotions as weights that can be given to the earth. Imagine the sun or lightning breaking up the tightness or tension. You are moving more deeply into the layers of your own imagination and visualization. In this sacred place, you are free to let go and surrender to a different kind of knowing and a different sort of experience. In the Shamanic tradition, this is known as "non-ordinary experience." It is a state of being that moves beyond cognition as we typically experience it. Allow yourself to move into openness, supporting yourself in having a new experience and trusting that someone greater than yourself—call it spirit, higher power, the great mystery, etc.—is with you in this enlivening of spirit. You are opening to the possibility of renewal. It is very important in this place to open to *intention* for your experience. Perhaps you are seeking peace. Perhaps you need comfort. Perhaps you have a very specific question that you are seeking some type of "answer" to. Perhaps you are simply seeking to feel love more deeply. Find your intention with clarity and stay focused on this intention. As you are connecting yourself to deepen into this intentionality of spiritual practice, stay connected to this image of yourself as a tree. Moving up into the area of your heart, imagine a bright golden sun or a full white glorious moon shining down upon you. Imagine this light penetrating your being, coming through your crown of head, into forehead, through throat and into heart area. Feel the pulsating of color through your body, and keep drumming, allowing for cleansing, shedding, releasing, relaxing, opening, transcending, and, finally, expanding into something greater.

As you feel yourself opening and relaxing, you may find yourself feeling expanded and more trusting. Pay attention to what you see and what words you hear. You may be visited by certain animals with gentle, supportive messages of ancient teachers, eager to offer you healing and support. It is very important that you remember your earlier defined intention and listen with "new ears" and see with "new eyes" in order to receive new information.

While this is happening, your drumbeat is consistent. Sometimes perhaps louder and other times softer, but always hearing clear the beat of the heart.

You will know when to stop. You will experience a sense of clarity. You will feel more whole. Perhaps more relaxed, more inspired, etc. At this point, it is okay to stop drumming and simply receive the fruits of fullness. You will feel full. Abundant. Peace. Trust…an experience of ecstasy, bliss and love is often felt.

Be sure to offer gratitude to spirit or nature (or whoever it is you offer thanks to) to remember that you recognize the gift of this experience. Remember that you can return to this ritual daily. The more often you practice this, the more comfortable you will become with this ritual. This place can be a sort of sanctuary and sacred place where you return daily to recharge, refuel, renew and elevate your downtrodden spirit.

Discussion/goals: Drumming for inspiration draws from the Shamanic tradition and earth-based spiritualities that seek to enliven the spirit and create a transcendent experience, offering a different perspective on the human journey.

Thought stopping

Materials: Drawing paper, scissors, glue, markers, oil pastels, pens and pencils.

Procedure: Discuss how thought stopping can help decrease stress and improve the quality of one's life. Clients will be asked to say "Stop" to themselves, quietly or out loud, and immediately change what they are thinking and change their activity in order to effectively stop irrational and/or troubling thoughts.

Ask group members to write out the word "Stop" using large colorful letters. Next have them cut the word out and place it next to them. Then suggest they draw or write a troubling and/or recurring thought on a sheet of drawing paper. Next ask clients to share their drawings and/or descriptions, and then have them glue the word "Stop" on top of the picture.

Discussion/goals: Discussion focuses on the obsessive thoughts and the way it felt to physically place the word "Stop" on top of them (symbolically gaining control). Goals include identifying uncomfortable feelings/thought, gaining mastery over obsessions and exploring coping skills.

A man named Joe glued the word "Stop" next to the figure he drew of himself. He stated that the "Stop" is large because he needs to stop feeling

sorry for himself and his "depression needs to stop." He included a smile on his face to represent his motivation to change.

A woman in her late 70s named Judith drew a mandala-like design filled with color and a variety of wavy, coiled, sharp and twisted lines. She stated it was a representation of her "chaotic brain." This client remarked that she wasn't thinking clearly and "this is how my mind looks." Judith placed a much smaller "Stop" near the brain because she didn't want the "Stop" to overlap it. She stated she didn't want to cover the brain because she was not ready to focus on her issues. Judith believed she needed a medication change and more support in therapy before she could feel "like my old self."

A widow in her late 70s named Lydia drew her smiling orange cat and a very large "Stop" pasted under it. She stated that the cat is smiling because "it refuses to be potty trained" and does what it wants to in her daughter's house. She complained that the cat is ruining her daughter's rugs and furniture. The "Stop" is massive because Lydia needs her cat to behave appropriately or her daughter "will get rid of it." The group members empathized with her and helped her think of ways to better train her cat so she could keep it. "Petunia the cat" was Lydia's "love" and helped her cope with loneliness and depression. It reminded her of her deceased husband who also adored it and helped care for it.

A woman named Evelyn drew a sad face with dollar signs surrounding it. She glued a large "Stop" on top of the bills to represent her need to be frugal. She remarked she is having financial problems, which are contributing to her depression. Group members suggested ways to save in the grocery store and in the department stores. They shared their own financial concerns, which gave Evelyn some comfort. Evelyn was able to joke after a while, saying, "But I love to shop and buy clothes."

Erroneous thinking

Materials: Drawing paper, writing paper, pens, pencils, markers, oil pastels and crayons.

Procedure: Discuss the following thinking errors and then ask clients to choose one error and write or draw about a time they used that coping skill to their disadvantage. On the bottom of the page ask the client to write or illustrate how they could have handled the situation in a healthier manner.

Thinking errors:

- *All or nothing thinking*—when someone sees things as black or white. There is no half way. If someone received an 80 percent on a test, he would see himself as a failure because it wasn't 100 percent.

- *Over-generalization*—an individual sees one negative event as precedent for all things to follow. For example, making an error during a presentation means that person thinks he will never be able to give "a good" presentation again.

- *Magnification (catastrophizing)*—exaggerating the importance of something (positive or negative). For example, a person accidentally spills his coffee during a meeting and he ruminates that his boss will think "he's a loser, and he won't promote him, maybe even fire him; everyone will be talking about him all day at work."

- *Jumping to conclusions*—when someone makes a negative conclusion, even though there are no definite facts to support it. For example, a person feels a small a lump on his neck and he immediately decides it is cancer.

- *Should statements*—individuals try to motivate themselves by using the words "should" and "shouldn't." The results are expectations that may be too high. Guilt, anger and frustration are often the result.

- *Personalization*—the individual sees himself as the responsible party for a negative event, even though this most likely is not true. For instance, Jane is at a party and Jill abruptly leaves. Jane blames herself, but there are many reasons that Jill might have left. Jane probably had nothing to do with it.

- *Labeling*—this happens when a person gives himself a negative label such as "idiot" instead of examining his mistake. For instance, if Jack is late for a date with Sarah and she leaves the movie theater before he arrives, he labels himself an "idiot" instead of processing that she left because he was not on time, not because of a specific character deficit.

Discussion/goals: Coping skills and healthier ways to process are explored. Goals include self-awareness and identification of erroneous thinking.

The sun

Materials: Drawing paper, markers, pastels, oil pastels and crayons.

Procedure: Ask clients to close their eyes and imagine that a large bright sun is emitting its rays down on them. Ask them to think about the warmth and feel of the rays. Suggest that the rays are penetrating all body parts: their head, face, neck, shoulders, back, arms, stomach, legs, feet and toes. Ask group members to feel the healing warmth and soothing comfort the sun provides. Next suggest clients draw the sensation of healing, their body as it becomes healthier and/or the sun emitting its rays.

Discussion/goals: Examine the verbal and creative responses to the imagery. Discuss how positive thinking and "warm" feelings affect the body and mind. Explore ways clients can nurture themselves. Goals include increased involvement of the client with regard to self-soothing, stress reduction and recovery.

Relaxation through touch

Materials: Textures that are soothing and gentle (fur, feathers, silk, creams, lotions, smooth stones).

Procedure: Have clients take turns feeling the various textures and describing their reactions to the experience. Next ask them to write about a time that a soothing touch reduced their stress and/or increased their sense of well-being. Examples might include touching a baby's skin, getting a massage, petting a dog.

Discussion/goals: Discussion focuses on the tactile experience and descriptions of previous experiences involving contact with people, pets and things. Goals include becoming aware of the effect that touch has on emotional and physical health and wellness.

Worry

Materials: Writing paper, pens and pencils.

Procedure: Discuss the meaning of the word "worry" with clients. Ask group members their thoughts and then share the following description:

Worry consists of future-oriented, often catastrophic thinking largely consisting of words rather than images. It affects how one behaves, thinks, feels and relates to others. It can be productive or non-productive. Productive worry leads to direct action to solve a problem or reduce a future threat. Non-productive worry paralyzes you and inhibits problems solving. People tend to worry about a variety of themes including finances, health, family, safety and relationships.

Have clients list five things they worry about. Next to the worries ask them to rate the level of stress associated with the worry on a 1–10 scale where 10 is the most stressful and 1 is the least stressful.

Next ask them to ponder and then share:

1. Is your worry productive?
2. Is the problem solvable?
3. Is the worry motivating you to take action?
4. Are you generating potential solutions?
5. Are you acting on those solutions?
6. What would be the pros and cons of mastering your worry?
7. List one worry that you can begin to control right now.

Discussion/goals: Clients explore realistic and unrealistic fears and how they affect their feelings, mood, behavior and actions. Goals include identifying concerns and then trying to adapt coping skills to help control worrying.

Self-soothing

Materials: Drawing paper, markers, oil pastels, crayons, pastels, pens and pencils.

Procedure: Begin the session by discussing the value of being independent, treating oneself in a positive manner and comforting oneself. Suggest that clients do not have to wait for others to make them joyful and fulfill their needs; they can do this on their own. For example, they can buy their own cake on their birthday or take themselves out to dinner or to a movie. Next ask clients to draw three hearts. Ask them to fill in each heart with things they do to comfort themselves.

Discussion/goals: Discussion focuses on the size and color of the hearts and the coping skills included. Goals include raising awareness of the importance of self-care and self-nurturance.

Mindfulness

Materials: Drawing paper, markers and colored pencils.

Procedure: Ask clients to divide their paper into six boxes or provide a sheet already divided. On top of each box write one of the following statements:

Box 1: Focus on your breathing.

Box 2: Focus on nature (beauty, fragrance).

Box 3: Listen carefully to others.

Box 4: Enjoy a warm shower or bath (become aware of sensations).

Box 5: Focus on your food (texture, smell, taste).

Box 6: Love yourself unconditionally (accept yourself for who you are).

Next suggest individuals illustrate each statement using colors, shapes and/or figures.

Discussion/goals: Discussion focuses on the mindfulness suggestions and the associated images. Suggest clients share other ideas and techniques that allow them to focus and be present. Share the importance of mindfulness as a way to decrease stress, lower blood pressure, "be in the moment," maintain a more positive attitude and enjoy life.

Clients were able to fully engage in this creative experience although they needed a few minutes to fully understand the concept. Examples of illustrations included a drawing of a pizza to represent "Focus on food." The client remarked that if she focused hard enough, she could actually smell the aroma of the pizza fresh out of the oven. Many clients drew their home shower to represent "Enjoy a warm bath or shower" and mentioned how lovely and soothing the warm water feels on their backs. Flowers and trees were often drawn to represent nature. Clients were able to share thoughts about the fresh smell of newly cut grass and the beautiful fragrances of various flowers. Most individuals drew themselves to represent "Love yourself unconditionally." They shared the importance of self-acceptance and the difficulty they have with it. Group members appeared to enjoy illustrating their breathing by using wavy lines and simple shapes. One woman drew a mouth with air blowing out of it. A brief breathing exercise that related to the drawings proved beneficial to clients and ended the session in a positive manner.

Sleep life

Materials: Drawing paper, markers, oil pastels and crayons.

Procedure: Suggest that clients create a design that represents their sleep life. For example, if they sleep well, they may want to use shapes and colors that are gentle and soothing; if they sleep poorly, a more chaotic design might be representative.

Discussion/goals: Discussion focuses on the way in which the drawings represent one's sleep patterns. Explore the importance of sleep:

- improved memory
- better mood
- less depression
- increased healing
- more energy
- longer lifespan
- healthier heart
- healthier diet/less calorie intake

- strengthened immune system
- more alert—fewer accidents of all types
- reduced stress.

Goals include exploring methods to improve sleep and focusing on the role sleep plays in reducing depression, anxiety and stress.

Stress relief kit

Materials: Drawing paper, markers, oil pastels and crayons; outline of a large suitcase or old fashioned doctor-type bag (leader can provide the outline by finding an image on Google Images or drawing it).

Procedure: Provide an outline to each group member. Suggest they are going to create a stress relief kit. Ask them to draw items needed to fill it (compare it to the medical emergency kits sold that include bandages, antiseptic, etc.). Examples might include a relaxation CD, warm milk, a tea bag, photo of grandchildren, mashed potatoes, soft pillow.

Discussion/goals: Discussion focuses on the items included in the kit and the way in which the client will utilize the items. Goals include exploration of methods to reduce stress and self-soothe.

A patient named Ida included her dog, flowers and music in her kit. She stated her dog is her friend and helps her cope during difficult times. Ida mentioned that she feels almost immediately relaxed and comforted when her dog sits by her side as she watches television. "Knowing there is someone in the house makes me feel more secure." Ida remarked that she tells her dog her sorrows and confides in him every day. "He won't judge me or say I should not think a certain way."

A woman named Jane added a cup of tea, a friend, a potato, a book, cheesecake and her cat to her bag. She remarked that her cat was the most important component of the bag. He was her companion and she stated she loved him very much. Jane's cat gave her a purpose to get up in the morning, something to take care of, hold, adore and spoil. The cat often slept with her, "warming my toes in the winter."

Weed garden

Materials: Drawing paper, construction paper, markers, oil pastels, crayons, scissors and masking tape.

Procedure: Instruct clients to draw a series of weeds and inside each weed write a negative thought. Have them cut out the weeds from the drawing paper, and, using masking tape, have them tape the weeds to the construction paper. Suggest clients create a garden of weeds. As the discussion begins, ask clients to begin pulling the weeds (negative thoughts) they want to eliminate out of their garden.

Discussion/goals: Discussion focuses on the type of garden, the number of weeds and the specific weeds pulled. Questions to ponder might include:

1. How long ago were the weeds planted?
2. Who planted them?
3. How did they grow?
4. How strong are the weeds?
5. How many weeds are there?
6. How will you get rid of the weeds?
7. How do the weeds affect your life?
8. What will replace the weeds?

Goals include self-awareness and examination of methods to stop negative thought patterns.

Komboloi (worry beads)

Materials: An assortment of beads, string and tassels.

Procedure: Briefly introduce the history of the Komboloi beads and how they are used.[3] The Greek Komboloi usually have an odd number of beads on the string such as 17, 19 or 23 (prime numbers). The length is often two palm widths. Have clients choose 17 beads and create what will look like a long bracelet. Connect the beads with a tassel and knot the end. If clients are able, they may use knots to divide the beads at regular intervals. Leave extra string on both sides of the Komboloi so that the beads will dangle. Connect the tassel by using one bead to connect it to both sides (eight beads on one side of the string and nine beads on the other side). Suggest clients utilize the beads when anxious by manipulating them, tassel end pointing downwards.

Discussion/goals: Discuss how the chain of beads gives clients a focus so they could stop worrying. It is a way to concentrate nervous energy on the worry beads and not on the actual worries. Support individuals to flip the beads back and forth. Manipulating and playing with them is considered to be calming and therapeutic.

Worry stones[4]

Materials: Non-toxic clay, Sculpey (can be bought in most art supply stores or purchased online), polymer clay (this clay is not powdery or dusty and remains workable until baked; it can be baked in a home oven), index cards, plastic knife and a tray.

Procedure: Have group members choose three different colors and cut small pieces of clay for them (three marble-sized pieces) or have clay ready beforehand. Ask clients to squish the colors together and twist the clay a few times. Have them create a sphere and place it on the index card. Ask clients to choose a thumb and press it down into the clay until the bottom is flattened. Ask them to etch their initials gently into the bottom of the clay and place the clay back on the index card. Clients can take the clay home and bake it themselves or the leader can bake the pieces and distribute back to clients.

Discussion/goals: Discussion focuses on the stones' healing qualities and the importance of keeping a positive outlook. Self-soothing, calming techniques are explored. Having a tangible object that can be used for healing is very therapeutic.

Mindfulness exercise

Materials: Paper, pastels, crayons and markers.

Procedure: Ask patients to close their eyes and relax, and listen to the sounds around them (birds chirping, sounds from the heater or air conditioner, wind blowing, etc.). Ask them to focus on the sounds and let all other thoughts float away. After a few minutes, suggest that they draw what they experienced. They may use color and shape or objects and figures to represent their thoughts and feelings.

Discussion/goals: Discussion focuses on the importance of becoming mindful in one's life. The importance of taking time to stop and smell the roses and not dwelling on the past or worrying about the future may be explored. Goals include stress reduction and relaxation.

Inner peace collage

Materials: Construction paper, scissors, glue, collage materials such as magazines, pom-poms, feathers, sequins, a variety of textiles and glitter; CD of tranquil music and CD player.

Procedure: Ask clients to take a few deep breaths and then close their eyes and listen to tranquil music for a few minutes. Suggest they relax their body and try to free their mind from all other thoughts. Next have them create a collage representative of the peace they felt while they were listening to the music.

Discussion/goals: Discussion focuses on the peaceful thoughts and feelings and the symbolism represented in the collage. Goals include self-awareness, mindfulness, relaxation, self-soothing and stress reduction.

Mindful drawing

Materials: Drawing paper, markers, oil pastels, watercolors, crayons and watercolor crayons; CD of soothing music and CD player.

Procedure: Encourage group members to listen to the music and relax. Ask them to take a few deep, cleansing breaths. Direct them to use markers, pastels, crayons and/or watercolors to create illustrations that relate to one or more of the following themes:

- a day at the beach
- floating on a cloud
- a walk in the park
- relaxing at home
- swimming in a lake or pool
- walking in moist, cool sand
- sitting in the grass, feeling the warm sun shine on you
- watching snowflakes gently fall to the earth
- watching a baby sleep peacefully
- flowers swaying in the breeze
- a waterfall in the rainforest
- a sunset or sunrise
- a tropical island

- relaxing on a sailboat
- sitting in a comfortable chair by a fireplace
- reclining in a float or in a pool
- a rainbow after a summer shower.

Suggest they feel free to experiment with shape, line and color. Have them think about the flow of the lines and the feelings elicited by the calming scenes.

Discussion/goals: Encourage group members to share their associations to the illustrations and explore peaceful sensations. Emphasize the importance of having a variety of relaxing imagery to utilize when anxiety becomes problematic. Goals include relaxation, focusing and being mindful.

A woman in her late 60s drew her mother and herself walking on the beach, the waves and ocean in the background. She thanked the writer for leading the group, saying, "I haven't thought about this memory in years; it was so nice to remember."

Bright side

Materials: Drawing paper, markers, oil pastels and crayons.

Procedure: Ask clients to fold their paper in half. On the first half of the paper have them draw a design or scene using very bright colors. On the other half ask them to write down at least five positive statements about life and/or themselves. Examples may include:

- I am worthy.
- I have a wonderful family.
- I derive joy from watching a baby smile.
- I am strong.
- I am feeling better every day.

Discussion/goals: Discussion focuses on the importance of having an optimistic attitude and the positive aspects of one's life. Goals include increased self-esteem and life satisfaction.

Peaceful mind

Materials: Drawing paper, markers, oil pastels, crayons and pastels.

Procedure: Instruct clients to write the word "Peace" in a way that symbolizes its meaning: tranquility and serenity. Suggest they think of serene colors and shapes to add to the word design. When the exercise is completed, ask them to try to find their "peace" by listening to the following brief meditation.

> Sit in a comfortable position. Close your eyes and breathe deeply in a slow and relaxed manner. Pay attention to your breathing. Block out all other thoughts and sensations. Keep your attention on your breathing. As you inhale, say the word "Peace" to yourself, and as you exhale, say the word "Calm."

Continue this exercise for a few minutes. Have clients describe their artwork and the peaceful feelings derived from the relaxation exercise. Finally, ask them to work together to create a list of stress-reducing activities. This directive might take up to two sessions depending on the length of the sessions and the abilities of group members.

Discussion/goals: Goals include exploration of relaxing activities and introduction to mindfulness and other methods to reduce stress.

The senses

Materials: Drawing paper, markers, oil pastels and crayons.

Procedure: Suggest that group members would benefit from becoming more cognizant of their surroundings. Ask them to take two deep cleansing breaths and then have them close their eyes for a minute or two. Direct clients to focus on any sounds they may hear. Next ask them to open their eyes and look carefully around the room. Instruct them to observe texture, shape, design and color. Instruct clients to draw or write their answers to the following:

1. List the colors you see.
2. List the sounds you hear.
3. List any scents you smell.
4. What is the temperature like in the room?
5. List at least three items you see.

6. Describe how your clothes feel against your skin.

7. How is your body feeling (e.g. headache, arthritis, stomach rumblings)?

Discussion/goals: Clients explore their surroundings in order to become mindful, decrease anxiety, clear their mind and learn to focus. Goals include stress reduction and self-awareness.

Fear (1)

Materials: Drawing paper, markers, oil pastels and crayons.

Procedure: Ask clients to draw their interpretation of fear. They might draw fear as an abstract concept using line, shape and color or draw a time in their life they felt afraid of someone or something.

Discussion/goals: Discussion focuses on various fears and the hold fear has on us. Have clients examine the size and shape of the fear. Ask them if it looks like something that can be managed or if it appears overwhelming and/or paralyzing. Discuss rational versus irrational fears. Goals include identifying and analyzing fears and exploring coping techniques.

This directive can be divided into two parts. During the second session, clients may choose to draw methods to minimize, manage and/or defeat their fears. Suggest they draw themselves battling or confronting their fear in some way.

Spiritual wellness

Materials: Writing paper, pens and pencils.

Procedure: Have group members share what spirituality means to them. Discuss how spirituality can go beyond religion to nature, art, the universe, strong beliefs and/or the belief in a higher power. Next have clients write brief answers to the following questions and then ask them to share their responses:

1. What customs do you follow (e.g. holiday customs or daily rituals such as drinking coffee every morning, reading before bed, etc.)?

2. What is your inner talk (what you say to yourself when undecided and in times of stress)?

3. How do you relax?

4. How do you find inner peace?

5. Do you have any special affirmations, mantras or prayers that help you cope?

6. Describe a few relaxation techniques that you find useful?

7. What things are you grateful for in your life?

8. What do you find beautiful in nature?

9. How do you stimulate your mind?

10. What is your purpose?

11. Whom or what do you love?

12. Do you believe in a higher power? Explain.

Discussion/goals: Clients share their ideas about spirituality and examine how spiritual beliefs can positively affect their lives. Group members focus on coping skills and examine what is meaningful to them.

"Good stress"

Materials: Writing paper, pens and pencils.

Procedure: Discuss "good stress" versus "bad stress." Examples of bad stress would include a loss, death, disability, operation, an unwanted move, losing a job. Good stress might include getting married, moving to a new home, graduating from high school and starting college, attending a child's wedding. Next ask clients to choose from the "good stress" list below or create their own list and draw a time they experienced "good stress."[5]

- moving to a new home
- wedding
- graduation
- beginning a new job
- taking a vacation
- retiring
- falling in love
- buying a new puppy
- getting a promotion at work

- learning to drive
- learning a new sport
- first date
- taking dancing lessons for the first time
- having a baby
- child leaving home to live on his own as a successful adult.

Discussion/goals: Clients share significant life events and reactions to the events. Goals include identifying behaviors, thoughts and feelings associated with "good stress" and examining coping skills.

Relaxation shaker

Materials: Clean baby food jars, water, mineral oil, glitter, assorted small shells, ribbon, waterproof glue such as Gorilla Glue[6] or glue gun.

Procedure: Have clients glue a few shells to the lids of the jars. Then ask them to fill the jars with about one tablespoon of glitter. Next, participants add water and a drop of mineral oil, leaving about a quarter of an inch of space at the top. Finally, direct clients to glue the rim of the jar and then place the lid on top and tighten. They may tie a ribbon around the lid for decoration if so desired.

Discussion/goals: Discussion focuses on the construction and specific use of the shaker. Explore how clients feel when they observe the glitter gently falling to the bottom of the jar after being shaken lightly. Goals include mindfulness and the creation of an attractive object to use as a focal point for relaxation and meditation.

Mindfulness: Nature study

Materials: Drawing paper, pens, pencils, markers, oil pastels and crayons.

Procedure: This directive needs to take place in a room with a window or outside, preferably in a park-like or woody setting. Have clients discuss the importance of being mindful and then ask them to take turns looking out a window, or, if outdoors, have them observe their surroundings. Direct each participant to study the trees, plants, etc. and focus on small details, relaying what they see—for example, a tree with a brown/beige bark, some of which is peeling from the bottom, small gray bumps lining the thick tree trunk, leaves composed of a yellowish green color that are swaying in the breeze. Next have group members draw part or all of what they have observed. They may draw just the bumps on the tree, the colorful leaves or the entire tree. The idea is to get a feel for things that compose the object and make it something unique.

Discussion/goals: Discussion focuses on the meditative experience, observations and the artwork. Goals include being in the here and now, increased awareness, focusing and relaxation.

Tabletop Zen garden

Materials: A tray, sand, assorted small rocks, a small rake, paint, markers, collage materials and glue.[7]

The tray can be a wooden, metal, plastic or ceramic item and not a tray at all. It could be a bowl. The sand should be clean, sterilized sand (white sand preferred) which can be purchased at a craft or hobby store.

The rocks could be polished stones, or even gems from custom jewelers. In addition to or instead of rocks, you could also use petrified wood, shells or sand dollars. The rake need only be a raking instrument such as a small fork or comb or other pronged instrument.

Procedure: Show a photograph of a Zen garden to clients and describe some of its benefits.

A Zen garden is a creative tool to calm anxiety, quiet the mind and relax an individual to relieve stress and be open to more creative and joyful thoughts. It can be meditative as well. It can simply slow one's mind down enough to focus on one thought at a time or cause one to explore a thought outside of a traditional line of thought, or 'outside the box'. A traditional Zen garden implements all natural elements, but this isn't absolutely necessary.

Distribute a tray to each group member and tell clients they may use paint, markers and/or collage materials to decorate the tray in any way they please. Then have participants place the sand in the tray and manipulate the sand and rocks and rake. They can write in the sand or just create patterns in lines or swirls. It is very easy to erase what has been done, start over and make a new design. Using a plastic container or tray with a closing lid is a great way to put it aside for storage until it is pulled out again to use.

Discussion/goals: Goals include stress reduction and pleasure through mindful manipulation.

Comfort collage

Materials: Drawing paper, magazines, markers, scissors and glue.

Procedure: Provide group members with a sheet of drawing paper that has a picture of a rocking chair in the middle of the page.[8] Briefly discuss the comforting feeling one may experience by rocking gently. Next ask clients to select additional photos of people, places and things that are conducive to feeling comfortable and relaxed. Examples include someone napping, relaxing in an easy chair, floating in a pool, petting a dog.

Discussion/goals: Explore methods to relieve stress and feel physically soothed. Goals include self-care and focusing on mindfulness.

Stress warning signs

Materials: Drawing paper, markers, oil pastels, crayons, pens and pencils.

Procedure: Instruct clients to create a sign that says "Warning: Stress." Next to the sign ask them to write various warning signs signaling that their stress level is rising. Examples provided may include difficulty breathing, indigestion, sleep difficulties, tension, headaches, stomach aches, restlessness, poor concentration, shaking, body aches/pains, excessive hunger, no appetite, panicky feelings, crying, emptiness, easily upset, feeling powerless to change things, forgetfulness, constant worry, loss of sense of humor, sweaty palms/hands, back pain, racing heart, light-headedness, tiredness, dizziness, excessive use of alcohol or other drugs, grinding teeth at night, nervousness, anger, sadness, boredom, trouble focusing, memory loss, feeling trapped and negative thinking.

Discussion/goals: Share with clients that, by identifying early warning signs of stress, they can be treated before a full-blown depression or anxiety attack ensues and recovery becomes more difficult. Self-help measures can often lessen and/or control the symptoms. Understanding warning signs allows individuals to get immediate help and decrease their discomfort. It helps give people control over their emotions and body. For instance, if a person is driving and feels panicky, he can say to himself, "This is just an anxiety attack; I must feel anxious. I can control it; nothing bad will happen to me." The awareness and positive self-talk will often help the person cope (practice is necessary to master the skill). If this individual continues to feel panicky, he can visit his doctor and discuss the issue. Knowing the warning signs proves most helpful.

The ocean: A relaxation exercise

Materials: Drawing paper, markers, oil pastels, pastels and crayons.

Procedure: Have clients share reasons they like to go to the seashore. Then ask them to draw their interpretation of the seashore including items or things that make them feel relaxed. Suggest to clients that this is a stress-reducing exercise; they may want to visualize themselves relaxing on the sand, on the boardwalk or in the water while they draw. They may use pastels to spread the color gently and represent the feeling of the seashore. Soothing background music may be played as an additional stress reducer.

Discussion/goals: Discussion focuses on the feelings elicited while drawing and the symbolism portrayed. Goals include stress reduction, focusing on positive imagery and self-soothing.

Clients usually create a list of reasons they like to visit the ocean. In recent groups, clients created the following list:

Tranquil, waves, freedom, cool water, sand, birds, the sound of the sea, seagulls, watching dolphins in Cape May, watching boats go by, salty fresh air, hypnotizing waves, especially at night, soft sand, 'reminds me of childhood,' warm, squishy mud, people smiling, watching children playing in the sand.

A widow in her 70s named Tania drew a beach scene. She remarked that in the sketch she is playing in the sand and is completely carefree. "The waves are gently washing ashore and I am watching people swimming and the birds in the sky. It is a sunny day and I feel the sun on my face." She related the picture to previous family vacations at the beach. Tania stated she remembered watching the boats going by and the brightly colored umbrellas: "There were so many umbrellas everywhere you looked." Tania remarked she wished her life now were "as carefree as it was in those days." When asked how she could attain a similar level of peace and happiness, she had to think for a few minutes. Tania then remarked that a friend invited her to Cape May, New Jersey, but she has felt too anxious to visit. She stated she hoped she might be able to visit within the next two months, but realistically she didn't think she'd be well enough for such a large step. Although Tania tried to draw a serene scene, her anxiety appears to emerge as depicted in the wavy sand lines, ambiguous expressions on the stick figures and choppy-looking water.

Relaxing at home

Materials: Pen and paper.

Procedure: Create a list of activities that can be done at home to ease stress. This can be created by the group leader and/or with the clients. The leader makes a copy of this list and distributes it to clients. Group members check off the items that appeal to them. Next, clients are asked to draw the activity that they find most helpful, and present it (temporarily) to the person sitting next to them. Have that person discuss how the activity could help him relax, and how he feels about receiving it.

Discussion/goals: Clients share ways to relax at home. Goals include sharing and exploration of coping skills. Examples include:

- taking a warm shower or bath
- watching television
- listening to the radio
- listening to a guided imagery CD
- doing a puzzle
- engaging in a hobby
- reading
- exercising
- working on a craft
- drawing
- baking
- journaling
- scrapbooking
- playing a computer game
- meditating/being mindful
- knitting/needlepoint
- sitting on one's front porch, terrace or deck, or peering out a window and people-watching.

Combating anxiety

Materials: Drawing paper, markers, oil pastels and crayons.

Procedure: Ask clients to examine the following list of ways to combat anxiety and create a collage of photos that represent items on the list—for example, a photo of someone in a yoga pose, someone mediating, a smiling person (being positive) or someone exercising or painting.

Methods of relaxation include:

- deep breathing
- guided imagery
- exercise (walking)
- journaling
- getting enough sleep
- eating in a healthy manner (including fruit and vegetables)
- having a positive outlook
- taking one day at a time
- taking tiny steps forward
- self-processing (self-talk)
- realizing things are probably temporary (just for now)
- trying aromatherapy or acupuncture
- finding support systems
- avoiding caffeine
- practicing yoga
- meditation
- focusing on the here and now (being mindful)
- if possible, avoiding people and/or situations that cause stress
- attending therapy
- having a pet
- taking medications as prescribed
- listening to music
- engaging in drawing, painting, needlework and crafts.

Discussion/goals: Clients explore a variety of ways to reduce stress so that they have a repertoire at their fingertips. Goals include self-soothing and identification of self-help measures.

Anxiety figure

Materials: Provide an outline of a figure that fills an 8.5 × 11 inch sheet of paper. The figure may be hand-drawn or taken from Google Images. Clients will need markers, colored pencils and oil pastels.

Procedure: Explore the feelings associated with anxiety (fluttering heart, dizziness, headache, stomach ache, headache, sweating, racing heart, nausea, etc.). Next provide the outlines and have clients fill them in with colors and shapes that represent their anxious feelings.

Discussion/goals: Clients explore the colors and shapes that compose the figure. Have them point out the parts of the body that are most stressed. By doing this they are better able to identify and understand their stress and associated symptoms and work on coping techniques such as being mindful and deep breathing.

Phases of anxiety

Materials: Drawing paper, markers and colored pencils.

Procedure: Instruct clients to draw three clouds with an arrow pointing from one cloud to another. Suggest that group members fill in the clouds with colors and/or symbols that represent the stages of their anxiety. For example, the first cloud may be dark, the second lighter and the third lightest. This would represent a decrease in anxiety over a period of time.

Discussion/goals: Clients share the clouds and explore how they symbolize their stress levels. Clients examine patterns in their mood and behaviors. Goals include self-awareness and identification of anxiety triggers, symptoms and occurrence.

One client named Frank drew a black cloud, a gray cloud and a light-gray cloud. He stated the dark one represented full anxiety, the gray represented moderate anxiety, and the light-gray symbolized the anxiety almost gone. He mentioned that he could go from dark to light in one day or sometimes in a few hours. He remarked that he would never achieve a white cloud; he will "never completely be rid his anxiety."

Anxiety triggers

Materials: Paper, pastels and markers.

Procedure: Ask clients to draw people and things in their environment that trigger their anxiety (e.g. being alone, sleeping poorly, ill health, a noisy neighbor).

Discussion/goals: Discussion focuses on the triggers depicted and the client's analysis of them. Suggest clients rate them on a 1–10 scale where 1 causes them the least anxiety and 10 causes them the most anxiety. Explore methods to create an awareness of the triggers before their anxiety escalates and to help clients cope with them in a healthier manner.

A woman in her 70s named Helena drew a large twenty-dollar bill to represent her stress. She gave it a number 10 on the anxiety scale and stated, "I need more money to make my life less stressful. I am always worrying if I will have enough money for food and medicine. I become very nervous when the bills arrive; they can be very confusing, especially the hospital bills. Sometimes I watch my friends buy fancy things and go on vacations, while I sit at home and worry." One group member observed that the face on the dollar bill looked like the patient's face; it had large eyes and curly hair. When asked about her reaction to this observation, Helena remarked that she wished she were on the bill because then she would be well known and rich. While exploring this anxiety trigger, Helena found the group feedback very helpful. She decided she would try to deal with a few bills a day and not let them overwhelm her. She also decided to be grateful for what she did have, which was a lovely apartment and a wonderful family. She was going to try not to dwell on the negative aspects of her life.

A widow in her 70s drew a figure with the emphasis on her back pain. She rated the pain a 9 on the stress scale and stated that when she's in pain she becomes tired, irritable and depressed. She immediately retreats to her bedroom and tries to sleep as much as possible. "This behavior can go on for days." This client was willing to receive feedback from group members. It was suggested that she engage in activities to get her mind off of her pain. Reading, listening to music and visiting with friends or family members were a few of the suggestions.

A widow named Wanda drew an oven with two large pots on top of it and stated, "The cooking gives me stress." This client rated her stress level a 7–8 "when she tries to cook." She remarked that she used to cook every day for her husband and herself; she enjoyed it very much. She cooked "every dish you could imagine." Now she cooks out of necessity because she is on a restricted diet: "I would never cook if I didn't have to." She says she feels too weak to cook most of the time and she thinks of her husband while she's preparing her meals. She states she feels so sad that he is not experiencing what she is experiencing during mealtimes. She says she misses conversing with him and seeing his smiling face. Group members empathized with her and suggested that, if possible, she do as much cooking as possible one or two days a week and freeze the rest. In this way she just has to warm up the frozen dinners, and it will be easier for her emotionally and physically. One woman suggested she buy pre-cooked meals or frozen dinners. Another group member suggested she eat out as much as possible. A widow named Beth suggested she have cereal or a sandwich sometimes instead of a formal meal. Wanda appeared to acknowledge these suggestions and said "she'll think about it."

Decreasing stress

Materials: Drawing and writing paper, pens, pencils, markers and pastels.

Procedure: Have clients share a variety of stress-management techniques and then provide a list for them (see below). Discuss the methods with clients and then have group members draw themselves engaging in one of the techniques discussed.
Self care techniques:

- take mini breaks throughout the day

- practice acceptance (like yourself)

- talk rationally to yourself

- get organized

- exercise

- focus on the "here and now"

- talk to friends

- watch habits (eat well, get enough sleep)

- meditate

- practice breathing exercises

- take one day and one task at a time

- be creative (draw, write, journal, do crafts, etc.)

- volunteer/help others

- reach out to friends and family for support

- read/watch a funny movie or television show

- keep learning (e.g. a new language)

- keep active (go out to dinner, to plays, museums)

- take your medication and see a doctor regularly

Discussion/goals: Discussion focuses on the artwork and methods to utilize the self-care techniques presented. Goals include stress reduction, the compilation of a repertoire of coping mechanisms and decreasing stress.

Notes

1. The CD may be purchased on the internet.
2. Roberta M. Pughe, EDS. MA
3. Misbaha Armenians also have their own worry beads, which serve the same purpose as the Komboloi and are also non-religious in nature. More information can be found on the internet. For clarification, search photos on Wikipedia and directions at Fire Mountain Gems (www.firemountaingems.com).
4. Worry stones are of ancient Greek origin. Rubbing was believed to lessen worry.
5. This project may also be used with "bad stress" as the focus.
6. Gorilla Glue is a very strong super glue that can be purchased online or at some art supply stores.
7. These items can be purchased at a craft or hobby store.
8. The picture of a rocking chair can be hand-drawn or taken from Google Images.

CHAPTER 6
MOVEMENT/MUSIC

According to the American Dance Therapy Association, dance/movement therapy is "The psychotherapeutic use of movement as a process, which furthers the emotional, social, cognitive and physical integration of the individual."

Dance/movement enhances sensory stimulation and the expression of thoughts and ideas. Clients socialize, reach out and connect with others through movement. They explore their inner and outer worlds, space, time and boundaries. Individuals discover the significance of body movements, facial expressions and gestures in forming and keeping relationships. They are able to enhance social skills and appreciation of their bodies while engaging in various movements. They discover their capabilities, strengths and limitations; powerful feelings and thoughts may be shared. In dance/movement the body and mind become more connected; self-confidence and a feeling of well-being is developed. Clients are given the opportunity to identify suppressed emotions and express them in a healthy, non-threatening manner.

Music helps individuals reduce stress and express fears, wishes and desires. Individuals may relive memories and enjoyable experiences while listening to certain tunes and melodies. Music helps people forget their problems and worries. It transcends time and affords people the opportunity to be young again. It helps promote positive changes, which may be demonstrated in physical, social and interpersonal development. Cognitive abilities, emotional and spiritual health may be enhanced. Music may ward off despair, promote healing and decrease pain and muscle tension; the production of endorphins is increased. Listening to music is calming and may lessen or even eliminate panic attacks. It helps individuals be mindful and self-aware. Soothing music can lower blood pressure and heart rates and decrease anxiety and tension. It can boost immunity and help clients think in a clearer manner; memory may improve. Listening to music is an enjoyable activity that increases joy and connects people to the past and present. It is something that almost everyone can relate to and appreciate.

My body

Materials: Markers, pastels and two outlines of the human body that fit within a 9 × 12 inch piece of drawing paper.

Procedure: Ask clients to fill in the first outline with colors that reflect how they feel about different parts of their body. For instance, if their shoulder aches, they may draw it red, or if they have a headache, they may emphasize the forehead. Next lead a series of chair exercises, which may include shoulders rolls (moving the shoulders forward and then backward), neck rolls (rotating the head gently), feet stamping, stretching of arms overhead and clapping. Then ask group members to fill in the second outline with color, again emphasizing any part of the body that feels better or still feels uncomfortable.

Discussion/goals: Discussion focuses on observing the effects that exercise has on body image and associated discomfort. This is done by examining the pictures and comparing the before and after images. Goals include relaxation through exercise, creative expression, body awareness and emphasis of the importance of exercise and movement as a way to increase energy and improve health and self-esteem.

Color mixing

Materials: Scarves of varying colors (may be bought in discount stores or made with material scraps), drawing paper, markers, pastels, a relaxing CD and CD player.

Procedure: Have clients sit or stand in a circle. Ask each client to select a scarf that best reflects their current mood and have them share the reason they chose the color. Next play the music and suggest that clients sway to the music and gently move the scarves as they sway. Encourage them to use movement to reflect how they are feeling. After a few minutes, ask group members to toss their scarves down in the middle of the room (either on the floor or table depending on the mobility of clients). Now ask them to observe the design the grouping of scarves created and encourage clients to produce their own unique image that incorporates the new design and their feelings about their combined movement/art experience.

Discussion/goals: Discussion focuses on feelings that emerged as a result of the movement exercise, thoughts about the transition to drawing and associations with the final sketches. Goals include creative expression, body awareness, identification of mood and feeling, freedom associated with the swaying motion and spontaneous and original movements.

Moods and feelings

Materials: Large ball with feelings written on it in various areas (this ball can be bought with words already written on it through catalogs such as S&S or a plain ball can be purchased in a discount store and feelings can be written on it with a permanent black marker).

Procedure: Have clients roll the ball to one another. The person who receives the ball selects one feeling written on it and then expresses how he communicates that feeling to others. Clients keep rolling the ball to one another until everyone has had at least one turn. This can be done on a table or clients may stand up and toss the ball to one another if they are in good physical shape.

Discussion/goals: Discussion focuses on how clients express their feelings and thoughts. Goals include communication with peers, socialization, self-awareness and a focus on relationships.

The winner

Materials: Drawing paper, markers, crayons and pastels.

Procedure: Ask clients to make a fist and, as they share something that is bothering them, ask them to punch outward. For instance, if the individual is troubled with anxiety, he says the word "anxiety," or says who or what is making him anxious as he punches out. Each client has a turn to do this. Then encourage group members to discuss how it felt to "punch away" their negative thoughts. Suggest they give themselves a pat on the back because they were able to begin to battle their problems symbolically. Share the idea of winning by fighting back; give the example of a boxing match: the fighter may go down but he usually gets up again in order to finish the match to the best of his ability. Next ask clients to think about their special challenges and have them draw themselves as the winner of their own personal battle (e.g. if the client is fighting anxiety, he might draw himself standing on top of a pile of anxiety, or if he is fighting worry, he might tie it up in a large knot).

Discussion/goals: Explore how group members portrayed themselves in the drawings. Discuss what it takes to win, to fight one's fears and troubling thoughts, problems and concerns. Goals include self-awareness, increased self-esteem and becoming more proactive in one's recovery.

Movement with partner

Materials: CDs of various types of music and singers (e.g. Benny Goodman, Frank Sinatra, Dean Martin, Broadway tunes, swing, classical hits, Bach, Beethoven) and a CD player.

Procedure: Divide clients into pairs and ask them to create one or more movements they can do together while listening to the music (e.g. clapping hands, swaying back and forth, moving their arms simultaneously to the beat of the song, dancing a waltz together, or dancing as they did in the past to music of the 1940s and 1950s).

Discussion/goals: Discussion focuses on the movements chosen and the way in which the clients worked together. Explore how they felt. Was there a flow to the movements, a pattern? What was each client's experience while participating in this exercise? Did he feel comfortable or awkward? Ask participants if a mood or feeling was conveyed through the movements.

Goals include making connections, sharing and communicating in a new and unique manner. Clients become more aware of body language and boundaries.

Jam fest[1]

Materials: CDs of a variety of lively and calming music and a CD player.

Procedure: Have group members form a circle. One by one, each person will be given the opportunity to stand in the middle of the circle and create a movement that other clients will imitate. When that individual feels he is ready to move on, he will point to another person who will also share a movement for the group to imitate. This will occur until everyone has had at least one turn.

Discussion/goals: Goals include socialization and enhancement of cognitive skills. Clients become more focused as they follow directions. Clients usually feel energized and joyful while engaging in this experience.

Memory/movement

Materials: Relaxing music and CD player.

Procedure: Group members are asked to sit in a circle and choose a simple movement such as tapping one's head, stamping feet, swaying or clapping. Next, each client demonstrates his movement, and the client next to him is asked to repeat that movement in addition to his own unique movement. As each person takes a turn, he is now doing his own routine in addition to all the movements that came before his movement. Eventually everyone will have to learn everyone else's movement.

For example, client A stamps his feet; client B is sitting next to him and stamps his feet and raises his arms up and down; client C decides to open and close his eyes, so Client C must stamp his feet and raise his arms up and down before he takes his turn. Clients are asked not to worry if they forget some of the motions; it's a creative exercise with the goal of improving memory and having an enjoyable experience.

Discussion/goals: Discussion focuses on the complexity and symbolism of the movement chosen and the ease or difficulty of following others. Goals include memory enhancement and socialization.

Moving to emotions

Materials: Drawing paper, markers, crayons, pastels, oil pastels and watercolors.

Procedure: Ask clients to draw their feelings using color and shape. Next ask them to create a movement that reflects all or part of their design. For example, if the artwork consists of wavy lines, the client might sway, or if it is rigid and consists of straight lines, the client might stand or sit very straight, perhaps with arms up in the air.

Discussion/goals: Discussion focuses on the relationship between the design and the movement and how both reflect the individual's feelings, mood and personality. Goals include creating an awareness of the connection between the physical and emotional self.

Stress reduction exercise

Materials: Soothing music, CD player, pencils and paper.

Procedure: Ask clients to rate their stress level on a scale of 1–10 (1 is the least stressed and 10 is the most stressed) and write the number on a piece of paper. Next ask them to create a movement or exercise that they find relaxing (e.g. shoulder rolls, gently moving head from one side to the other). Have clients share their movements with the group. After everyone has a turn, ask clients to rate their stress level once again.

Discussion/goals: Discussion focuses on the exercises created and the clients' attitude about doing them. The similarities and/or differences in the stress levels before and after the exercises are examined. Goals include moving for emotional and physical health and developing a repertoire of stress-reducing techniques.

Conveying emotions

Materials: None required.

Procedure: Ask each client to convey an emotion using facial expressions and body movements. Group members guess which emotion each individual is conveying.

Discussion/goals: Discussion focuses on the emotions shared and the method by which they were communicated to group members (were they clear, emphasized, difficult to decipher, overly exaggerated; were facial expressions and body movements used?). Socialization, communication and expression of thoughts and feelings are examined. Body language and boundaries are explored.

Ball of anxiety[2]

Materials: Drawing paper, markers, oil pastels and crayons.

Procedure: Tell clients they will pretend to throw a ball of their anxiety to the person sitting next to them. As clients throw the ball, they are asked to describe how they feel at that moment. They are also asked to share if they are throwing away all of their anxiety, throwing part of it away or keeping it. After everyone pretends to throw the ball, ask clients to draw the part of their anxiety they did not throw away. If an individual chose to keep all of the anxiety, ask him to draw a representation of it;

if he threw all of the anxiety, away ask him to draw how it feels to be stress-free.

Discussion/goals: Discussion focuses on how clients felt about the imaginary play, the anxiety they threw to their peers and the resulting artwork. Goals include identifying and exploring how to cope with stress.

Dance and life

Materials: Paper, pens and pencils; CDs of music for various time periods (1930s, 1940s and 1950s) and CD player.

Procedure: Ask clients to discuss which specific dances and dance crazes represent different phases of their life. Suggest they write down the dances and then, if they feel comfortable doing so, demonstrate all or part of the dance for group members.

Dance ideas:

• ballroom dancing	• jitterbug
• folk dancing	• Lindy Hop (swing)
• polka	• line dancing
• swing (Cakewalk)	• tap dancing
• bunny hop	• ballet
• waltz	• tango
• Charleston	• Macarena
• circle dancing	• Mambo
• conga	• Twist
• country/western dance	• rumba
• foxtrot (ballroom social)	• salsa
• hokey pokey	• samba
• hora	• square dance
• hula	• two-step
• Israeli folk dancing	• Kalamatiano.

Discussion/goals: As clients share the dances, they also share life experiences. Goals include life review and identification of enjoyable experiences.

Optimism (1)

Materials: Drawing paper, markers, oil pastels, pens, pencils; cheerful music and CD player.

Procedure: Clients listen to upbeat songs such as "Happy days are here again," (Judy Garland) "Don't worry, be happy," (Bobby Mcferrin) "What a wonderful world" (Louis Armstrong) and "I got rhythm," (Ella Fitzgerald and Ethel Merman) and list the positive words and phrases that they detect in the lyrics. Next ask them to illustrate at least two of the words or phrases.

Discussion/goals: Clients focus on being positive. Goals include uplifting of mood, increased self-esteem and enjoyment.

Circle of movement

Materials: CDs of lively music such as polkas, country tunes and ethnic songs such as "Hava Nagila" and the Tarantella.

Procedure: Clients stand in a circle, hold hands and move to the left for a minute or two, then to the right, and then everyone comes forward towards the center of the circle and then back to their original position. This is repeated for a few rounds. Next, clients take turns deciding which way the group moves. Finally, clients take turns choosing various movements everyone will follow.

Discussion/goals: Group members share reactions to moving and emotions that may have been elicited from the movements. Goals include stretching, connecting with others, release of tension and socialization.

Move to the music

Materials: Octaband™ (stretchy material that extends to as many as 16 clients and allows for movement and group cohesiveness)[3] and music with a lively, but moderate beat, familiar to the elderly.

Procedure: Participants bounce and stretch the Octaband as they move in synchrony with the music and each other. Group members may use the band in a number ways that include:

- making small bouncy movements in time to the music
- coordinating breath with movement as everyone raises their arms up on the in-breath, and brings their arms down on the out-breath

- shaking arms to release tension

- swinging arms from side to side

- crossing both arms in front and then out to the sides

- bringing one arm up while bringing the other arm down

- lifting one arm up diagonally across the body and bringing it down, then repeating this exercise with the other arm

- pulling on the arms, bending elbows and releasing, then extending arms

- leaning one's body toward the center and, as client grasps his arm, he puts one fist in front of the other.

When the group is cohesive, in good control and has the required skill level, clients may:

- stand in a circle, and walk to the music clockwise

- reverse directions and walk to the music counterclockwise

- change the pace of walking

- stand still and repeat the movements that were experienced while they were seated

- vary the pace of moving together up and down, sometimes suddenly, sometimes slowly. When participants are following instructions and working together as a group, have them move freely while still holding on to the Octaband. Experiment by allowing the spontaneity of individual group members to emerge.

Discussion/goals: This exercise builds awareness of others, enhances liveliness, heightens spontaneity, increases self-expression and reinforces resilience. It magnifies recognition of one's effect on others.

Moving sculpture[4]

Materials: None required.

Procedure: One person designated "the model" strikes a pose. He then transforms into "the sculpture." Group members may add to the sculpture if desired. They may do so by standing or sitting next to it, lightly touching it (if given permission by the model) and/or continuing it with some sort of body movement such as stretching next to it. The sculpture is in process and continues to develop until group members decide it's completed.

The "mechanic" (the person chosen to be in charge of the sculpture) pushes an imaginary button and the machine (the sculpture) begins to move once it is fully constructed. Clients will be asked to move in any way they wish with the mechanic's approval. They may wave their arms, stretch, sway, etc. The mechanic has the power to speed up the machine (clients create quick movements) or slow it down (participants make small, gentle movements).

Discussion/goals: Group members discuss their ability to form and change positions and connect to peers. Goals include socialization, increasing flexibility, following directions and body and boundary awareness.

Energy[5]

Materials: None required.

Procedure: Clients are asked to share their vitality with each other. Direct them to share their energy with the person sitting to their right, and then that individual will share his energy with the person to his right, etc. This occurs until everyone has been given their neighbor's energy. Next, clients may be asked to share their happiness or other emotion using body movements. Group members may use their full body, arms, hands, breath, words, gestures and facial expressions to share their emotions and energy.

Discussion/goals: Group members discuss how it felt to give and receive energy. Goals include connection, communication and motivating clients to move, experience and revitalize.

Notes

1. Modified version of a directive submitted by Joy Schoffer.
2. Modified idea from Alan Shapiro, LCADC, LPC.
3. The Octaband can be found at www.octaband.com. Designed by Donna Newman-Bluestein, MEd, BC-DMT, LMHC, Adjunct Faculty, Lesley University.
4. Modification of a directive suggested by Susan O. Cohen, MA, BC-DMT. This directive may be changed according to the health, needs, flexibility and mobility of clients.
5. Modified from a suggestion by Evelyn Sutkowkis, NCC, LPC, Princeton House, University Medical Center at Princeton.

CHAPTER 7
CREATIVE EXPRESSION

Creative writing, journaling and poetry provide clients with the opportunity to share feelings and experiences in a very personal and artistic manner. They are in control as they put their thoughts and dreams on paper. The author is in charge of what he writes and how he writes; he can be truthful or fanciful if he wishes. Experiences that are too painful to share verbally can be written and shared only if the author chooses to do so. He can hide his notes and refer to them, as he feels comfortable. Creative writing allows the client to reach out to others in a non-threatening manner. It permits him to communicate his feelings and gain a more realistic perspective. After expressing troubling thoughts, the client can view his feelings from a distance and not "own them" so much. He can gain more perspective and analyze his work at his leisure. The writer is given the opportunity to identify, recognize and process his feelings. Poetry, for instance, becomes a vehicle for sharing happiness, sadness, fear, frustration, love and hope. It can lift one's spirits and free the mind. Self-awareness and self-esteem are enhanced. Creating poetry can help clients who are stuck to gain more freedom as they learn to think more abstractly.

Journaling allows the client to keep a diary of his experiences and associated thoughts. It can be considered a written reflection of his achievements, questions, fears and day-to-day activities. Writing "gradually eases pain and strengthens the immune system" (Woolston 2000). Some studies show that it helps to relieve stress and depression and may heal illnesses such as arthritis, asthma and even cancer. Creative writing assists people with interpersonal conflicts and problems. It enables individuals to organize their thoughts, relive pleasant memories and remember achievements. It allows for self-exploration, insight and reflection. Creative writing is a healing art that helps clients to reconcile conflicts, express emotions and share beliefs and values.

Group list: Seasons

Materials: Pen, writing and drawing paper, markers, pastels and crayons.

Procedure: For each season (do one list for each season), have group members take turns listing the reasons they enjoy that season. Ask one group member to take notes, or the leader can do this. When the list is complete, ask one or more group members to read the list aloud. Then suggest that clients choose one of the descriptions and represent it on paper.

Discussion/goals: Discussion includes sharing of positive experiences and memories associated with the season. Goals include reminiscing, awareness and group cohesiveness.

This is an autumn list that a group of seniors composed in a creative expression group therapy:

The leaves turn beautiful colors.

The weather is crisp and cool.

Halloween is fun and we love to watch the children wear their cute costumes.

The trees are stunning.

It is fun to drive upstate to look at the fall foliage.

The mums are so pretty in colors of yellow, purple and pale orange.

Thanksgiving is right around the corner!

"Who Am I?"

Materials: Writing paper, pens and pencils.

Procedure: Suggest that clients write a paragraph answering the question "Who Am I?" After they write their paragraph, ask them to draw a self-portrait in any way they wish. Emphasize that an abstraction (line, shape, color) is perfectly acceptable.

Discussion/goals: Discussion focuses on the descriptions (ask clients to read them aloud) and the associated representations. Goals include self-awareness and identification of strengths and weaknesses. It is important for clients to view themselves in a variety of roles (mother, friend, teacher, helper, sister, etc.), and not just as a client or someone who has depression or bipolar disorder.

Descriptions of written work:

"Who Am I?"

I am a mother of two,

I am a wife; I like making friends,

I am a person who enjoys music and going to concerts,

I enjoy eating in restaurants.

I am a mother, grandmother, and cousin,

I like to read,

I like to draw and paint,

I like to play with my grandchildren,

I like to cook,

I am a mother-in-law,

I am an aunt,

I am a friend; I like to travel,

I like certain games.

I am a grandmother who played concert piano in my younger days, and plan to try to remember and collect more of my earlier songs.

I have a grandson in the air force who I am particularly proud of, and a granddaughter (his sister) who is a lawyer of excellent quality.

I live with my married daughter and my pets (dogs and horses).

My favorite pastime is reading.

I am a woman, lady, a lover of nature,

I love cats and dogs, and I am the mistress of a kitten who is sweet and intelligent.

I am going through a process from depression to wellness, one small step at a time.

I must remember, people suggest, to be less harsh on myself.

I am attracted to people—men and women, who are intelligent, kind thoughtful and honest.

Acrostic poems

Materials: Paper and pencils.

Procedure: An acrostic poem uses the letters of a word for the beginning of each line of the poem. The poems do not need to rhyme. For example:

CAT

C: Chloe sat under a tree

A: And the sky was bright blue

T: Two birds chirping a lovely song.

Ask clients to think of a simple word and write a poem using that word as the outline.

Discussion/goals: Discussion focuses on the poem and symbolism within it. Goals include creative expression, focusing and sharing of ideas and feelings.

Client examples:

Home:
Home is where the heart is,
It is filled with plants, love and colorful flowers,
My plants grow beautifully,
Every one of them is amazing.

Bill:
Back some twenty years ago,
I took a wrong turn in the road,
Leaving the familiar path,
Later I saw my mistake and returned.

Hi:
Here I sit under a tree looking up at the sky hoping to fly like a bird,
I know my thoughts cannot be heard.

Cat:
Come, let us all go away,
And let us all enjoy ourselves,
The trip is so far away.

Love:
Let me try to write a poem,
Only I would understand it,
Volume will not be included,
Even though it took so long.

Happy:
(Group acrostic poem)
How do you appreciate life?
Are you mindful?
Perhaps you meditate,
Perhaps you sing, dance or draw.
You are special to me.

Achievements

Materials: Writing and drawing paper, pens, pencils, markers and pastels.

Procedure: Ask clients to list their achievements. Then have them create a trophy for their greatest accomplishment. Emphasize that accomplishments can include a wide variety of things such as graduating from school, having a child, serving in the military, being married any years, keeping one's house clean.

Discussion/goals: Discussion focuses on the achievements listed and the design of the trophy. Examine the size, shape and colors of the trophy. Ask questions such as:

1. Is the trophy deserved?
2. Is it heavy/light?
3. How does it specifically represent the achievement?

Goals include identifying strengths and increasing self-esteem.

Group list:

I planned a bridal shower for my daughter. My self-esteem was the highest when I was raising my daughter.

I am proud of my previous job in an accounting department. My self-esteem was highest as a child.

My greatest achievement is my daughter. My self-esteem was highest when I graduated from high school.

My greatest achievement has been my three boys and two girls!

I like to cook meals; my family is my highest achievement.

My highest achievement is my family.

The Little Engine That Could[1]

Materials: Writing paper, pencils and pens.

Procedure: Clients take turns reading this book aloud or the leader reads it. When the story is finished, ask clients to share their thoughts and reactions to the story. Next ask them to write a brief essay about a time when they needed extra strength to achieve a goal.

Discussion/goals: Ask clients to read their stories. Then suggest group members explore one or more of the following questions:

- What is the moral of the story?

- Which of the engines/trains can you best relate to?

- How do you "push" to move ahead?

- Has there been a time in your life when you had difficulty pushing?

- What is the difference for you between the phrases "I think I can" and "I can?"

- Describe what it means when you use the words "I can't."

- Is there a difference between "I can't" and "I choose not to?"

- What changes in your life can be made by shifting your thinking from "I can't" to "I can?"

- What are the benefits of "standing still" (in other words, staying the way you are and not changing)?

- What changes would you like to see in your life in the near future? What changes would you like to see in the more distant future?

- How can you achieve these changes?

Missing you

Materials: Plain white envelopes, writing paper, pens, pencils, markers, crayons, pastels and 8.5 × 11 inch typing/computer papers.

Procedure: Suggest that clients write a letter to someone they love and/or have strong feelings about. It could be someone alive or dead, someone who lives close to them or someone who lives far away. When they have completed the letter, ask them to decorate the envelope in such a way that it represents their feelings toward that person. Goals include sharing of relationships, connecting to loved ones and healthy expression of love and loss.

Aging (2)

Materials: Writing paper, pens, pencils, coffee can or large container.

Procedure: Ask clients to make a list of what they like about getting older and a list of what they don't like about getting older (most likely the negative list will be much longer). When the lists are completed, ask group members to read them aloud. After each group member reads the negative list, give him the opportunity to hold on to it or part of it, or throw it in the coffee can (get rid of it). Ask him how it felt to throw the negative thoughts away.

Discussion/goals: Discussion focuses on the lists and attitudes of the clients. If the clients kept the negative list, ask him the reasons why it was kept. Goals include exploration of coping skills relating to aging and accepting and dealing with change.

Benefits of aging list from a group of clients:

grandchildren
freedom
memories—a focus on positive memories
acquired wisdom
retiring—sleeping later
respect
movie discounts
social security benefits
less responsibility—will choose responsibilities
less self-conscious
we say what's on our mind more often
less cooking and cleaning
more time for leisure activities like reading and golf
better able to get a seat on the bus or train.

Group newsletter

Materials: Writing paper, pencils and pens.

Procedure: Have clients decide on a name for the newsletter as well as the contents. Suggestions include poetry, memories, thoughts about the seasons, humorous anecdotes, recipes, reminisces, achievements and coping skills. Writing sessions take place once a week, if possible, and each client chooses a topic to write about. Towards the end of the session they share what they have written (if they feel comfortable doing so). Then they decide if they want their essay, poem, etc. published. After enough expressive writings are finished, type them, edit, organize, staple and distribute the completed newsletter to group members. Clients take turns reading their contribution aloud and then critique the publication as a group. They decide what they want to put into the next publication and if any changes are needed.

Discussion/goals: Clients greatly enjoy seeing their work and names in print. Goals include focusing, problem solving, creative expression, communication, making connections and increased self-esteem.

The following are group poems created by clients and printed in one of the newsletters, titled "Bits and Pieces." Group members worked together to think of the newsletter name.

Fall reminds me of colors,
When winter comes I feel cold and lonely,
When spring comes I hope for warm weather,
My favorite flowers are daisies,
It's good to think about life.

I love life,
Beauty is within,
My eyes widen when the sun rises,
Hope is eternal,
Happiness is forever.
The sun is warm,
The wind is cold,
The rain is damp,
The snowflakes are beautiful,
The snow is white.

She is perfect,
Her heart is made of gold,
My heart beats,
My eyes sparkle,
My thoughts are happy.

The newborn is beautiful,
I was astounded,
My heart runneth over,
My smile is contagious,
A teardrop falls.

Photograph

Materials: Writing paper, pens, pencils and a photograph of a friend or family member. If a client does not have a photograph, he can sketch a picture or symbol representing that individual.

Procedure: Encourage clients to share their photograph with others. Next ask them to use the photograph as their reference point and write a poem, story, essay or just a few lines about the person in the photograph and/ or something related to that individual. For example, if the photograph is of the client's husband, she might write about the time he surprised her with a party on their 25th anniversary.

Discussion/goals: Discussion focuses on important people in the client's life and the effect those people have on the client's present mood, attitude and life circumstances. Goals include sharing of relationships and self-awareness.

Lifestyle balance

Materials: Writing paper, pens and pencils.

Procedure: Discuss ways clients take care of themselves (e.g. meditation, aerobics, eating healthy). Next have them write a brief story about an individual who chose to nurture himself after a period of self-neglect. Inform clients that the story could be imaginary or based on reality.

Discussion/goals: Discussion focuses on the narrative and the significance of it. Ask participants if they relate to the main character in the story. Goals include greater self-awareness and identification of self-care techniques.

An 87-year-old man named Moe wrote the following. He remarked that it was based on his true life experience.

> My wife left me after 13 years of marriage. I was 39 years old. I was devastated and in disbelief. I couldn't believe she would do something like this to me. We had two children at the time and I knew they would be very upset. I was still in love with her and felt extremely depressed, angry and betrayed. I thought I was a good husband and an excellent provider. She wouldn't share much with me, which made things worse. Later I found out she was having an affair with someone from her office. I couldn't believe it. I fell into a depression. I wasn't able to eat or sleep, and I stayed away from friends. I just wanted to sleep and be by myself. For days I laid on the couch like a mummy. My best friend saw what a mess I was and urged me to see a therapist. He almost had to drag me to see the psychiatrist. I was put on an antidepressant, which seemed to work a little. I had to go back to work because money was running short, so I had no choice. My friend helped me by encouraging me to move on with my life and inviting me to his house for dinner and taking me to the movies and ball games. I knew I had to get well for my children, who had gone through enough. Eventually I started to feel better and I began a new life for myself. I found a new woman who I have been married to for 45 years. She is the love of my life.

"I Don't Know"[2]

Materials: Writing paper, pens and pencils.

Procedure: Ask clients to complete the phrase "I don't know..." three to five times in a row. Additionally, they may choose to write a brief poem using this phrase.

Discussion/goals: Discussion focuses on clients' questions, doubts, uncertainties and potential answers to problems and fears. Goals include self-awareness and introspection. Coping skills may be explored.

"Acceptance Poem"[3]

Materials: Writing paper, pens and pencils.

Procedure: Read the poems "Reflections" and "Those Hands" by AlmaMaria Rolfs.

"Reflections"
My mother once told me
I was just like her.
What did she mean?
Was it a triumph?
Was it a curse?

She glimmers at me now
From store windows,
Unexpected mirrors, sudden
Reflections. Always.
She takes me by surprise.

"Those Hands"
Chopin and Brahms I recall:
My mother at the piano,
Lullabies poignant in the night,
Her small hands fluid
As the northern rivers she loved.
And Scrabble: her fingers
Placing the polished letters
In elegant combination, how
She loved to play with words...

Other hands move across
My memory now:
Another rhythm, equally old,

A layering not of chords but threads,
As I watch her mother,
My namesake, a weaver,
From untidy handfuls of color
Bring order, texture,
A shawl, a patterned blanket, a room.

And mine? Though my own hands
Move over the page, releasing words,
And in the earth, bringing forth
Blossoms and herbs,
Arranging tapestries,
Symphonies of touch and color,
Singing the songs of the hands
Of my mothers, still…

Today,
I would gladly turn from these,
To hold in mine, those hands.

Discuss the poems and then ask group members the following:

- Alma's poem names specific things that are part of both her earlier and present experiences, such as lullabies, Scrabble pieces, a shawl, a blanket, blossoms, herbs and tapestries. What objects/things can you specifically name that were/are an integral part of a family member's life? What feelings are connected to those things?

- What did this person give to you of himself? What in his life—and in your own—would you like to celebrate?"

- Things my family member loved or did well…

- Object/things I associate with this person…

- Things I can name about myself that I do well, and things I love in myself that connect me with this person…

Discussion/goals: Discussion focuses on exploration of memories and associated feelings. Goals include increased self-awareness and self-esteem.

Love yourself

Materials: Writing paper, pens and pencils.

Procedure: Read the poem "Always Love and Accept Yourself" to group members. Explore the clients' associations with it. Next ask participants to list the ways they demonstrate love and respect for themselves.[4]

"Always Love and Accept Yourself"
I accept myself completely.
I accept my strengths and my weaknesses,
My gifts and my shortcomings,
My good points and my faults.
I accept myself completely as a human being.
I accept that I am here to learn and grow,
and I accept that I am learning and growing.
I accept the personality I've developed,
and I accept my power to heal and change.
I accept myself without condition or reservation.
I accept that the core of my being is goodness
and that my essence is love,
and I accept that I sometimes forget that.
I accept myself completely, and in this acceptance
I find an ever-deepening inner strength.
From this place of strength, I accept my life fully
and I am open to the lessons it offers me today.
I accept that within my mind is both fear and love,
and I accept my power to choose
which I will experience as real.
I recognize that I experience only the results
of my own choices.
I accept the times that I choose fear
as a part of my learning and healing process,
and I accept that I have the potential and power
in any moment to choose love instead.
I accept mistakes as a part of growth,
so I am always willing to forgive myself
and give myself another chance.
I accept that my life is my expression of my thought,
And I commit myself to aligning my thoughts,
more and more each day with the Thought of Love.
I accept that I am an expression of this love.
Love's hands and voice and heart on earth.

I accept my own life as a blessing and a gift.
My heart is open to receive, and I am deeply grateful.
May I always share the gifts that I receive
Fully, freely and with joy.
(Author unknown)

Discussion/goals: Goals include focusing on self-care and strengths, increasing self-esteem and positive thinking.

Keys (2)

Materials: Construction paper, outlines of keys of varying sizes, glue, scissors, lined writing paper, pens, pencils, markers, crayons and oil pastels.

Procedure: Provide outlines of keys of various sizes and shapes. The leader might draw the outlines on one or two sheets of 8.5 × 11 inch paper and make copies for clients. Have clients color in at least three keys and then glue them on a piece of construction paper. Next ask clients to create a brief list and describe what each key might open (e.g. one key might be the key to someone special's heart, another might be the key to an old home, another might be the key to good health or to a Cadillac).

Discussion/goals: Discussion focuses on the design and symbolism of the keys. Goals include exploration of needs and wishes. Realistic versus non-realistic desires/goals may be examined.

The discussion

Materials: Drawing paper, lined writing paper, pens, pencils, markers, crayons and oil pastels.

Procedure: Ask clients to draw two people having a discussion. On a piece of writing paper or on the back of the sketch, ask them to describe what the people are talking about.[5]

Discussion/goals: Generally, one or both of the figures depicted represent the client in some way. Clients' issues and concerns often become apparent by exploring the figures and the written descriptions. The facial expression, size and position of the figures may be examined. Goals include exploration of communication skills, sharing of relationships, feelings and concerns.

Perception

Materials: Drawing paper, markers, pencils, oil pastels and crayons.

Procedure: Ask clients to divide their page into four boxes. The first box is labeled "Inner self" and the box next to it is labeled "Outer self." The box below "Inner self" is labeled "I like" and the box below "Outer self" is labeled "I don't like."

Next, clients draw and/or write their private thoughts/feelings in the "Inner self" box. Clients draw/write the way they present themselves to others in the "Outer self" box. Clients draw/write things about themselves they admire (e.g. smart, thoughtful, good cook) in the "I like" box. Clients draw/write characteristics they'd like to change and/or improve in the "I don't like" box.

Discussion/goals: Discussion focuses on clients' strengths and weaknesses. Goals include self-awareness and greater understanding of the way clients view themselves versus the way others view them.

Loss

Materials: Drawing paper, markers, crayons and oil pastels.

Procedure: Ask clients to fold their paper in half. On one side of the paper have them draw something, someone, a goal or dream they have lost in their life, and on the other side of the paper ask them to describe their drawing. Encourage group members to include their feelings and the magnitude of the loss in their description.

Discussion/goals: Discussion focuses on the loss and the effect the loss has had on the client's mood, attitude, focus and life events.

This directive helps clients to express their sadness, and allows them a chance to grieve the many losses that seniors often experience. Widows will often draw their husbands and talk about the many things they miss about them. Although they usually begin sharing with tears in their eyes, they frequently end up smiling and sharing amusing anecdotes.

Healing words[6]

Materials: Writing paper, pens and pencils.

Procedure: Ask clients to create a list of healing words and phrases (e.g. one day at a time, be patient, I'm strong). Next ask them to create a simple poem or imaginative paragraph (writing whatever they please if a poem is too difficult) using the words/phrases as the basis of the poem. Clients are told the poem doesn't need to rhyme or have the correct rhythm; anything they create is fine.

Discussion/goals: Discussion focuses on the significance and usefulness of the words/phrases for emotional well-being. Poems are read aloud and feedback is elicited from clients. Goals include socialization and creative expression for healing and support.

In the moment[7]

Materials: Writing paper, pens and pencils, drawing paper, markers, crayons and oil pastels.

Procedure: Ask clients to complete the phrase "Right now I feel..." Suggest they write at least three statements reflecting how they feel at the present moment. Next ask them to draw one or all of the feelings represented in any way they please.

Discussion/goals: Discussion focuses on the written descriptions and associated artwork. Goals include identifying and expressing current feelings and increased self-awareness.

Time (1)

Materials: Writing paper, drawing paper, pen, pencils, markers and oil pastels.

Procedure: Discuss the statement "Everybody looks, thinks and feels differently as time goes by." Then ask clients to write a response, create a poem or draw an image related to its meaning.

Discussion/goals: Discussion focuses on the significance of the words, symbols and pictures presented by group members. Clients explore their past, present and future and how they are affected by change. Goals include acceptance and self-awareness.

A female client wrote this poem titled "The Golden Years."

There is a special time in life
Filled with special cheers,
Known as your retirement
In "The Golden Years."

Some are quite lucky,
To have reached this high goal
And have now set back,
With a different soul.
In "The Golden Years"
We all play flute and sax,
Give out a "Thank you all,"
Just sit back and relax.
Some people miss out
On reaching this fine aim,
For through disease or illness
Things are never quite the same,
So, forever remember,
Life through its good cheers,
Live life freely each day,
And enjoy "The Golden Years"!

"I Used to be a Person" was written by an 87-year-old man.
I used to be a person,
I used to be handsome,
I used to be strong,
I had energy,
I went places,
I did things,
I could see; I could hear,
I had all the time in the world,
Now I am old, I am nothing,
There is no time left.
Where did the time go?
Where did the time go?
I don't know if I'll be here in the morning,
I hope, I pray,
Just one more day,
Where did the time go?
Where did the time go?

A 67-year-old woman wrote "The Hospital Room."
I sit in my hospital bed,
Feeling achy and half dead.
I hate being in this place,
Illness is difficult to face.
I felt fine before I came,
I guess there's no one to blame.

As soon as I put on the hospital gown,
I felt sick, depressed and down.
I'd much rather be sitting outside,
But I guess I'll do my best,
To obey orders and get some rest.
When I get out of here,
My life I will hold dear.
Never take for granted your life,
Your children, family or wife,
For one never knows,
Life easily comes and easily goes.

Exchange

Materials: Writing paper, drawing paper, pens, pencils, markers, crayons and oil pastels.

Procedure: Ask clients: "If you could trade one characteristic you have for another, what, if any, qualities would you exchange?" For example, changing a good sense of humor for high intelligence, or a sense of direction for creativity. Instruct group members to write down the qualities they would exchange and then write or create a cartoon or sketch about how this exchange would change their life.

Discussion/goals: Clients explore satisfaction or dissatisfaction with traits and desired characteristics. Goals include exploration of self-esteem and methods to increase it.

Myth/strengths

Materials: Writing paper, pens and pencils.

Procedure: Ask clients to write down myths associated with old age on one side of the paper and strengths that older adults possess on the other side. Discuss the lists. Next suggest group members write a brief story or poem using one or more of the strengths listed.

Discussion/goals: Acknowledging myths allows clients to examine and dismiss them. Clients become more self-aware regarding the biases that seniors face and the erroneous beliefs (e.g. older adults lose creativity and productiveness, have little to offer, are incapable of learning and growing and are disinterested in life). Self-esteem increases with self-awareness and recognition of strengths and potential.

Knowledge

Materials: Writing paper, pens and pencils.

Procedure: Suggest clients create a list of their mentors or "life teachers" and describe what they have learned from them. Ask questions such as "How have these teachers affected you and how has the information/ wisdom helped and is presently helping you cope with life?" Direct clients to write their thoughts on paper and share with group members.

Discussions/goals: Support and wisdom acquired over the years may help clients better cope with problems associated with old age. Many clients have a stable base of wisdom to lean on when times are rough. This exercise helps individuals find their base and remember skills that were taught long ago. With resources comes strength; the goal is for individuals not to be victims but active participants in life.

Relationships (1)

Materials: Writing paper, pens and pencils.

Procedure: Ask clients the following questions and have them verbalize and/or write down their answers.

1. Discuss a close relationship you presently have or have had in the past.

2. What do you look for in a friend? What would be your friend's special qualities?

3. What qualities do you bring to a relationship?

4. Can you think of a television or movie couple you admire? Why do you admire that couple?

5. Can you think of a *real life* couple you admire?

6. What role do television and movies play in our searching for that perfect relationship?

7. How are relationships nurtured?

Next suggest they write a poem or brief description of their ideal relationship.

Discussion/goals: Discussion focuses on group members' relationships, specifically their interactions with acquaintances, friends and family.

Goals include exploration of ways to form and maintain bonds with others. Clients share what they look for in a friend, mate or partner.

A group participant who is not married and lives in an assisted living facility wrote the following poem:

"Relationships"
To have a perfect relationship,
With family or friend,
Gives you the strength and courage,
To live to the very end.
People should care and respect,
For each other every day,
For when you help the other person,
You have a lot to say.
Respect and understanding,
Should go hand in hand,
For when you try your very best,
You will feel very grand.
Remember to listen,
And hear the other out,
Try to be loyal,
In what you talk about.
So just do your best,
Every single day,
And try to get along,
In your own best way.

"Don't Quit"

Materials: Writing paper, pens and pencils.

Procedure: Read the poem "Don't Quit" with clients.

Next ask them to describe a time that persevered and/or have them describe how they are presently working toward wellness and recovery.

"Don't Quit"
When things go wrong, as they sometimes will,
When the road you're trudging seems all uphill,
When the funds are low, and the debts are high,
And you want to smile, but you have to sigh.
When care is pressing you down a bit,
Rest if you must, but don't you quit.

Life is queer with its twists and turns
As every one of us sometimes learns,
And many a failure turns about,
When he might have won had he stuck it out;
Don't give up though the pace seems slow,
You may succeed with another blow.

Success is failure turned inside out,
The silver tint of the clouds of doubt,
And you never can tell how close you are,
It may be near when it seems so far;
So stick to the fight when you're hardest hit,
It's when things seem worst,
That you must not quit.
(Author unknown)

Discussion/goals: Discuss the meaning of the poem, the client's responses, his written work and his attitude toward working hard. Goals include supporting clients to keep moving forward and helping them recognize their inner strength.

I am

Materials: Writing and drawing paper, pens, pencils, markers, oil pastels and crayons.

Procedure: Have clients complete the following:

I like . . . .

I love . . . .

I am . . . .

I will . . . .

I have . . . .

I want . . . .

I need . . . .

Next ask them to choose one of the sentences and illustrate it. For instance: "I want a husband." Have the client draw an image of a desired husband.

Discussion/goals: Discussion focuses on the meaningfulness of the answers and illustrations. Goals include self-awareness and identification of desires and needs.

Healing (1)

Materials: Writing paper, pens and pencils.

Procedure: Have clients answer the following: "Share a time that your words healed someone else. What did you say? How did it feel to be supportive?"

Ask them to list at least five encouraging words and then draw a picture, write a poem or description symbolizing the feeling gained from helping another person feel better.

Discussion/goals: Discussion focuses on the responses, drawings, descriptions and poetry. Clients share ways they have helped others. Goals include encouraging a feeling of power, helpfulness and purpose and increase of self-esteem.

Client poems:

"Grandson"
I love you grandson,
I support you in every way.
Keep up the good work,
You add delight to my day!

"Friend"
You look great,
I hope you are feeling well.
Things will get better,
I am so sorry,
May I help you?
Please call me,
I am here.
Always with you,
Always near.

"You"
You're doing much better,
Glad you could come today,
I love you because of who you are.
You made my day.

Just knowing you has been my pleasure,
The TV you fixed,
Works better than ever!

"My Dear"
Feelings of warmth, happiness,
Good thoughts.
Pleasant, satisfied, joyful.
Good job,
Good helper.
You.
Start my life all over again.

Love letter

Materials: Pens, pencils, envelopes, writing paper, markers and crayons.

Procedure: Suggest group members write love letters to themselves. Encourage them to add a lot of self-praise and support. Next suggest they decorate the letter and envelope to reflect the positive words included in the letter.

Discussion/goals: Discussion focuses on the importance of having self-worth, being present (being aware of ourselves) and self-acceptance. Goals include increasing self-esteem and confidence.

Look at me

Materials: Writing paper, pens and pencils.

Procedure: Ask clients to answer the question "What do you see when you look at me?"

Have them write what they think others would see if they opened their eyes wide enough. For example: "You would see a mother, grandmother, wife, ex-school teacher, loving person, sister, someone who was once a happy-go-lucky teenager, a New Yorker, etc."

Discussion/goals: Many seniors vividly recall the past and sometimes feel as if they are still 25 years old "inside." Unfairly, they may be judged as slow, incompetent, fragile and unworthy by younger individuals. Our society often promotes these attitudes; youth is widely worshipped, especially in the media. Discussion focuses on the complexity of people and the many aspects of their personalities. Seniors are supported to be assertive and focus on their strengths instead of their weaknesses. Goals include acceptance and assertiveness. Seniors are encouraged to be aware of biases and confront others, if possible, when they make judgments based on appearance, race, religion or age.

Introspection

Materials: Writing paper, pens, pencils, drawing paper, markers, oil pastels and crayons.

Procedure: Introduce the Chinese proverb "We naturally see the beauty of youth, but we must learn to see the beauty of age." Ask clients to explore the meaning of the proverb and then write or draw their reactions to it. Suggest they might list the positive aspects of aging and/or describe the beauty of older individuals. Encourage group members to think about inner as well as outer beauty.

Discussion/goals: Examine how our society views aging and how other groups, such as Asian people, view it (much more accepting and respectful). Explore how many individuals allow culture and a strong emphasis on youth to determine their value. Encourage clients to share the benefits, wisdom and grace that come with aging. Goals include increased self-esteem, self-awareness and validation.

Motivation (2)

Materials: Writing paper, pens and pencils.

Procedure: Read the brief story "The Young Man and the Starfish: A Motivational Story about Making a Difference."

Once upon a time there was a wise man who used to go to the ocean to do his journal writing. He had a habit of walking on the beach before he began his work.

One day he was walking along the shore. As he looked down the beach, he saw a human figure moving like a dancer. He smiled to himself to think of someone who would dance to the day. So he began to walk faster to catch up.

As he got closer, he saw that it was a young man and the young man wasn't dancing, but instead he was reaching down to the shore, picking up something and very gently throwing it into the ocean.

As he got closer he called out, "Good morning! What are you doing?"

The young man paused, looked up and replied, "Throwing starfish in the ocean. The sun is up, and the tide is going out. If I don't throw them in, they'll die."

"But, young man, don't you realize that there are miles and miles of beach, and starfish all along it. You can't possibly make a difference!"

The young man listened politely. Then he bent down, picked up another starfish and threw it into the sea, past the breaking waves and said, "It made a difference for that one."

There is something very special in each and every one of us. We have all been gifted with the ability to make a difference. And if we can become aware of that gift, we gain through the strength of our visions the power to shape the future. We must each find our starfish. And if we throw our stars wisely and well, the world will be blessed.

(Author unknown)

Explore the meaning and the clients' reactions to the story. Next suggest that group members write about a time that they made a difference in someone's life. Emphasize that it does not have to be a great feat; it can be a favor, a show of empathy or affection, a suggestion or support.

Discussion/goals: Discuss the butterfly effect.[8] Emphasize how one person can make a huge impact on the life of others. Explore how everyone, regardless of age, has a lot to share, give and teach. Examine ways in which clients have helped others in the past and can be of help in the future. Goals include increased self-esteem and motivation to volunteer, interact with others and become more active.

Perseverance

Materials: Writing paper, pens and pencils.

Procedure: Share the story of the "Two Frogs" and explore its meaning. Ask clients to write about a time they worked hard to reach a goal.

"Two Frogs: An Inspirational Story about Perseverance"

Two young frogs fell into a bucket of milk. Both tried to jump to freedom but the sides of the bucket were steep and no foundation was to be had on the surface of the liquid.

Seeing little chance of escape, the first frog soon despaired and stopped jumping. After a short while he sank to the bottom of the bucket.

The second frog also saw no likelihood of success, but he never stopped trying. Even though each jump seemed to reach the same inadequate height, he kept on struggling. Eventually, his persistent efforts churned some milk into butter. From the now hardened surface of the milk, he managed to leap out of the bucket.

The moral of this little inspiring story: Those who don't give up and persevere may be in for a surprise!

(Author unknown)

Discussion/goals: Discussion focuses on determination, tenacity and past accomplishments. Goals include increase of resolve and spirit.

Sharing (1)

Materials: Drawing paper, pens, pencils and markers.

Procedure: Ask clients to fold their paper in half and write and/or draw feelings they usually share with others on one side of the paper and emotions they tend to hide from others on the other side of the page.

Discussion/goals: Discussion focuses on how expression of feelings and lack of expression affects mood, socialization and behavior. Clients examine their outer and inner worlds. Goals include self-awareness, revealing (at least to oneself) problematic emotions that have been kept hidden and identification of problems that need to be addressed.

A woman in her late 60s drew a flower on the "can share" side of the page and wrote, "I can share funny stories, how I feel about my cat, the weather, a cup of tea, how I feel about a person, and today's fashions." She sketched a sad face on the other side of the page and wrote, "I can't share how I feel when I am in pain."

A widow in her late 60s drew a full red heart on the "can share" side of the page and a broken heart on the other side. The broken heart had many cracks in it. She remarked that she often hides her great sadness about her husband's death; she "puts on a smile" but often doesn't feel it.

A very stoic woman in her early 70s wrote on the "can share" side, "I plan how I feel physically and emotionally. I plan how I feel about my family—those who are deceased and those who are alive and still a part of my life." On the other side of the page she wrote, "My deep sadness is not shared and it comes across by the way I look (not smiling). I don't share how deeply fearful and sad I am of the future. The future terrifies me."

A recent widow wrote, "I share my feelings with my children." On the other side of the page she wrote, "I try to hide my feelings from my grandchildren when I'm depressed. But when I'm happy I share with them all." She added three tiny stick figures (her grandchildren) on the bottom of the page.

Emotions

Materials: Pens, pencils and pre-written list of emotions:

Happiness

Anger

Boredom

Sadness

Fatigue

Fear

Loneliness

Depression

Anxiety

Procedure: Ask clients to draw a symbol that will represent each emotion, and then have them write the way they express the emotion under the symbol. They may use shapes, figures, lines, color and design to create the symbol. For example, one client drew a fireball to represent anger and then stated he "blows up" when he becomes very angry. Another individual sketched an empty box to represent loneliness and stated she sits home by herself when she's lonely and doesn't reach out to others.

Discussion/goals: Discussion focuses on the relationship between the symbols and the associated feelings. Clients share how expression and/or non-expression of their emotions affects behavior, self-talk and attitude. Goals include self-awareness and identification of healthy and unhealthy communication skills.

Expressing feelings

Materials: Writing paper, pens and pencils.

Procedure: Provide a list of feelings and ask clients to write one or more sentences describing a situation in which they experienced that feeling. The list may consist of a few or many emotions.

Feelings:

Joyful

Excited

Confident

Appreciated

Comfortable

Loved

Capable

Sad

Afraid

Anxious

Undecided

Discussion/goals: Clients share their behaviors, mood and reaction to specific feelings. Goals include increased communication self-awareness and expression of emotions.

Feeling letter

Materials: Drawing paper, markers, oil pastels, crayons, pens and pencils.

Procedure: Direct clients to think of a feeling they are currently experiencing and represent it as some type of figure using line, color and shape. Have them personalize the feeling by giving it a name—for instance, Joe Fear. Next ask clients to write a letter to the feeling. They may let the feeling know their associations to it, how it affects them, whether they wish it would go away or remain in their life, and what they are planning to do to the feeling (e.g. keep it, keep part of it or throw it away).

Discussion/goals: Clients share their symbols, and personal letters if they are comfortable doing so. Goals include acknowledging and identifying fears, examining methods to master them and exploring coping techniques such as meditation, deep breathing and self-processing and positive self-talk. When clients draw and write to their fears, they begin to gain control over them; the fears are out in the open, ready to be examined, and not hidden where they create anxiety and physical symptoms.

"The Road Not Taken"

Materials: Drawing paper, markers, oil pastels and crayons.

Procedure: Read the poem "The Road Not Taken" by Robert Frost (1916).

"The Road Not Taken" by Robert Frost
Two roads diverged in a yellow wood,
And sorry I could not travel both
And be one traveler, long I stood
And looked down one as far as I could
To where it bent in the undergrowth;

Then took the other, as just as fair,
And having perhaps the better claim
Because it was grassy and wanted wear,
Though as for that the passing there
Had worn them really about the same,

And both that morning equally lay
In leaves no step had trodden black.
Oh, I marked the first for another day!
Yet knowing how way leads on to way
I doubted if I should ever come back.

I shall be telling this with a sigh
Somewhere ages and ages hence:
Two roads diverged in a wood, and I,
I took the one less traveled by,
And that has made all the difference.

Participants are encouraged to discuss the meaning of the poem. They are then asked to draw the road they took in life and the road they didn't take. Clients are asked to draw symbols representing life events on both roads (e.g. a wedding gown and children representing the road taken, a painter's easel representing the road not taken).[9]

Discussion/goals: Clients discuss which road they chose in life and feelings about their choice. They also discuss the road not chosen. Clients assess their life and reflect upon accomplishments and regrets, and explore future plans.

Coffee identification

Materials: Writing paper, pens and pencils.

Procedure: Share the list of coffee flavors below, and ask clients to choose the coffee that represents them the most. Have them write a description of why their personalities may be similar to the chosen flavor. For example, someone who likes caffeinated coffee might say he is a traditionalist, a decaf person might be anxious or a health enthusiast, an espresso person might be someone who likes parties, a cappuccino type might be someone who likes the finer things in life. Have clients problem solve to associate personality characteristics to the coffee.

Coffee types:

- latte
- cappuccino
- ice coffee
- instant coffee
- espresso
- caffeinated coffee
- decaf
- hazelnut
- amaretto
- mocha
- "Dunkaccino"
- "Tropical Orange Coolata"
- Irish coffee
- French vanilla
- Hawaiian Kona coffee
- "Mocha coffee with cream"
- iced caramel swirl latte
- dark roast
- cinnamon spice
- vanilla bean
- "LatteLite"
- hot chocolate mix
- (Tea).

Discussion/goals: Clients share personality characteristics. Goals include self-awareness, introspection and enjoyment.

Exploration

Materials: Writing paper, pens and pencils.

Procedure: Have three boxes (five questions to a box) of the open-ended statements placed on the page. Ask clients to fill in the answers and discuss.

1. If I . . . .
2. Then I . . . .
3. And I . . . .
4. So I . . . .
5. Sorry I . . . .

1. When I . . . .
2. It was . . . .
3. I was . . . .
4. I felt . . . .
5. I had . . . .

1. Now I . . . .
2. It is . . . .
3. I am . . . .
4. I feel . . . .
5. I will . . . .

Discussion/goals: Clients share positive and negative aspects of their life, personality, actions, mood and behaviors. Goals include self-awareness, sharing, communication, introspection and assessment of needs and desires.

Group stories

Materials: A variety of objects placed in a box. Examples might include a tea bag, a ring, a dishrag, soap, a watch, a band-aid, a doll.

Procedure: Each client chooses an object. The first participant begins a story using his object as the theme of the story; the second person continues the story incorporating his object into the story. This goes on until everyone has had a turn and the narrative is completed. To begin a new tale, clients put their item back in the box and choose a new one.

Discussion/goals: Clients usually enjoy this exercise; it gives them a chance to socialize and laugh. Goals include problem solving, abstract thinking and creating connections with peers.

Gratitude (1)

Materials: Drawing paper, markers and pens.

Procedure: Read the following poem and discuss the meaning.

Be Thankful
Be thankful that you don't already
have everything you desire.
If you did, what would there be to look forward to?
Be thankful when you don't know something,
for it gives you the opportunity to learn.

Be thankful for the difficult times.
During those times you grow.
Be thankful for your limitations,
because they give you opportunities for improvement.
Be thankful for each new challenge,
because it will build your strength and character.

Be thankful for your mistakes.
They will teach you valuable lessons.
Be thankful when you're tired and weary,
because it means you've made a difference.

It's easy to be thankful for the good things.
A life of rich fulfillment comes to those who
are also thankful for the setbacks.
Gratitude can turn a negative into a positive.
Find a way to be thankful for your troubles,
and they can become your blessings.
(Author unknown)

Suggest group members draw and/or write ways in which they are thankful. Examples might include illustrations of their family, a sun, trees, flowers to represent nature. They may write about being healthy, having a home to live in, friends, lovely memories, etc. Life's battles and lessons learned may be examined.

Discussion/goals: Clients share their "riches" and things that are enjoyable in their life. They may explore how problems and challenges have enriched their life in various ways. Goals include exploring coping skills and methods to optimize happiness in their lives.

Autobiography

Materials: Writing paper, pens and pencils.

Procedure: Instruct clients to write an autobiography of their life. Suggest they include details such as where they were born, the important people they have met over the years, their family, significant experiences such as graduations, births and marriages, and achievements.

Discussion/goals: Clients share their descriptions and fond memories. Goals include communication, self-awareness, self-reflection and increased self-esteem.

Real and ideal

Materials: Writing paper, pens and pencils.

Procedure: Ask group members to write four statements about their life that are true and four statements that they wish were true.

Discussion/goals: Discuss the similarities and differences between the real and ideal statements. Ask group members:

1. Are the wishes very different from reality?
2. Are the wishes attainable?
3. How would you feel if they came true?
4. What would you do if the wishes came true?
5. How do you feel about your present reality?

Beauty

Materials: Writing paper, pens and pencils.

Procedure: Group members work together to list everything they find beautiful in life. Next they create a poem from the word list. They may add additional words and phrases if they please. The poem doesn't have to rhyme or be within any specific type of form. It will be personal and unique.

Examples of words that might be used include: sun, flowers, roses, raindrops, rainbow, gold, children, glitter, sunset, smile, blue sky, diamonds, mountains, babbling brook.

Discussion/goals: Clients share their poems and their associations to them. Goals include working together (teamwork), socialization, problem solving, creative thinking and looking at the positive aspects of life.

Goodbye letter to symptoms

Materials: Writing paper, pen and pencils.

Procedure: Ask clients to write a goodbye letter to their symptoms and/ or illness.

Discussion/goals: Encourage group members to share their letters with their peers. Ask them to describe their feelings about saying goodbye to their illness and symptoms. Explore whether clients are allowing their symptoms to control them and/or scare them. Goals include acquiring power and control over symptoms and exploring attitude and work in therapy. Clients examine the role they play in regards to their illness and symptoms, and identify methods to gain control of their life.

Notes

1. *The Little Engine That Could*, 1930, Watty Piper.
2. "I Don't Know" written by John Fox, CPT.
3. "Acceptance Poem" written by John Fox, CPT.
4. An addition to this directive might be to draw a self-portrait that illustrates self-acceptance.
5. This directive may be more specific. Clients may be asked to draw themselves with specific people in their life such as their spouses, children, neighbors and/or friends.
6. Modified from a suggestion by John Fox, CPT.
7. Modified from a suggestion by John Fox, CPT.
8. Chaotic processes, such as the weather, can be affected by small changes in initial conditions, so that the flapping of a butterfly's wings in Tahiti can, in theory, produce a tornado in Kansas. See Gleick (1988).
9. As an alternative, if the group is less focused you could just have them draw the road that was taken.

CHAPTER 8
COLLAGE

Collage work allows clients to express themselves freely using a variety of resources. They are able to experiment with texture and touch and to manipulate materials such as paper, photos, magazine pictures, fabric, foam shapes, felt, wood pieces, construction paper, pipe cleaners and cotton. Collages may be presented in numerous ways. A theme may be presented, specific materials may be used and the collage might be structured or non-structured. A structured approach might include having group members create a themed magazine collage, such as an emotions collage by cutting out pictures of faces; a non-structured approach might include having clients use a variety of materials such as wool and beads to represent inner feelings.

Individuals are often more willing to participate artistically when asked to design a magazine collage. It provides structure and a relatively non-threatening means of expression. This is partly because the pictures are easily accessible, there is not a right or wrong way to do this and the photos just need to be torn or cut out. Clients have an array of ideas right in front of them. They can find photos representing their feelings, family members, hobbies, likes and dislikes, and just glue them on the paper in any way they please.

The collages provide non-threatening methods of representing thoughts, concerns, attitudes and feelings. Clients usually feel free to share symbols represented in the collages. It is noteworthy to observe how the clients create their collages—whether they are full or empty, organized or disorganized, glued neatly or haphazardly. The therapist can observe fine motor skills by the way in which the client cuts and glues his pictures on the paper. Many clients state feeling "more relieved and relaxed" when cutting and pasting meaningful pictures in an organized manner. Elderly clients who are normally guarded and defensive about drawing will usually participate fully and share their feelings more readily during a collage art experience. The way a client works may reflect his physical and psychological state.

Body collage

Materials: Magazines, markers, glue, scissors and drawing paper.

Procedure: Suggest that clients find pictures of body parts (arms, feet, face, legs, eyes, etc.) from the magazines and create a collage of the pictures, emphasizing body parts that serve them well. Clients may add words or their own sketches if they desire.

Discussion/goals: Discussion focuses on exploration of one's body, its strengths and weaknesses. Goals include self-awareness, coping with change, having an outlet to express feelings about one's body (aches and pains) and a focus on what is in the client's control.

Children (2)

Materials: Magazines, markers, glue, scissors and drawing paper.

Procedure: Suggest that clients find photos that remind them of their children, grandchildren or friends or relatives when they were young. Clients may add words and their own sketches if they desire. Ask them to glue them on the paper in any way they please.

Discussion/goals: Discussion focuses on memories and positive thoughts. Goals include increased self-esteem, appreciation of one's gifts and review of experiences, responsibilities and strengths.

Torn paper design

Materials: Colored construction paper, glue and white drawing paper.

Procedure: Direct group members to choose one or two sheets of paper in *one color*. Ask them to choose the color that best represents their current mood. Suggest they tear the colored paper into a variety of shapes and glue the shapes on the white drawing paper (the background) in order to create a design.

Discussion/goals: Discussion focuses on the meaning of the color used and the way the design was approached. For instance, did the client use large or small pieces of paper, is the sheet filled up or empty, are the shapes dull or exciting? While the clients are working, observe if they tear the paper timidly or with gusto. Explore how their work style could represent their mood.

Number design

Materials: Drawing paper, markers, crayons, oil pastels, colored pencils, scissors, glue, glitter, sequins, buttons, beads and feathers.

Procedure: Direct clients to create a number design by using a significant year or decade as the basis for the picture. For instance, if a client's daughter was born in 1983, he might use those numbers in any way he wants to create a design. The numbers could be upside down, next to each other, large, sideways, colorful, monochromatic, decorated with glitter or beads, etc.

Discussion/goals: Discussion focuses on the significance of the year or decade represented, the symbolism in the artwork and the client's reaction to it. Goals include exploration of life experiences, problem solving and increased self-awareness.

A widow named Ada drew dancing music notes, birds flying in a sky of gold glitter and the years 1951–1964 written boldly with bright pink marker. She incorporated the words "Music and Dancing" into her design. She shared that those were the best years of her life. Her daughter was born in 1964 and she got married in 1954. She reminisced about a lovely large wedding and her very handsome husband whom she adored. She shared that her husband was incredibly strong and stubborn. Half laughing, half crying, she told group members a story about a time he was severely wounded but survived. She stated, "No, it did not happen in the war, it happened in his own store. A robber shot him. My husband tried to catch him; he was always brave, and sometimes a fool."

A client named Don wrote the year 1959 in bold, colorful letters and added a smiling person holding a large diploma, an oak tree, a bright yellow sun and the words "Happy, positive, enjoyable, college graduate." He included a sign that reflected his high school name and logo. Don shared that graduating from high school was a huge feat for him; he was the first person in his family to be a graduate and he was extremely proud of this accomplishment.

Another client drew a bride and groom peering into each other's eyes. The groom is holding the bride's hand. She's wearing a long, flowing dress and he's in a tuxedo. The year 1958 is written at the top of the page and under it are the words "The Year I Got Married—The Best Year!" This individual spoke about the strong connection he has with his wife and the support she provides. He stated she accepts him even when he's depressed and isolated: "I have to get well for her."

A client who likes to joke (usually used as a defense mechanism) drew a large baby and the year 1924 on top of it. The baby is wearing a diaper and has one hair coming out of its round head. It has a large smile on its face. Next to the year 1924 is the word "Born" written in bold blue marker with three exclamation marks next to it. This individual stated, "If I weren't born, my children and grandchildren would not be here and I wouldn't be sitting in this group right now." Group members chuckled, delighting in this reprieve from more serious therapy.

Hand collage (1)

Materials: Construction paper, drawing paper, pencils, markers, oil pastels, crayons, glue, scissors and magazines.

Procedure: Direct clients to outline their hands and then fill the outlines in with self-representative photos from magazines.

Discussion/goals: Discussion focuses on the pictures chosen and their meaning to the client. Goals include sharing likes and dislikes with others (greater communication and socialization), self-awareness and increase of self-esteem.

Hand collage (2): Self-esteem

Materials: Drawing paper, construction paper, scissors, glue, markers, oil pastels and a list of affirmations to be distributed to each group member. Examples of affirmations may include: I am at peace, I love and accept myself, I am worthwhile, take one day at a time. The affirmations should be printed in large, bold letters and underlined, if possible, so that they are easy to cut out.

Procedure: Direct clients to outline their hands and fill the outlines in with colors, shapes, symbols and/or figures that represent happiness, admirable characteristics and positive aspects of their life. For instance, they may use bright colors to represent a lively personality or they may include people in their life who raise their spirits. When the hands are filled in, have group members cut them out and glue them on the construction paper. Lastly have participants select affirmations from the list, cut them out and glue them on the paper surrounding the hands.

Discussion/goals: Clients share their hand designs, focusing on the way they symbolize the client's personality and life. The affirmations are read, shared and analyzed. Goals include increased self-esteem, self-awareness and positive thinking.

Clients enjoyed this exercise because it was structured and helped them highlight their strengths and the joy in their life. They smiled and joked as they tried to outline their hands or their neighbor's hand. Working together strengthened connections.

A woman named Claudette created a very busy and colorful hand with many attributes surrounding it. She stated that the hand represented the way she'd like to be and the affirmations symbolized hope. Claudette remarked that she wants a rich, full life and she wants to have friends and enjoy her family, but she "is not there yet." She shared that she doesn't "feel the affirmations" at this time. She specified the statements "I am worthy" and "I bring joy to others." She did point out a small symbol drawn on her hand, which represented an award she received when she was in high school for helping others. Claudette described herself as "someone who was strong and popular in the past, but weak and frail in the present." It was suggested that she focus on present strengths; group members supported her by saying, "Maybe you are stronger than you think."

Wisdom collage

Materials: Construction paper, magazines, markers, oil pastels, crayons, scissors and glue.

Procedure: Ask clients to reflect on some of the experiences they have had over the years. Suggest they share the lessons and knowledge gained from these experiences through their artwork. Instruct them to draw, write and/or cut out pictures, words and phrases from the magazines that reflect some of the wisdom they have acquired. For example, if an individual regretted not going to college, he may cut out a picture of a diploma; if a woman believed she wasn't an attentive mother, she might find a picture of a mother hugging or playing with her child.

Discussion/goals: Discussion focuses on the symbols represented and insight shared. Goals include increasing self-esteem and self-awareness, socialization and focusing.

Aging (3)

Materials: Construction paper, magazines, markers, crayons, scissors and glue.

Procedure: Ask clients to draw and/or find pictures, words and phrases from the magazines that represent what aging means to them. For example, a popular phrase found on posters and in some advertisements is "Aging is Not For Sissies."

Discussion/goals: Discussion focuses on the pictures/words chosen and the clients' associations with them. Goals include identifying changes in one's body, mind and environment, and the development of coping skills to help clients understand and accept the changes.

Max, a rather spry and very intelligent 95-year-old man, had recently lost his wife. He had lost much of his family during World War II. He had been in a prison camp and survived because "of pure luck." He stated that if he had had to wait a few more days to be released, he would have been dead. He didn't attribute his survival to anything in particular. Max did not believe he did anything special: "Nothing more than anyone else did." When Max's wife died, his heart died with her. He felt he had seen enough death and endured enough loss; he tried to take his own life. His children were horrified and supported him to get immediate treatment. He stayed in an inpatient facility for a few weeks and then graduated to our outpatient facility where he got along well with the other clients. He hid his feelings behind a wonderful sense of humor, but he was able to share genuine feelings through his artwork. Max drew this empty-looking picture, which consists of a small stick figure rubbing his head as if he's thinking about what to do next, a bed and end tables. The items are outlined but not filled in. The lamps on the end tables appear almost as question marks. He titles his work "Nobody Here to Share."

A widow named Carolina drew a picture of herself standing next to her bed and titled the sketch "Not to Be Able to Sleep." This individual stated that since her husband died she has slept poorly. Lack of proper sleep has affected her mood, motivation and mental state. Carolina remarked that she and her husband had a bedtime ritual of having cookies and milk, watching the news and reading briefly before falling to sleep. Sometimes he would hold her hand as they fell asleep. She stated she misses everything about her husband, but this ritual is what she misses most. Carolina stated, "Now that he's gone and I'm getting older and weaker, I feel lost and lonely much of the time." She believed her children and grandchildren were visiting less often. She knew she had to start looking for happiness in her life and find new ways to feel comfort and peace. She started by joining the local senior center and socializing with other people who were in similar circumstances. She was beginning to enjoy aerobics and exercise classes.

Another client, Claire, drew her small apartment (represented by a tiny house with one window and a little doorway) and stated, "I don't like living here because it is not my previous home, which was large, beautiful and filled with loving memories of my family." She remarked that she hates being alone. She is still living with much clutter and many large cardboard boxes because she refuses to accept circumstances as they are and unpack. Claire doesn't want to stay but she has nowhere else to go. She feels trapped. The mess and drabness of the apartment increases her depression, but she can't get herself motivated to do anything about the mess. She won't even hang up pictures, not one print. Claire remarked, "If you saw my home, you wouldn't believe it."

A widow named Deirdre drew a bright red sports car, apparently going very fast. She remarked that "aging means no more money problems, at least not for me." She stated she feels financially secure and that pleases her. She stated she is able to travel, help her children and buy what she wants, including a new sports car. Deirdre stated she would not sit home and dwell on sadness. She makes sure to look attractive, structure her days and enjoy life to its fullest: "You are only as old as you feel or allow yourself to feel."

Eye collage

Materials: Magazines, markers, oil pastels, construction paper, scissors and glue.

Procedure: Ask clients to find a variety of photographs of eyes from the magazines and have them glue the photos in any way they like on the paper. Clients may add sketches of eyes to the collage if they desire.

Discussion/goals: Discussion focuses on the feelings evoked by examining the various eyes chosen to create the collages. The significance of conveying emotions through facial expression and the impact of eye contact is explored. Goals include self-awareness and communicating with others.

Employment

Materials: Magazines, scissors, glue, markers, construction or drawing paper.

Procedure: Ask clients to cut and glue pictures that show people performing a variety of jobs. For example, add a photo of a nurse, doctor, engineer or teacher.

Discussion/goals: Ask clients to share their collages and discuss the various jobs selected. Suggest that group members describe which photos, if any, represent their previous occupation. Have group members explore their thoughts about the transition from working person to retiree. Goals include sharing accomplishments and skills and examining and contrasting the past and the present.

Well-being

Materials: Magazines, construction paper, drawing paper, scissors, glue and markers.

Procedure: Direct the group to form a design with pictures and/or drawings of people engaged in healthy behaviors (exercising, bicycle riding, brushing teeth, etc.).

Discussion/goals: Discussion focuses on the significance of the photos chosen, the way they are placed on the paper and their meaning for the client. Goals include supporting a healthy lifestyle and self-care.

Heart mosaic

Materials: Construction paper, drawing paper, magazines, scissors, glue and markers.

Procedure: Ask clients to cut out a large heart from construction paper and glue it onto another sheet of construction or drawing paper. Next instruct them to cut out small squares or other small shapes from construction paper and/or magazines (these will be the mosaics). Suggest group members fill the heart with the mosaics.[1]

Discussion/goals: Discussion focuses on the design of the heart, the colors and shapes utilized and its significance. Goals include focusing, problem solving and sharing thoughts and feelings about love.

This is a constructive Valentine's Day project; it celebrates the occasion without focusing on having a partner, husband or wife, which can be especially painful for many seniors on this particular day. Many clients find that working with mosaics is calming and helps them be mindful.

Maps[2]

Materials: All types of maps (e.g. road maps, maps of the world and charts), glue, scissors, construction paper, magazines, markers, crayons, oil pastels and paint if desired.

Procedure: Provide maps to clients (maps may be copied and distributed). Have clients build images over the lines, waterways, states, cities and boundaries. They may draw, paint and/or use cut paper or photos to decorate. Suggest that clients think of the map as a coloring page that they will fill in however they please.

Discussion/goals: Discussion focuses on the uniqueness of the collages and the ways in which clients utilize color and shape to create new compositions. Relate the way the designs connect to the client's "new life map," which is developed as he utilizes new and enhanced coping skills. Goals include focusing, problem solving and self-awareness.

Dream collage

Materials: Magazines, construction paper, glue, scissors and markers.

Procedure: Suggest that clients cut, glue and/or illustrate various aspects and symbols reflected in their dreams and daydreams. For instance, a photo of a magnificent mansion might represent a client's wishful daydream; a lovely brook might symbolize an aspect of a comforting dream.

Discussion/goals: Clients focus on the representations and composition of the collage. Goals include self-awareness and expression of thoughts, wishes, fears and fantasies.

Animal collage

Materials: Construction paper, tissue paper, sequins, magazines, scissors, markers, glue and other collage materials.

Procedure: Provide an outline of a variety of animals such as a lion, horse, cow, monkey, dog, cat, bird. Ask clients to choose the animal he can identify with the most and fill it in with color, shapes, magazine photos, sequins, etc.

Discussion/goals: Encourage clients to relate characteristics of the chosen animals to their own personality traits. For instance, if a client chose a lion, perhaps he has "a roar" like a lion or likes to be king of his domain. Goals include focusing, decision making and creative expression.

Life stages collage

Materials: Magazines, scissors, glue, markers and paper.

Method: Suggest that clients find photos from various magazines that represent different stages of their life and have them glue the pictures on a piece of 11 × 14 inch paper in any manner they please.

Discussion/goals: Discussion focuses on examining how one's past affects present attitudes, beliefs and circumstances. Goals include increasing self-esteem and self-awareness by reminiscing about past experiences, achievements and strengths.

Amusing collage

Materials: Magazines, glue, scissors and markers.

Procedure: Ask clients to search for photos that they find uplifting, amusing, entertaining and enjoyable. Instruct them to glue the photos on the page in order to create a pleasing arrangement.

Discussion/goals: Have group members share their work and point out pictures that amuse them. Encourage clients to keep the collage on display at home to brighten their mood. Explore the benefits of keeping positive, smiling and making time for leisure and enjoyment.

People collage

Materials: Construction paper, markers, scissors, glue, magazines, cut-outs of people of various professions and ages.

Procedure: Provide various figures of all shapes and sizes (drawn by leader or taken from Google Images). Ask clients to cut out magazine photos, use the figures distributed and, if they like, add their own sketches to create a collage of people engaged in various activities.

Discussion/goals: Discussion focuses on the clients' associations to the figures, relationships presented and collage construction. Goals include exploration of relationships and examination of the different roles clients play in their life.

Questions to explore:

1. What professions are represented (e.g. teacher, doctor, lawyer, homemaker)?

2. Which figures can you relate to? Why?

3. Do any of the figures remind you of someone special in your life (past or present)?

4. Observe and share thoughts regarding the connectedness of the figures.

5. Are you represented in the collage?

Photo collage[3]

Materials: Various family photos, glue, scissors, markers, construction paper or other colorful cardboard or paper, sequins, glitter, buttons and stickers.

Procedure: Ask clients to bring in an array of photos and arrange them on construction or other attractive paper, adding words, descriptions, collage materials (e.g. sequins and glitter) and illustrations to create a personal collage.

Discussion/goals: Clients share photos of family, friends and assorted memories. Goals include life review and creation of a special keepsake that can be framed and displayed in the home to lift the client's mood and spirit.

Feeling/shape collage

Materials: Pre-cut shapes from construction and other assorted paper, glue and scissors. Some of the shapes may be wavy and round, while others might be sharp and jagged.

Procedure: Distribute a variety of shapes to each individual. Direct them to choose shapes that represent their feelings and thoughts. Next have them place and then glue the shapes on a sheet of construction paper in order to create a pleasing design.

Discussion/goals: Clients share the ways the colors and shapes reflect their mood and attitude. Goals include creative expression, decision making and abstract thinking.

Spice collage[4]

Materials: White or colored construction paper (8 × 11 inch or 12 × 16 inch), glue or glue stick, pre-cut pieces of construction paper, pre-cut pictures of various food items or family meal settings cut from magazines, aromatic spices (e.g. cinnamon, allspice, garlic powder, nutmeg), magic markers, colored pencils or oil pastels, water colors, various food items (e.g. pasta, grains, beans and spices).

Procedure: Ask clients to think of a favorite recipe. Next have them sniff the spices and try to remember how they used these spices in their own cooking. Then, with glue, paste, construction paper and other art materials, have clients create a mixed media collage or piece involving the use of spices. Ask them to write down their favorite recipes to the best of their ability. Distribute a few simple recipes to follow; the recipes may help clients remember some of the ingredients they used in the past.

Discussion/goals: The goal of this directive is to engage clients on a sensory as well as visual level, to have them recall their abilities and build ego strength by reviewing their accomplishments in areas such as running a home, cooking and raising children (many of the elders of today were full-time homemakers). Memories of childhood may also be explored.

Teardrops

Materials: Construction paper, scissors, glue, pre-cut teardrop shapes of all colors and sizes.

Procedure: Distribute the teardrops and ask clients to select as many of them as they please in order to create a teardrop collage.

Discussion/goals: Explore the compositions and the feelings elicited from the teardrops. It is frequently difficult for clients to share feelings of grief and loss in front of other group members. This project allows them to associate sadness and sorrowful events with the teardrops in a way that is typically less threatening.

A client name Mandy created a very large blue teardrop and then added five more teardrops within the blue one so that the teardrops overlapped and became increasingly smaller and lighter. She stated that the drops represented her disappointment in herself for being so weak. She felt guilty about needing extra help at this stage in her life. She saw herself in the middle of the drops: "Not as bad as I was, but I still have a long way to go until I am cured."

An 81-year-old male client drew a face and cut and glued tiny teardrops near the eyes. The face represented another client who was going to be leaving the program the next day. On the picture he wrote, "You are going to be sorely missed; you are smart and kind. You are one great lady and I'm glad I had the pleasure of knowing you. What will I do here without you?"

Some of the clients decided to create abstract designs with the drops and associated the designs with a variety of topics and themes such as "A Rainy Day" and "Fish in the Sea."

One client chose to create an optimistic design with the drops. She began to glue the pieces haphazardly, but soon a butterfly appeared in the abstraction. She took a black marker, outlined the butterfly and was very pleased with her work. She remarked that she saw the drops as positive and beautiful: "I don't want to cry anymore." This individual associated the butterfly with "brighter days."

Flower arrangement

Materials: An assortment of pre-outlined flowers, glue, scissors, white drawing paper, markers, oil pastels, pastels and crayons.

Procedure: Have clients choose a variety of flowers to fill in and cut out (all shapes and sizes). Then ask them to glue the flowers on the white paper in order to create an arrangement, bouquet or collage.

Discussion/goals: Discussion focuses on the variety of flowers, the arrangements, compositions and colors utilized. Many clients will share gardening techniques, their own gardens and their love of flowers. It is a topic that most adults can relate to and enjoy. Goals include decision making, problem solving and socialization.

This is a popular directive; the clients usually enjoy relaxing and listening to calming music as they fill in the flowers. The completed collages are generally bright and colorful. Self-esteem is raised as clients admire their work and the work of their peers. It is a directive that is guaranteed to work well for most individuals.

A client named Ellen was extremely pleased with her artwork. She stated, "I never did anything like this before; I didn't know I could do something so beautiful." She related the vibrant, lively flowers to her psychological

growth. She was developing a positive sense of self (something she hadn't had for a very long time). Ellen was living temporarily in her son's home, which was often a challenge for her. She mentioned that his garden was lovely and peaceful. When she was anxious, she would sit on his porch and enjoy the garden, using its beauty and tranquility to meditate and relax. The pink rose in the center of the picture caught her eye. Ellen was able to relate it to the fact that she was finally "blossoming."

Observation (1)

Materials: Drawing paper, pastels, oil pastels, crayons, markers and watercolors.

Procedure: Provide a few objects to draw such as fruit or a vase. Ask clients to divide their paper in half and draw the objects with distinct lines (contour-like drawing) and bright colors on one side of the page (more realistic), and on the other side, have clients use pastels or watercolors and draw/paint the objects hazy, indistinct, abstract and/or distorted.

Discussion/goals: Compare the clear and blurry illustrations. Suggest that the same objects can be drawn in different ways but they are still the same objects. Relate this concept to realistic and erroneous thinking. Ask clients if they have ever misinterpreted what others said to them or the reality of a situation. Examples include catastrophizing, blaming, over-generalizations and labeling. Goals include self-awareness of erroneous thinking and mistaken beliefs.

Doily collage

Materials: Doilies of varying sizes, paint or food coloring, small bowls, paper towels, water, brushes, glue, construction paper and rubber gloves.

Procedure: Instruct group members to paint or dye their doilies. If painting, clients may choose to experiment with watercolors. If dying the doilies, clients will place the doilies one at a time in a shallow bowl of water that has been colored with a few drops of food dye (red, yellow, blue and red). Have group members dip the doilies in and out of the dye quickly and then dry them by laying them flat on paper towels.

Next, clients will glue the doilies on the construction paper to create a colorful, appealing design. If doilies are too wrinkled, they can be pressed with an iron on low heat.

Discussion/goals: Review the procedure of dying the materials and/or how it felt to use a brush to paint the intricate details of the doilies. Explore the colors and patterns. Goals include experimentation, organization, problem solving and increased self-esteem. Most clients will be pleased with the outcome of this project due to the beauty of the shapes and colors.

Vision board

Materials: Poster board or cardboard (about 12 × 18 inches), magazines, markers, oil pastels crayons, scissors and glue.

Procedure: Introduce the vision board as a collection of photos, drawings and words that represent the clients' visions for the future. Group members will select photos, draw pictures and/or use symbols that represent things they'd like to do, places they'd like to go, people they'd like to socialize with, how they'd like to feel, etc. in upcoming years.

Discussion/goals: Discussion focuses on the composition of the vision board and items included in it. Methods to obtain those items, aims and desires are examined. Goals include identifying objectives, organizing thoughts and supporting a positive outlook.

Goodbye card collage

Materials: Magazines, printed affirmations, the word "goodbye" printed in a variety of styles, scissors, glue, drawing paper, sequins, glitter, buttons, other collage material if desired, markers, pens and pencils.

Procedure: Have clients fold 8.5 × 11 inch drawing paper in half so that it resembles the shape of a card. On the outside of the card ask group members to glue affirmations, words and positive images. Inside the card ask them to either write their own thoughts, include a poem or glue words from magazines to bid farewell.

Discussion/goals: The client who is leaving listens as each group member shares the images on his card and reads the affirmations and positive thoughts. Clients are given the opportunity to say goodbye in a creative and heartfelt manner. The individual who is completing the program has a remembrance of his peers and usually feels encouraged, admired and connected to other group members.

Cupcake paper collage

Materials: A variety of cupcake paper liners,[5] construction paper, markers, scissors and glue.

Procedure: Clients choose which paper liners they want to use; they may leave the paper as is or flatten it out on the construction paper. Group members may cut or tear the liners in order to create the design they desire. They may add their own artwork in addition to the papers.

Discussion/goals: Clients share their collages and associations. Connect the collages to cupcakes and the cupcakes to memories. Encourage group members to think about times they baked cupcakes for various events such as parties, school activities, block (street) parties. Goals include creative expression, abstract thinking, decision making and reminiscing.

Stamp collage

Materials: Construction paper, pictures of stamps from various countries and/or original stamps, glue, scissors, markers and pens.

Procedure: Collect stamps and/or make copies of photos of stamps from Google Images. Have clients cut out the stamps and glue them on the construction paper in any way they wish. Suggest they add words or additional artwork that may assist in the creation of the collage.

Discussion/goals. Explore associations with the stamps; encourage clients to share places they have visited in the past and/or places they'd like to go in the future. Goals include sharing of experiences, expanding one's boundaries (by designing the collage in one's own unique style and by thinking about places to visit in the future), problem solving and focusing.

Menu collage

Materials: Construction paper, a variety of menus from different restaurants, scissors, glue and markers.

Procedure: Make copies of the menus and distribute to clients. Direct group members to cut out sections of the menus that attract them and create a design on the paper. They may select foods that they like, eye-catching menu designs, healthy options, value meals and/or house specials.

Discussion/goals: Discussion focuses on the method used to create the collage and the parts of the menus utilized. Encourage clients to share foods they like and restaurants they have visited in the past. Goals include sharing of experiences, finding commonality among clients and enjoying lighthearted conversation, which may reduce stress.

This is a popular directive among clients. Usually a lot of discussion, sharing and laughter takes place. Participants usually enjoy speaking about food and places they have visited in the past. Clients frequently compare positive and negative stories and share experiences of eating in all types of restaurants.

They speak about unusual cuisine they have eaten as well as their favorite dishes. Vacations, family get-togethers and celebrations are often shared.

A man named Henry created a collage filled with menus from Italian restaurants and shared his honeymoon experience in Italy. He spoke about the wonderful food, museums, architecture and restaurants. Henry reminisced about the love he had and still has for his wife of 50 years. He smiled as he shared the amazing scenery and the friendly people they met on their trip.

A client named Maggie related her collage to her love of food. She stated she often treats herself "to dinner out," especially since her husband died. Maggie remarked that she used to cook every evening but doesn't see the point anymore. "What's the point in cooking a whole chicken or roast, it's only me now." She stated that dining in various restaurants helps her cope with loneliness and boredom. It gives her something to look forward to and something she is comfortable doing by herself. She stated that in the past she would not eat by herself, but she has learned to enjoy dining alone. Through therapy, Maggie realized that she is valuable, strong and worthy of enjoying herself. This new-found realization has helped her cope and become increasingly independent.

Coupon collage

Materials: Construction, paper, scissors, glue, a variety of coupons and markers.

Procedure: Make copies of coupons and distribute to clients. Suggest they trim the coupons as desired and glue them on the paper to create a collage. Participants may add their own artwork or writing to the collage.

Discussion/goals: Clients share the way the coupons form a design. Discussion focuses on food, shopping and savings. Goals include self-care, practical issues such as saving money and maintaining a healthy diet and communication among group members.

Multimedia collage on canvas

Materials: Small canvas boards approximately 5 × 7 inches, glue, scissors, collage materials such as buttons, beads, glitter, sequins, feathers, felt, foam shapes, colored paper, etc. Paint and/or markers are optional.

Procedure: Direct clients to experiment with the collage materials and create a design on the canvas (realistic or abstract). Encourage them to express themselves in any way they please.

Discussion/goals: Clients share their designs, the materials utilized and their thoughts and feelings pertaining to their artwork. Goals include experimentation, problem solving, thinking outside of the box, emotional expression and enjoyment.

Clients benefit from this directive because it is easy, relaxing and guarantees success. Self-esteem is automatically raised. Group members who are worried about their artistic abilities relax as they glue bright attractive beads and baubles on the canvas. The materials are lovely to look at and conducive to creative work.

A client named Fran used foam pieces to create the collage. She was attracted to the vibrant colors and soft texture of the foam. She stated she had no particular idea in mind when she began working, but after examining her collage she noticed "a smiling face with hearts for eyes." Fran remarked that she has been feeling better and she is smiling for the first time in six months. She stated the X on the left side and the heart on the right side of the canvas represent her children, whom she loves very much. The two tiny dots in between the X and heart represent "my grandchildren whom I adore."

Movement collage

Materials: Magazines, glue, scissors, markers and construction paper.

Procedure: Suggest group members create a collage of people in movement (e.g. running, walking, swimming, bicycling, exercising, doing yoga, Tai Chi).

Discussion/goals: Discussion focuses on the importance of being active and vital; various exercises and methods of keeping fit are explored. Goals include awareness of the impact that exercise has on our physical and emotional health.

Movie stars

Materials: Drawing paper, markers, glue, scissors and photos of movies stars (selected from Google Images).

Procedure: Copy and distribute photos of movie stars from the 1940s and 1950s (such as Marilyn Monroe, Burt Lancaster, Katharine Hepburn and Sophia Loren). Ask group members to select a variety of the photos, glue them on the paper to create a design and, if desired, add their own drawings, phrases or descriptions to the pictures.

Discussion/goals: Discussion centers on nostalgia and what the photos "bring up" for the clients. Goals include focusing on memories, youth and positive times. Movie posters may be used in addition or instead of the movie stars as described in the "Movie poster collage" directive next.

Movie poster collage

Materials: Drawing paper, small copies of movie posters of the 1940s, 1950s and 1960s, glue, scissors, markers, pens and pencils.

Procedure: Go to Google Images and print photos of old movie posters (most of the images are not more than six inches). Copy and distribute the photos in stapled booklets to clients. Have clients choose the posters that appeal to them, cut them out and create a collage on half of a sheet of 18 × 24 inch drawing paper. On the other side of the page ask clients to write and/or draw their memories of the years these movies were popular.

Discussion/goals: Discussion focuses on the movies chosen, the clients' reaction to the movies, their memories of the movie stars and their recollections of that period of time. Goals include reminiscing, enjoyment and sharing of thoughts and feelings with others.

Love myself collage

Materials: Drawing paper or construction paper, magazines, tissue paper, felt, sequins and other collage materials, scissors, glue and markers.

Procedure: Ask group members to find pictures that represent ways to nurture, soothe and show love and respect for oneself. In addition, participants might choose to cut out a variety of shapes (e.g. hearts and flowers) from construction and/or tissue paper. They might use words from the magazines to help emphasize thoughts. Photos might include healthy and/or delicious food, people smiling, families showing affection, people enjoying vacations, someone sipping tea, etc.

Discussion/goals: Clients discuss the positive photos that comprise the collage and their associations to the photos. Goals include increased self-esteem and identification of ways to cherish oneself.

Arrow collage

Materials: Construction paper, drawing paper, scissors, glue, markers and cardboard.

Procedure: Clients cut a variety of arrows (all shapes, sizes and colors) from construction paper. (The client can draw the arrows or the therapist may draw and cut them out beforehand if necessary.) At least 8–10 arrows per person are needed. Group participants are asked to arrange the arrows on paper or cardboard in such a way that they represent the direction of one's life (e.g. are all the arrows pointing downwards? Are they going in many different directions?). The arrows are then glued onto the paper or cardboard.

Discussion/goals: Discussion focuses on exploring one's life direction, goals and the obstacles to achieving one's goals. Objectives include achieving greater self-awareness, focusing and problem solving.

Walk in my shoes[6]

Materials: Drawing paper, construction paper, magazines, scissors, glue and markers.

Procedure: Suggest that clients share with others what it's like "to walk in their shoes." Have them draw or cut out a picture of a pair of shoes and glue it in the center of the paper. Next direct clients to choose pictures from the magazines that represent their lifestyle, struggles, problems, experiences and goals. Suggest that those pictures are placed so that they surround the shoes. Clients may include sketches and/or write feelings or other ideas on the collage.

Discussion/goals: Clients share issues, problems, losses, changes in their life and various experiences. Goals include self-awareness, sharing, empathy, identifying problems and expressing concerns.

Thinking out of the box

Materials: Magazines, construction paper, scissors and glue.

Procedure: Have clients find groupings of pictures that make unusual or strange statements. Examples may include a woman holding an elephant, a man dancing with a flower, a dog with the head of a cat. The idea is to think outside of the box—to design something unusual that will create conversation and encourage creative experimentation. Work of abstract and modernistic artists such as Picasso and Chagall may be used as examples.

Discussion/goals: Clients share the work and discuss what it feels like to design something out of the ordinary. Discuss their comfort level and generalize their reactions to the way they respond to change and unusual happenings in their lives. Goals include abstract thinking and loosening of rigid ideas and boundaries.

Stencil collage

Materials: A variety of stencils, construction paper, glue, pencils and scissors.

Procedure: Clients outline a variety of stencils (both shapes, figures and words if desired) and cut them out of the construction paper. Then they glue the shapes onto another sheet of paper to create a design. Have group members title their work.

Discussion/goals: Clients share the title and meaning attributed to the work. Encourage identification with shapes and colors utilized. Goals include problem solving, focusing and increased self-esteem.
This project is easy and guarantees success.

Empty/full

Materials: Drawing paper, magazines, markers, glue and scissors.

Procedure: Have clients fold their paper in half and ask them to find pictures and words that represent themselves feeling full (full of hope, love, friendship, food, etc.) on one side of the page and pictures that represent themselves feeling empty (feeling lost, lonely, black, little hope, saddened by world affairs, etc.) on the other side.[7]

Discussion/goals: Clients share what leaves them feeling empty and what fills them up. Examine what they have and what they are missing. Goals include identification of wants and needs and appreciation for the positives in one's life.

Healing mandala collage

Materials: Drawing paper, markers, magazines, glue, scissors and paper plates.

Procedure: Have clients create a circle by outlining a paper plate. Direct them to fill in the circle with photos that represent ways in which they are healing. They may add figures, phrases and words. Examples may include a sun to represent increased energy and happiness, flowers to symbolize beauty and a river to represent serenity.

Discussion/goals: Discussion focuses on the photos, words and symbols chosen. Encourage clients to share their feelings and reactions to the collage and ask them whether or not it is self-representative. Support group members to title the collage and explain the reason/s for the title. Goals include identifying objectives, positive feelings, needs and ways to gain support.

Most clients chose to represent things that made them feel joyful as opposed to specific healing representations. They were supported to go with the theme in any way they chose. Group members appeared very relaxed and focused when working on this directive. The healing came from the actual choosing of the photos, cutting and gluing as well as processing the completed work.

A 72-year-old woman named Kate titled her mandala "Relationships." She was very focused on creating the collage and carefully chose photos that represented people in all types of relationships. She included families, couples, a man and woman dancing, pictures of mothers and daughters and a large photo of a smiling baby. The mother is not seen, but her hand is holding the baby, covering her stomach. The baby has a wide smile, as does everyone in the photos. At the bottom of the mandala is a woman dressed in a white robe looking up "at the baby" and praying. Kate highlighted her head with bright yellow marker to emphasize her spirituality and desire for happiness. She remarked that the yellow line drawn around the entire mandala represents hope. Kate stated the woman in the photo is praying for friends and family: "She would like to have a baby in her life." Kate stated she regrets never marrying "because I don't have a husband or grandchildren to hug and cherish." She stated she would feel better if she had people in her life to love. She desperately wants a relationship but doesn't know how to meet people; she is fearful of rejection. Group members praised her artwork and helped her explore various ways to make friends.

A woman in her 80s created a collage titled "Inspirations." She included people and items that gave her pleasure. She included flowers, a mother and son talking, a photo of *The Wizard of Oz*, a family having a picnic, a large piece of lemon cake, books, a spotless kitchen, strawberries and children napping. She remarked that she felt comforted by the photos and hoped that she'd see her family more often; her son lived in another state and didn't visit as often as she would have liked. She stated she missed her four grandchildren.

A woman named Esther titled her collage "Happy." She included in her collage a large chocolate chip cookie, blueberries, flowers, a baby, a dog, children, a woman sipping coffee and reading, a woman smiling and a butterfly. She stated the cookie symbolized that she is baking again and the flowers symbolized that she is able to engage in gardening again. She stated the smiling woman "is me" and the baby "is my grandson." She remarked "for a while I was not able to enjoy my grandchildren because I was too depressed, but now I am able 'to feel again' and begin doing what I used to do in the past." She stated she never thought she'd be able to appreciate nature again.

Storytelling

Materials: A multicolored ball of yarn.

Procedure: Clients work together to think of a theme for a group story. One group member holds the yarn, unwinds it and begins telling the story. That person speaks until the yarn color changes, and then the person sitting next to him unwinds the yarn and continues the story until the color changes again. This goes on until everyone has had a chance to contribute to the story.

Discussion/goals: Clients assess the story and decide if the theme prevailed. Goals include socialization, sharing, communication and creative thinking.

Sharing (2)

Materials: Writing paper, pens and pencils.

Procedure: Clients are asked to write five things about themselves, some true and some false. Each person reads their list and group members guess if the descriptions are accurate.

Discussion/goals: Clients share characteristics, experiences and relationships. Goals include socialization, communication and connecting with peers.

Home life

Materials: Pre-outlined house, magazines, glue and scissors.

Procedure: Leader provides an outline of a house that fills an 8.5 × 10 inch sheet of paper. The house may be hand-drawn or taken from Google Images. Group members are asked to fill in the house with photos that represent the items, treasures, pets, friends and family members that inhabit their house. They may also include furniture, flowers, food, etc.

Discussion/goals: Clients explore the representations of their homes and possessions and share thoughts about their living situations. The difference between a house and a home and feelings about past and present homes may be discussed. Goals include sharing, communicating with peers, and exploring the effect one's home, belongings and family, or lack thereof, have on attitude and behavior.

Clients enjoy this exercise because it is easy, enjoyable, structured and reflects their feelings about their home life. They like to share the photos that fill the house outline.

A client named Betty filled her house outline with a woman drinking coffee while sitting by a computer, a rabbit, a man and small child, flowers, a half-eaten apple, pots and pans, dog food and a large brown dog. Betty remarked that her home is ordinary but comfortable. She stated she preferred the house she lived in for over 25 years, but it was too large and too much work to maintain. The man and child represented her husband and "her daughter long ago." Betty mentioned that they used to laugh a lot and go to the movies on Saturdays together. She sighed as she stated that her daughter now lives in another state and she doesn't see her too often. Betty remarked that she misses her and her two beautiful grandchildren.

Robert, a widower in his 70s, included all of his pets in his home outline: two dogs, three cats, a parrot, rabbit, tropical fish, a white mouse and an iguana. Robert remarked that his pets are his family: "They keep me from feeling too lonely." He stated he feeds them well, even frequenting fast-food restaurants to buy his dogs the fried chicken they enjoy. He stated that taking care of his pets gives him something to do and a reason to get out of bed in the morning: "It takes me a long time to feed and care for them." Walking the dogs affords him the opportunity to socialize and greet his neighbors while getting much-needed exercise. He joked with his peers that his house is turning into a zoo.

Collage of tears

Materials: Drawing paper, magazines, scissors, markers and glue.

Procedure: Clients create a collage with pictures that represent their feelings of loss and/or sadness. They may also use words and phrases from the magazines or they might write their own.

Discussion/goals: Clients examine their illustrations and associations with them. Goals include expression of sorrow and loss. It is often difficult for clients to share their anguish; this project offers a relatively non-threatening way of beginning a dialogue on this theme. Clients can explore their entire collage or one small aspect of it. It is a way for them to begin to identify their losses and feelings of grief and share those feeling with others. Sharing the feelings allows clients to begin to move on with their life and helps to relieve and/or minimize anxiety symptoms such as headaches, anxiety attacks, dizziness and stomach aches. Some people have kept their sorrow bottled for years; this directive often proves very cathartic for these individuals.

Profile collage[8]

Materials: Large outline of a profile, pre-drawn on poster board or light cardboard. This will be used as a template. An optimal size would be approximately 14–16 inches. Pencils, magazines, drawing paper, glue, markers and scissors will also be utilized.

Procedure: Clients place the template on a sheet of drawing paper and follow the outline using a pencil. When the template is outlined, have group members cut it out. If this is difficult for clients, the therapist may do the cutting and/or the outlining. Next, participants are asked to fill in the head with pictures that are self-representative. They may include photos of people, nature, food, children, advertisements, words, phrases and anything that they can relate to in some way.

Discussion/goals: Individuals share the way in which their profile reflects their personality, characteristics, likes and dislikes. Goals include self-awareness, sharing with others, introspection and identification of desires, achievements, talents and goals.

Notes

1. A modification of this project would include having clients fill the heart in with colored squares and then write affirmations, phrases or words that describe themselves positively in each square.
2. Modified from a project by Dean Nimmer (2008).
3. If this project is adapted in a psychiatric facility, it is important to make sure that it is acceptable for clients to use personal photos (confidentiality).
4. Suggested by Rita Klachkin, MS, EdS, ATR-BC, LAC LCAT. Enhancements to this directive include giving out pre-made items for group members to eat afterwards or baking simple treats if cooking hotplates are available.
5. Many supermarkets and art supply stores sell these papers in a large variety of colors and designs, usually in packs of 50–100.
6. Modification of a project by Mary Beth Bauernshub, Mitchville, MD.
7. This project has also been successful in mask design (half of the mask is empty, the other half full). Clients will often represent life as they wish it to be.
8. Modification of a directive utilized by Tracylynn Navarro, MA, ATR-BC.

CHAPTER 9
CHANGE/
TRANSFORMATION

Accepting change is very difficult for most individuals. Older adults are faced with many unpleasant changes and losses. Clients have to learn to accept changes that might include retirement, loss of friends and family, loss of one's home and loss of health and energy. Transformation aids personal growth, healing and recovery. It entails having the clients challenge old beliefs and attitudes. Transformation involves turning losses into something people can cope with and accept. For instance, when an individual has to move to a small apartment after living in a large house for many years, he is usually very upset. To help with this lifestyle transformation, the client may be supported to make the new home as attractive as possible and focus on its benefits. Some of these might include the fact that it is easier to clean, it's cozy and bright, and all the rooms are on one floor. Perhaps everything is new and spic and span. When clients are not physically able to do what they did in the past, they can transform their skills. For example, someone who was a piano player and now has arthritis may be able to guide others and assist them in learning how to play the piano. Individuals discover that they have the choice of adjusting to new circumstances or remaining angry and sad. It is a continuous process of redefining and refining relationships and lifestyle. Moving on is difficult but not impossible. It takes patience, support and hope.

Individuals learn what is and what is not changeable, and what is and what is not in their control. They learn that sometimes they need to find new ways to achieve pleasure. Perhaps new experiences and meeting stimulating people can create feelings of satisfaction, similar to pleasant feelings one had in the past. Some clients learn a new skill or volunteer and help others to find satisfaction and joy in their life. Clients discover how skills and insights gained over the years can be used to help them cope.

Pain

Materials: Drawing paper, markers, crayons and oil pastels.

Procedure: In order to decrease pain, it is helpful to first form a mental image of the discomfort. Ask group members to close their eyes, take a deep cleansing breath and visualize their pain. Have them focus on the size, shape, color and intensity of it. Next distribute two sheets of paper per person and ask clients to draw their pain on one sheet of paper using color, shape and/or design and then transform their pain on the second sheet of paper to a friendlier, more soothing color, shape and design.

Discussion/goals: Discussion may focus on questions such as:

1. How long has the pain been a problem?
2. On a 1–10 scale, where 1 represents the least pain and 10 represents the most pain, what number is the pain?
3. How often does the pain express itself?
4. Is there a pattern to the pain?

In addition to these questions, explore ways to relax the pain away—for example, talking to it and/or having it talk to you (using the symbols sketched).

The pictures drawn may be visualized in a relaxation technique where clients attempt to "draw" the pain out of their body. They visualize the symbols flowing out of their bodies via their arms, legs, even mouths.

Past and present (2)

Materials: Writing paper, drawing paper, magazines, construction paper, glue, scissors, markers, oil pastels, pens and pencils.

Procedure: Ask clients to describe themselves in the past (write about the way they looked, what they liked to do, who their friends were, their jobs, etc.). Next ask them to create a drawing and/or collage representing their life in the years to come. They may include friends, family, jobs/volunteer positions, possible vacations, desires and dreams.

This project may be divided into two sessions if necessary.

Discussion/goals: Discussion focuses on comparing the past with the present and future. Clients explore how change can be exciting, providing opportunities for enjoyment, insight and growth. Goals include accepting and coping with change while increasing insight and hope for the future.

The move

Materials: Drawing paper, pens, pencils, writing paper, scissors, glue, markers, oil pastels, crayons and colored pencils.

Procedure: Suggest that group members draw a house (outlines may be distributed if the leader wishes to do so). Have participants fill in the house and cut it out. Next ask clients to write a brief essay or poem about the house they just designed (a short paragraph will suffice). Finally, ask clients to trade their house with someone else in the room. No one should keep his original picture.

Discussion/goals: Discussion focuses on the houses created, how it felt for group members to part with them and how it felt to receive new ones. Clients will then relate their experience to past, recent and/or possible future moves. Goals include self-awareness, coping with change and acceptance.

Empty nest

Materials: Drawing paper, markers, crayons, oil pastels, writing paper, pens, pencils, scissors, glue and magazines.

Procedure: Ask clients to draw a large nest or provide an outline of one. Suggest that clients fill it with pictures, sketches, photographs and words.

Discussion/goals: Discussion focuses on questions including:

1. What items are in the nest?
2. Is the nest full, moderate or empty?
3. How did it feel to view the empty nest at the beginning of the session?
4. Does the nest need to be full at all times?
5. How can the nest be connected to being alone or a decrease in family members living in the home?
6. How did it feel when your children left for college, began to work outside of the home or decided to live on their own?

7. How have you coped with the "empty nest syndrome?"

Goals include expanding on coping skills and exploring how change affects mood, attitude and behavior.

A widow named Arlene drew herself with her family in a "comfortable nest." She sadly stated, "My husband should be in the nest, but he passed away two years ago." She included her daughter, her granddaughter and her daughter's dog, Sandy. She remarked that the family is close and safe in the nest. She didn't place her son-in-law in the picture because her daughter may separate from him in the near future. She stated, "I never really liked him anyway."

Strengths/weaknesses

Materials: Drawing paper, writing paper, pens, pencils and markers.

Procedure: Ask clients to draw or write about things they are not able to do now but were able to do in the past—for example, play piano, participate in sports, hike. Next ask them to transform these "inabilities" into something that is different but can still provide pleasure. For example, someone who can't play piano anymore because of arthritis or poor eyesight could now listen to music or attend piano recitals; someone who is not fit enough to play tennis or baseball can watch ball games on television.

Discussion/goals: Discussion focuses on the importance of substituting one activity for another and being flexible. Goals include examining ways to cope with change and exploring ways to enjoy leisure activities and life to its fullest.

Physical transformation

Materials: Drawing paper, markers, oil pastels and crayons.

Procedure: Ask clients to draw themselves at a young age (perhaps in their 20s or 30s) on one side of the paper and their present age on the other side of the paper.

Discussion/goals: Discussion focuses on the similarities and differences between the two pictures. Encourage clients to share thoughts about physical changes such as thinning hair, wrinkles, perhaps weight gain or needing to wear glasses, a hearing aid, needing to use a walker or cane. Goals include learning acceptance and dealing with disabilities. The therapist helps clients work toward finding a new definition of beauty and strength.

Victim to hero

Materials: Drawing paper, markers, oil pastels, pastels and crayons.

Procedure: Suggest that clients draw themselves in the victim role (helpless or weak) and then change the drawing so that they become the hero (strong and powerful). For example, a client might draw himself in a row boat lost at sea (victim) and then transform the drawing (or create a new drawing) to put him in the role of captain, in charge of a large ship. Another example might be of a client depicting himself alone in a large room (victim) and then changing the drawing so that he is standing in the center of a large crowd giving food or money to the people surrounding him (hero).

Discussion/goals: Clients share their transformation and the feelings associated with the change. They explore how people can change their roles in life with the right attitude and behavior. Goals include instilling strength, awareness and increasing self-esteem.

Opposites

Materials: Drawing paper, markers, oil pastels, pastels and crayons.

Procedure: Ask clients to fold their paper in half. Have them draw a feeling, emotion, movement, person, description and/or activity on one side of the paper and its opposite on the other side. Provide a description of opposites to choose from if desired. Some examples include:

- brave/cowardly
- bright/dull
- dark/light
- everything/nothing
- girl/boy
- happy/sad
- fearless/fearful
- hope/despair
- huge/small
- kids/adults
- man/woman
- neat/messy
- old/young
- past/present
- rise/set
- straight/wavy.

Discussion/goals: Discuss the differences between the two pictures and then relate the theme of contrast to one's emotional and physical life. Explore how an individual can experience more than one feeling at a time. For instance, a person can feel both anger and love; he can be strong and independent during certain parts of his life and more dependent, perhaps needing extra assistance, during other parts of his life. People can like some characteristics of a friend but find other characteristics distasteful; part of one's day may be delightful and other parts of it may be unpleasant. By accepting contrasts in life, people are better able to cope and see "the big picture" and keep an open mind. Goals include self-awareness and development of critical thinking skills.

A client named Tamar drew a woman and a man and titled her picture "Happy Girl and Sad Boy." The illustration depicts a woman who is fully clothed and appears much stronger than the man. She is wider and heavier than the man and her mouth is emphasized. His mouth is thin and slanted downward. Her eyes brows are also slanted, which gives her an angry appearance. The man looks weak. His body is composed of a series of small unconnected lines and his eyebrows are lifted up, giving him a sad and almost surprised appearance. While the woman's feet are placed flat on the ground, the man seems to be floating and he appears off balance. Tamar stated that the woman represents her and the man represents her husband. She remarked that she might divorce him after 45 years of marriage. She explained that he is not interested in going anywhere or doing anything with her and hardly speaks to her: "We never go on vacation." She wants to move to a small condominium and he doesn't want to move, but he won't help clean the large house. "He's a chauvinist," Tamar remarked, "he just doesn't care." Group members suggested she express her feelings to him using "I" statements. Tamar is usually too unsure of herself to speak up and let others know her true feelings. She agreed to try but wasn't optimistic about her husband's response.

A client named Toni drew an angel and a devil. The angel is smiling and its arms are extended outward as if it's ready to hug someone. The devil appears angry and one arm is holding a pitchfork. He's filled in with black crayon. Toni remarked that she can sometimes be an angel, but she's also capable of being a devil. She related the devil in her to her bipolar disorder, which sometimes "makes me act in ways that aren't very nice. Sometimes I yell too much or accuse people of doing things they have not done. I can get out of control." She attributed the devil to overspending and having affairs when she was younger. She felt the angel was the stronger figure because of its light blue halo and yellow wings. Toni stated she is trying to find a happy medium but she's afraid she will return to being the devil again. This is a great fear for her, but she was able to say that she will fight against this happening again.

Time (2)

Materials: Pre-drawn clock, drawing paper, scissors, glue, markers, oil pastels, crayons and pencils.

Procedure: Provide the outline of a clock to each participant; make sure the time of day is not marked. Ask clients to fill in the time, cut the clock out and glue it on another sheet of paper. Next suggest group members draw or write their response to the saying "Time goes by too quickly." Clients may create an environment surrounding the clock or decorate the clock if so desired.

Discussion/goals: Discussion focuses on the passage of time and thoughts associated with it. Life events, achievements and regrets may be explored. Examine the time of day that was chosen and associated meanings. Goals include sharing feelings about change and aging.

A client named Francine drew a clock with brightly colored squiggles surrounding it. The time on the clock was 3.30 p.m. Next to the clock she placed her three grandchildren and wrote, "Time goes by so quickly; my grandchildren have gotten so big. I love spending time with them, but I am afraid that soon they won't have time for me. They will want to be with their friends and they will have other interests. That will make me very sad and lonely." Francine chose 3.30 p.m. because that is the time the children arrive home from school. She brightened as she described how she hugs the children and gives them cookies and milk when they arrive home.

A widow named Mandy created a brightly colored clock and wrote, "Make each day special. Keep your memories special." She choose 6 p.m. because "that is my dinner time." She stated she usually has a large dinner with her family. "It is the time of day that everyone shares what they did during day; I feel happiest when I am with my family."

A divorcee named Clarissa drew a heavily outlined clock. When asked about the outline, she stated, "It represents the very slow passage of time for me." The time placed on the clock was 2 p.m. Clarissa remarked that "2 p.m. is in the middle of the day; the time of day when I feel lonely and bored." She included many phrases and words surrounding the clock. Some of the phrases included " Tick Tock! Tick Tock! Time passes slowly when I am bored; Time just passes, Time passes so slowly, so slowly, emptiness." Clarissa was not responding well to antidepressants and was in the process of considering electroshock convulsive therapy to help her severe depression. She was very indecisive because she was afraid of the treatment and she "was not sure if she really did want to change."

A 69-year-old man named Daniel drew a clock outlined in blue and emphasized 4 p.m. The blue represented "a peaceful feeling," and 4 p.m. represented "when I get home from the program." He said this with a wide grin. He titled his picture "Time Flies By So Quickly." He wrote, "I cannot believe that it has been 45 years ago that I was in the Navy. I cannot believe where the time went from age 40–60. I cannot believe I recently had my 50th reunion from high school. I cannot believe it has been ten years since I was in Ireland."

A 66-year-old woman named Bonnie created a heavily outlined clock with layers of "armor." She drew a bright orange layer ("hope") and then a layer of dashes with straight lines ("uncertainty") intersecting it, then a thin layer lined with black marker and finally "a layer of arrows." Bonnie remarked, "the layers are protective; I want time to stop." She expressed fear of getting older and possibly getting ill. She expressed concern that she might have no one to take care of her in the future and she might be alone. The clock is stopped at 12.15 p.m. because "that is lunchtime." Bonnie

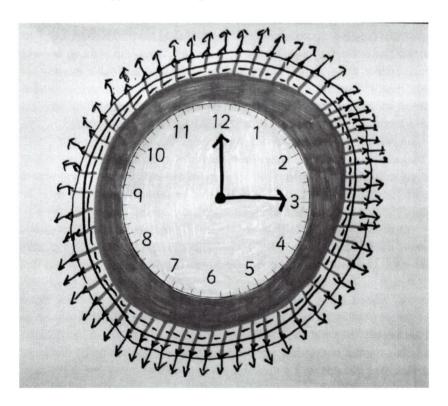

remarked she feels most at ease during lunch when she is not thinking about her problems and just focusing on what she is eating and what she will do for the rest of the day. While participating in the outpatient program, she remarked that "she loves to chat with other group members while she eats and sips her tea."

Fear and its opposite

Materials: Writing paper, drawing paper, pens, pencils, colored pencils, markers, crayons and oil pastels.

Procedure: Have clients fold their paper in half and create a small symbol representing fear on one side of the paper toward the top of the page (e.g. a bolt of lightning, a large snake, spider or an angry-looking face). Next have them create a symbol representing boldness, confidence or courage on the other side of the page (e.g. a lion, eagle, unicorn, shield or sword). Now ask group members to write things they are afraid of under the fear symbol (even the most minor fears) and things they are not afraid of under the bravery symbol.

Discussion/goals: Discussion focuses on comparing and contrasting the symbols and the lists. Goals include self-awareness, relief due to expression of fears and exploration of coping skills.

Change (1)

Materials: Drawing paper, pastels, crayons and markers.

Procedure: Ask clients to fold their paper in half. Have them draw things they can't change (e.g. their age, perhaps a physical disability) on one side of the paper and things they can change (e.g. attitude, mood) on the other side of the paper.

Discussion/goals: Individuals often focus on what they can't change and aren't in control of in their life. This exercise helps clients to observe the differences between what is and what is not changeable. It helps them refocus by becoming aware of self-defeating thoughts and behaviors, and then transforming negative behaviors into more positive ones. Clients begin to understand what to accept and what to challenge in their life.

Past and present (3)

Materials: Drawing paper, markers, oil pastels, pastels and crayons.

Procedure: Ask clients to fold their paper in half. Have them draw what they enjoyed about the past on one side of the paper and what they find strange or unpleasant about present-day life on the other side.

Discussion/goals: Discussion focuses on differences between the past and present and how clients cope with change. Examine how the artwork reflects positive life events and experiences. Explore ways in which the skills and insights gained over the years can be used to help clients cope with life as it is today.

This is a helpful directive for older clients. It helps them express thoughts about changing times. Issues such as electronics, the internet, cellphone abuse, aloofness, isolation, rudeness and differences in how people act towards one another are often examined. It gives clients a chance to vent about the differences in family relationships, the negative way in which many elderly people are treated, and fear associated with war and terrorism. Clients usually speak about "the old days" when a person could walk in the street any time of day and ride the subways late at night without fear. They speak about years gone by when families stayed close and children didn't move far away from their parents: "People were able to get together and see their grandchildren often or even live with them." Many categorize today's children as disconnected, selfish and unfocused. They see this "new world" much the same way. Clients usually feel comforted when their peers express similar opinions and share similar experiences.

In response to this exercise, one patient remarked she felt more in control when she was younger. She was aware of the popular music, movies and trends. She knew what was expected of her (housewife) and she knew what to expect from others (respect and support). She was in charge of her home and her family. Family gatherings were frequent and enjoyable. The world felt safe. Her picture of a large primitive-looking computer represented a change in her life she wasn't prepared for and disliked. She wanted to go back to the past when "times were simpler." Most group members agreed fully.

An 85-year-old woman named Ethel disagreed. This woman joined the Peace Corps at age 80 and worked in Europe for two years. She was a major contributor to women working in the service during World War II. She drew a dishwasher and washing machine and stated that appliances are amazing. She felt life is easier today because of advances in medicine, cancer therapies, drug therapies and surgical procedures. She spoke about improvement in car manufacturing, she loved air conditioning and she expressed appreciation of computers because they allow her to communicate with others who live far away.

Change (2)

Materials: Drawing paper, markers, pens and pencils.

Procedure: Ask clients to fold their paper in half. Have them draw something difficult to change (e.g. attitude, move to a smaller house, getting out of bed) on one side of the paper. Next direct them to list on the other side of the paper the first three steps that will help create the change.

Discussion/goals: Discussion focuses on lifestyle and attitude changes. Goals include acceptance and exploration of coping skills such has taking "one step at a time; taking baby steps."

Redefining happiness

Materials: Drawing paper, markers, crayons and oil pastels.

Procedure: Explore the process of change and the way we adjust to life's circumstances. Discuss how our definition of happiness may need to be transformed during different periods of our life depending on our age, situation and experiences. Loss of a loved one or long-time job, for instance, may push us to recreate another way of finding joy and fulfillment. After the group discussion, ask clients to draw how they can redefine their happiness.

Discussion/goals: Discuss ways to find joy in small pleasures and methods to make transformations. Goals include being mindful and making the most of what we have at the moment.

Blending of emotions

Materials: Watercolors, watercolor paper, cups for water, brushes. If clients do not choose to paint, oil pastels or chalk pastels will serve nicely.

Procedure: Review the meaning of being mindful (living in the present moment, focusing, being aware) with clients. Remind group members that mindfulness includes the ability to allow feelings to come and go;

they do not have to work to control them. Suggest that participants use color and shape to represent feelings they have recently experienced. Suggest they blend the colors to demonstrate transformation from one feeling into another. For example, red might represent excitement or anger and that might be transformed into a more mellow pink by adding white, and then that color might be transformed into a stronger purple by adding red and blue.

Discussion/goals: Clients share the transformation of colors and shapes that compose the artwork. Goals include expression of feelings and observation of change. Clients are encouraged to relate transformation to various areas of their life.

Healing (2)

Materials: Drawing paper, markers, oil pastels and crayons.

Procedure: Have clients draw symbols, figures and sketches to represent ways in which they are healing. For example, drawing a smile may demonstrate increased happiness, sketching someone walking or jogging may represent more activity in one's life, and a heart may symbolize being able to feel love again.

Discussion/goals: Clients examine their progress in therapy by exploring the artwork, which depicts healthy behaviors, activities, moods, movements and actions. Goals include focusing on progress, strengths, recovery and positive thinking.

Expressing emotions

Materials: Drawing paper, markers, pens and pencils.

Procedure: Provide clients with the outline of five heads (blank ovals). Instruct them to fill in the ovals with various expressions. Ask group members to write the reason the character has a specific expression. For example, if the face is smiling, maybe the smile is a result of positive self-talk or thinking about someone special such as a grandchild.

Discussion/goals: Discussion focuses on the ease or difficulty of expressing emotions and reasons for expressing specific emotions such as anger or frustration. Goals include greater self-awareness, a focus on communication skills and relationships and identifying one's inner and outer self (how we really feel and how we come across to others).

Old and new

Materials: Drawing paper, markers, oil pastels and crayons.

Procedure: Have clients fold their paper in half and draw "What I will allow into my life" on one side of the page and "What I can release (let go)" on the other side of the page. Suggest they allow the new in and release old patterns.

Discussion/goals: Discussion focuses on healthy change and attitudes toward new experiences. Goals include identification of barriers and exploration of ways to embrace growth, innovative ideas and creative thinking.

Life's changes[1]

Materials: Pens, pencils, drawing paper, magazines, scissors and glue.

Procedure: Have clients answer the following questions and share their responses.

1. What changes in your life are you experiencing at the present time?
2. Have you moved recently?
3. Have you changes jobs or volunteer positions recently?
4. Have you recently retired?
5. Has someone close to you moved away?
6. Has someone close to you recently passed away?
7. Do you notice a change in your strength?
8. Is there a change in what you can physically manage at home?
9. Has there recently been a change in your skin, body, hair or weight?
10. Has the state of your health changed?
11. Have any of your relationships changed over the last few years?
12. Have you noticed a change in your mood or attitude?
13. Are there changes coming up in your life that you are anticipating (good or bad)?

Then ask them to find one or more photos that represent their attitude toward change and glue the photos on the paper—for example, a frowning person (negative outlook), someone joyfully dancing (feeling positive).

Discussion/goals: Discussion focuses on the responses to the questions and identification of anxiety/unhappiness associated with transitions. The mini collages are explored and attitudes toward change are examined. Goals include helping group members deal with and better accept physical, emotional, social and environmental changes.

Young/old

Materials: Drawing paper, markers, crayons and oil pastels.

Procedure: On one side of the paper direct clients to draw things about themselves that make them feel young (e.g. walking/exercising, good sense of humor, their grandchildren), and on the other side of the page have them draw things about themselves that make them feel old (e.g. aches and pains, too serious, no goals or purpose, living in a small apartment versus a large home). Items drawn may be physical, emotional and/or environmental.

Discussion/goals: Explore ways in which the artwork relates to one's attitude and behaviors. Goals include awareness of strengths and weaknesses and exploration of skills needed to maintain strength and a positive outlook.

Change (3)

Materials: White paper (8.5 × 11 inches), markers, oil pastels, colored pencils and crayons.

Procedure: Use Google Images to find an outline of a person (or draw one yourself) that fills an 8.5 × 11 inch sheet of paper. Make four copies of the figure. Label the first figure "Teenager," the second figure "Young adult," the third figure "Middle age" and the fourth figure "Older adult." Create a booklet that includes theses four figures and make as many copies of the booklet as there are clients in the therapy group. Next ask group members to represent themselves during various periods of their life by filling in the figures in any way they please. Clients may add faces, hair, clothes, accessories, words, phrases, other people and an environment surrounding the figures if they wish.

Discussion/goals: Using the artwork as a springboard, explore the way clients have changed over the years. Discussion focuses on the meaning of change, beliefs about change and ultimate acceptance. Goals include acknowledgement and understanding of life transitions. Encourage clients to focus on being positive and strong.

Notes

1. This directive may need two sessions to complete.

CHAPTER 10
MURALS

Mural making is beneficial for clients because it promotes togetherness, unity, cooperation and socialization. It provides a forum for discussion, decision making and problem solving. It is often less threatening for clients because everyone contributes equally. Creative thinking is enhanced as group members decide on the theme for the mural and the way it should be approached. Clients are given the opportunity to observe and reflect on their own work as well as the work of others. They feel free to comment because of the non-threatening nature of the directive and because clients understand that each group member is an integral part of the artistic process.

Groups may be led in a variety of ways. Murals may be placed on the wall, floor or table, depending on the flexibility of the clients and layout of the art room. In general, seniors prefer the paper to be placed on a table so they don't have to move about; they feel more comfortable and at ease while seated. The clients or therapist can decide whether participants will draw at the same time or take turns, one person drawing at a time. A theme may be given, clients may decide on a theme or a mural may be drawn in a spontaneous manner. Any number of materials may be utilized, but, with older adults, markers, pastels, magazine photos and collage materials are most desirable. When the mural is hung up after it is completed, clients often enjoy observing it, pointing out their contributions and analyzing it with peers. Their self-esteem and sense of belonging greatly increase.

Universality

Materials: Mural paper, markers and crayons.

Procedure: Discuss with clients how we all have a lot in common with each other (e.g. pain, loss, love). Ask clients to create a list of things they have in common with other group members. Next suggest that they create a mural to represent the theme of universality.

Discussion/goals: Discussion focuses on commonality within the group and the ways in which it is represented in the mural. Goals include connecting with peers, problem solving and socialization.

Protest mural

Materials: Mural paper, markers and crayons.

Procedure: Clients are directed to draw and/or write anything they would like to protest about in their life. For example, someone might draw a slice of pizza to protest that they have to watch their diet or someone might draw a stethoscope to protest about too many doctor visits.

Discussion/goals: Discussion focuses on the design of the mural, what is being protested about and the strength of the objections. Goals include connecting with others, identifying concerns, voicing discontent and developing coping techniques.

Connections (1)

Materials: Mural paper, scissors, glue, construction paper and markers.

Procedure: Ask clients to cut out colorful strips of paper in varying sizes. Next ask them to create a design where their strips interconnect with other group members' strips so that all the pieces are linked in some way and an abstract design is formed.

Discussion/goals: Discussion focuses on connecting with others. Goals include socialization, problem solving and cooperation among group members.

Needs

Materials: Mural paper, markers, oil pastels and crayons.

Procedure: Ask clients to draw what they need from the group as a whole or from individual group members. For example, a client might need more respect, more suggestions or love from the group.

Discussion/goals: Discussion focuses on needs and desires, one's position and role in the group and the relationship between group interactions and communication at home.

Group life mural

Materials: Mural paper, markers, oil pastels and crayons.

Procedure: Ask clients to draw symbols that reflect what goes on in the therapy group or in the program throughout the day. Suggest they represent things such as exercise or gathering together for tea or coffee at the beginning of the day.

Discussion/goals: Discussion focuses on the clients' attitude toward the program and their participation. Goals include identifying attitudes toward recovery and self-awareness.

Connections (2)

Materials: Large sheet of mural paper, markers, outlines of figures, markers, crayons and oil pastels.

Procedure: Provide an outline of a figure for each individual. Ask clients to fill in the figure so that it represents them in some way. Next direct clients to glue their figure on the paper and connect it to at least one other figure by writing a positive word, phrase or statement as the method of connecting one figure to another.

Discussion/goals: Discussion focuses on the figure created (explore facial features, expression, clothes, style and colors used), the way it is situated on the paper (in the middle, bottom, top, end of the paper) and the words used to connect the figure to the other figures. Goals include socialization, awareness of self in relation to others and greater self-awareness.

"Believe in yourself"

Materials: Mural paper, markers, oil pastels and crayons.

Procedure: Discuss with clients what it means to believe in yourself. Suggest they work together to create symbols that represent this concept. They may use words and phrases in addition to pictures.

Discussion/goals: Clients explore the overall mural and then the individual contributions. Examine the theme of self-acceptance as it is reflected in the artwork. Goals include increase of self-esteem and connecting with others.

This project has been presented a variety of times. During one session a group of seniors worked independently and drew various symbols. Then clients decided (with support) to connect the individual drawings with colorful wavy lines. Symbols included two people holding hands, a face with a large smile, a heart, the phrase, "I'm okay, you're okay," flowers, a sun and a figure of a large, bright woman (representing the group member).

During another session clients chose to decide on a unified idea and worked together to design a mural of a woman (the group was composed of women) taking a walk in the park. Trees, grass, flowers and bushes surrounded her, and there was a large yellow sun and a butterfly in the sky. The woman had a bow in her red hair, glasses and a wide smile. Her shoulders appeared large and strong, and her feet were firmly planted on the ground. Clients were very pleased with the outcome of the mural and especially with the way they worked together. Everyone felt that there was much cooperation and flexibility in the group. It was of interest to note that a leader was chosen (the "best artist" according to clients). She was also the most personable individual in the group. It wasn't the leader, though, who directed the other group members; it was another client who was very detailed oriented and diagnosed with obsessive-compulsive disorder. Participants didn't appear to mind taking direction; they were too focused and enthusiastic about the imaginary person they were creating.

Clients remarked that the woman in the picture believed in herself and "had a strong sense of who she was." They stated she was 35 years old, a doctor and had two children. She was married to a wonderful man, but she was very independent. They remarked she decided to take a stroll in the park by herself on a sunny Saturday morning. Most clients were not able to relate to her but hoped they would be able to possess similar qualities of self-acceptance and self-worth in the future.

Baking

Materials: Mural paper, markers, oil pastels, crayons, magazines, scissors and glue.

Procedure: Suggest clients work together to choose pictures from magazines and/or draw things they have baked/cooked in the past and/or present.

Discussion/goals: Baking is a common denominator for many of the clients. A great many individuals used to bake/cook for their families daily and for special occasions, birthday parties, holidays, etc. The theme of baking often evokes memories of family and enjoyable get-togethers.

It assists in reminiscing about joyful times and helps clients to remember strengths (being in charge, organizing, providing, sharing, having a special purpose). Encourage clients to think about the smells, tastes and experience of cooking. Ask them to remember who they were with when they baked and how they felt. Goals include increasing self-esteem and self-reflection. Clients focus on strengths instead of weaknesses.

Mural of hope

Materials: Mural paper, oil pastels, markers and crayons.

Procedure: Suggest clients work together to create a mural that represents hope. Have them draw images of expectations, wishes, goals and desires.

Discussion/goals: Explore the symbols presented and their significance. Support clients to maintain a positive attitude while striving to achieve good mental health and recovery from depression and anxiety. Help clients identify realistic goals.

Spirituality

Materials: Mural paper, oil pastels, markers and crayons.

Procedure: Ask clients to share their personal definition of spirituality and then have them illustrate their thoughts. Suggest that spirituality can focus on religion, but it can also be a belief in nature, love, art, music, the universe, a higher power, etc.

Discussion/goals: Explore how spirituality helps people handle problems, losses, illness and life's uncertainties. Examine the symbols and the meaning of the artwork presented. Observe similarities and/ or differences in the representations. Goals include exploration of the healing power of spirituality, its diversity and its significance for many individuals.

The following list, compiled by clients, incorporates the benefits of being spiritual:

Gives you a purpose.

Raises self-esteem.

Something to believe in.

Better sense of self-worth.

Helps get you through the hard times.

Gives you more faith and confidence.

Can calm you down.

Gives you hope.

Faith, hope and charity, three theological virtues.

Connects you with others, like when you go to church or synagogue.

"My home town"

Materials: Mural paper, markers, oil pastels and crayons.

Procedure: Suggest group members represent something about their home town on the paper. They may add houses, stores, parks, restaurants, their childhood home, schools, favorites spots, etc.

Discussion/goals: Discussion focuses on memories and places of interest. Compare and contrast towns and explore how one's environment affects behavior, mood and interactions with others. Goals include reminiscing and connecting with others.

"Splash of happiness"

Materials: Mural paper, markers, watercolors and brushes.

Procedure: Ask clients to draw or paint symbols associated with the theme "Splash of happiness." Suggest they paint (if they are comfortable doing so) splashes of joy on the paper.

Discussion/goals: Discussion focuses on the images, colors and shapes. Goals include focusing on positive aspects of one's life.

Art tape mural

Materials: Mural paper, assorted colors of masking tape and scissors.[1]

Procedure: Demonstrate how to cut and place the tape to form a simple image. Next ask clients to work together to create a group mural using the colored tape. Encourage clients to decide together how the design will be formed. Will it be completely abstract or will the tape be used to outline realistic subjects such as houses or trees?

Discussion/goals: This is a very easy and non-threatening art form. It is a beneficial project for clients who are not comfortable with more complicated media. Goals include problem solving and making connections emotionally and artistically.

Full body mural

Materials: Mural paper, markers, oil pastels, pastels and crayons.

Procedure: Provide the outline of a full body tracing (you may trace a client's body if he is comfortable enough to let you do this, or have someone trace the outline of your body before group begins). Lay the paper out on a long table so that clients can clearly see the paper and comfortably draw on it. Have them work together to create a person, filling in and decorating, if desired, all parts of the body. Clients may draw together at one time or each group member may receive a specific job (one person draws the hair, another the face, another a dress, eyelashes, shoes, etc.).

Discussion/goals: Clients share their thoughts about the figure. They may give it a name, age, profession, etc. They may choose to decide if it is female or male, married or single, content or depressed, working or unemployed, etc. Explore which group members associate with the figure or with various aspects of it. Suggest clients observe the expression (emotions) and stance (physical presence). Observe if the figure is smiling, angry, sad, etc. Examine which clients participated actively and which ones took a lesser role. Goals include cooperation, communication and self-awareness among group members.

"Senior power"

Materials: Mural paper, markers, oil pastels, pastels and crayons.

Procedure: Suggest that group members work together to create a mural representing things that make older adults powerful. They may use pictures, phrases and words. Examples may include grandchildren, wisdom, teaching/guiding others, patience, stamina and positive memories and experiences.

Discussion/goals: Encourage clients to share the symbolism expressed through their artwork and support them to focus on what is in their control. Goals include looking at the positive side of aging and focusing on strengths instead of weaknesses.

Joint mural[2]

Materials: Large mural paper, cut shapes of integrated design (e.g. a flower arrangement, street scene), oil pastels, glue, markers and a possible still life or pictures available for reference.

Procedure: Clients are assigned one part of the mural to complete and told that their portion must integrate with that of their fellow group members. Clients are then given their allotted number of shapes to draw on, whether flowers or buildings, etc. Clients complete their portions and must, through discussion, integrate with their fellow group members and discuss how each piece will be placed and coordinated on the mural. As the mural fills with drawn-on and glued-on elements, clients work on lessening space. They place each element, with the agreement of other group members, on the paper until the mural is completed.

Discussion/goals: The goal of this directive is to encourage each group member to participate, interact and help decide how the mural will be completed. Seniors tend to isolate even more than others when facing depression and anxiety. The idea of drawing on small areas and gluing them on the paper lessens the anxiety of finishing and filling a large space of paper.

A slice of life

Materials: Each client receives a 4 × 4 inch square of white paper, markers, crayons, oil pastels and glue.

Procedure: Ask clients to draw "a slice of their life" in their square. Suggest they include something about themselves such as hobbies and interests, present or previous jobs, their home and/or important people in their life. Ask them to fill in the entire square. Once the squares are completed clients will be asked to glue the individual squares together to create a group mural.

Discussion/goals: Everyone will share their individual square and then assess the mural as a whole. Goals include self-awareness and sharing of one's life and relationships.

Clients spent a long time putting this small mural together. They elected a leader and she emphasized the need for balance in design and color. The group members decided that each person would glue one of the squares on the paper, but everyone would need to approve the placement. They worked slowly and deliberately, making sure each square was placed in the correct position and contained enough glue so that it would remain stuck to the paper. An apparent bonding took place during this period of time. When the mural was completed, one client asked if she could write the title on the paper. Clients were pleased with the results, and when it was hung on the wall they pointed out their individual square to people who didn't have the opportunity to participate in the project. An obvious sense of pride and self-esteem was derived from each individual's participation.

Group story

Materials: Mural paper, markers, oil pastels and crayons.

Procedure: Group members decide on a theme for a story and associated mural. Each participant adds to the narrative and at the same time illustrates his contribution on the mural paper. The artwork should relate to the ongoing storyline. This keeps occurring until everyone has had an opportunity to contribute at least once. Usually participants have about three to four turns, depending on the size of the group and the enthusiasm of clients. When group members decide the story and mural is completed, discussion begins.

Discussion/goals: Clients discuss their reactions to the story and artwork. Everyone has the chance to share their contributions. Goals include socialization, problem solving, cooperation and creative expression.

Pattern/texture mural

Materials: Large sheet of mural paper, magazines, scissors and glue.

Procedure: Clients cut out patterns from magazines—for example, the patterns from curtains, furniture or a dress. They glue the photos on the paper, deciding together on the placement and whether or not the pictures will overlap. When the mural is completed, it will be composed of many different patterns, colors and designs, creating an abstract, eye-catching piece of art. Unless they choose to focus on a specific method, clients are told not to worry about organization. They are free to glue the pictures in any way they please as long as their peers agree.

Discussion/goals: Clients share their specific contributions and reactions to the competed work. They are asked how it felt to take part in this group project. Goals include cooperation, working together, experiencing artistic freedom, making choices and problem solving.

Clients greatly enjoy this project. It gives them a sense of unity and togetherness. One client remarked, "It's like we are one big family; I never did anything like this before!" It is interesting to note how clients work. Observations, which may be used for greater self-awareness, may include:

- Placement—for instance, one narcissistic gentleman placed his texture photo right in the middle of the page, while many other participants choose the outer corners.

- The way clients place their photos on the mural. Do they work neatly? Does it take them a long time to decide on placement? Are they applying the paste on the correct side of the photo?

- Are they fearful of placing the photo in the wrong place? (This is common among group members.)

- Are group members patient or impatient while waiting their turn?

- Are clients unwilling to overlap others' work even thought they are given permission to do so (fear of angering or hurting others)?

- Can they work well with peers?

- Do they dominate the mural and take over, or are they meek and withdrawn?

- Do they follow directions appropriately?

- Do they see the exercise as a chore or do they find it enjoyable to create with their peers?

- When the work is completed, how do they feel? Are they proud of their participation or apathetic?

- How do the clients' reactions relate to their experiences and relationships with friends and family?

Graffiti mural

Materials: Large sheet of mural paper, markers and oil pastels.

Procedure: Explore what graffiti is, why it has been so popular over the years and where one might see it (on a train, bus, car, billboard or the side of a building in the city, even on a mountainside of stone located on the highway). Next instruct group members to write and/or draw whatever they want on the mural using bright colors and imaginative designs. They may doodle, scribble and add their signature and/or messages. Suggest participants might include affirmations, comments on news and current events, things about themselves or family members or random thoughts. Religion and politics are forbidden because they can cause too much controversy, anger and offense. Suggest the clients "let themselves go" and have fun. Encourage spontaneity.

Discussion/goals: Clients share their contributions and associated meanings, as well as reactions to the entire mural. Goals include self-expression, artistic freedom and enhancement of creativity and communication skills.

Road to recovery

Materials: Mural paper, markers, oil pastels, magazines, scissors and glue.

Procedure: A client or the group leader outlines a large road that fills most of the paper. Participants are asked to add to the road people, places and things that are important for one's recovery. Everyone has a turn to add drawings and/or photos such as smiling people, men and women exercising, healthy foods, a photo of a doctor and a patient, a dog or cat. The pictures may be drawn or cut out from magazines.

Discussion/goals: Clients share significant items on the road and the way in which they are helpful. Goals include connecting with peers and identifying needs, progress and goals for recovery.

Decades mural

Materials: Large sheet of mural paper, markers, crayons and pastels.

Procedure: Have clients decide which decade they wish to focus on. This will depend on the ages of the group members—for example, seniors will most likely choose the 1940s or 1950s, and baby boomers may select the 1960s or 1970s. Suggest that participants draw items, clothes, symbols, words and things they would find during that period of time. For example, if the 1960s were chosen, symbols might include bell-bottom pants, a guitar, flower (flower power), a hippie, the Beatles.

Discussion/goals: Discussion focuses on the era, the symbols drawn and reminiscing about that period of time. Goals include socialization, cooperation and unity. Reminiscing brings individuals together, enhances self-awareness and often brings about positive feelings.

Notes

1. Tape may be purchased from S&S Worldwide and Amazon.com.
2. Directive suggested by Rita Klachkin, MS, EdS, ATR-BC, LAC, LCAT. This directive can also be adapted for seniors facing cognitive conditions such as Alzheimer's or dementia.

CHAPTER 11
COPING SKILLS

"Coping skills" is an umbrella term for many different types of therapeutic interventions. Coping skills may include cognitive behavioral therapy, dialectical behavioral therapy, communication skills, behavior modification, leisure skills, time management, self-esteem skills, anger management, art therapy, dance/movement therapy, music therapy, journaling, etc. Clients learn how to express feelings and to think and behave in a healthy manner. They learn how to adjust to life's changes and to accept loss and rejection. Individuals discover methods to decrease stress and worry. They become acquainted with ways to be mindful, hopeful and calm; they learn how to set goals and attain them. Clients are taught to focus on their own issues and not just the issues of family and friends. They explore ways to be independent and take care of their physical and psychological health.

Many people have never acquired the skills needed to handle life's trials and tribulations. They use poor techniques such as black and white thinking, denial and avoidance. It is important that these clients explore methods to be more open-minded. Eventually clients begin to realize that erroneous thinking such as negative self-talk is harming them. With support, they work to implement new techniques such as positive self-talk and mindfulness.

Seniors use various coping skills to deal with issues such as disability, illness, loss, moving to a smaller home or assisted living, retirement and depression. They explore ways to make sense of their life as it is at the present and they discover ways to develop and find new skills, friends and hobbies. Sometimes older adults have to find a new purpose in life to keep them motivated and energized. They examine how to adjust to challenges such as arthritis, aging and living alone. Seniors examine methods to enjoy activities and live each day to the fullest.

While practicing coping skills, people come to realize they have choices; they can decide how to react to issues and problems and they can choose their battles. Coping skills help individuals to increase self-awareness, break down barriers and lessen and/or alleviate loneliness. Clients begin transforming themselves into happier, more functional individuals. They learn to focus on the positive instead of the negative and increase their self-esteem. Self-realization and self-actualization occur as individuals discover and employ new skills.

Self-care (1)

Materials: Drawing and writing paper, pencils, pens, markers and pastels.

Procedure: Ask clients to write a few lines about the way they take care of themselves. Have them read aloud what they wrote. Then ask them to work together and create a mural which reflects the self-care descriptions.

Discussion/goals: Discussion focuses on the written descriptions and the mural. Ask clients to share their view of the mural and specific symbols/ figures represented. Encourage a discussion about self-care and the importance of exercise, proper nutrition, self-esteem, etc. Goals include socialization, problem solving and exploration of methods to take care of one's body and mind.

Examples of self-care descriptions:

- I like to cook healthy meals; it is healthier for your mind and body. I like to go with my friend to the mall, to see funny movies and to visit her family. When I am home alone, I plan for what to do next.

- I practice my breathing exercises. I am happy when I drive more and get to the places I need to go without other friends and relatives taking me. I finally got a much-needed haircut, which made me feel better about myself. I look younger and healthier.

- I go to the opera.

- I love swimming in New Hampshire.

- I like to travel and I sleep seven hours a night.

- I walk one half-mile a day and I play ping-pong.

- I sing in the choir and I have Thanksgiving with my entire family.

- I eat a low-fat diet.

- I love America and I love my wife.

Self-care (2)

Materials: Writing paper, pens and pencils.

Procedure: Provide a sheet with the following written questions:

1. How do you take care of yourself physically? For instance, do you exercise?

2. How do you take care of yourself emotionally? For instance, do you try to reduce stress in your life?

3. What do you do to treat yourself?

4. What is your "self-talk?"

5. What do you do in your leisure time?

6. Who do you talk to when you need to share thoughts and feelings?

7. What do you do to keep yourself busy when you are alone?

8. How do you maintain a healthy diet?

9. What are your comfort foods?

10. What do you do when you don't feel well?

11. How do you keep from becoming sad?

12. What type of people do you try to surround yourself with to make you feel positive?

13. How do you try to improve your sleep patterns?

14. How do you keep your home safe and comfortable?

15. What do you do when you become anxious?

16. How do you remember to take your medicine on time, and keep doctor appointments?

Give clients a few minutes to answer each question (or as many as you think suitable) and then have them share their answers with each other. Next ask clients to choose one answer and illustrate it. For example, if a client chose question number 9, he might draw an ice-cream cone or mashed potatoes or pizza to illustrate comfort foods.

Discussion/goals: Clients share their artwork and their responses to the questions while exploring their lifestyles, self-care strategies and new coping skills. Goals include self-awareness and identification of strengths, weaknesses and goals.

Self-awareness (2)

Materials: Writing paper, pens, pencils and index cards.

Procedure: Write the following questions on index cards and put the index cards in a box.

Questions to include:

1.   Describe a typical day at home.

2.   What is your favorite time/part of the day? What is your least favorite time/part of the day?

3.   What are your strengths?

4.   What are your weaknesses?

5.   What do you need in order to be happy? What changes do you need in order to be happy? What is stopping you from achieving your goals?

6.   What do others expect from you? What do you expect from yourself?

7.   How do you need to improve as a person?

8.   Who are you? What type of person are you? Describe yourself.

9.   Describe ways you are good to yourself.

10. What makes you angry?

11. What qualities do you admire in others?

12. When do you feel safe?

13. Describe an ideal friend.

14. What was the nicest thing ever said about you?

15. What is your favorite childhood memory?

16. What does wisdom mean to you?

17. If money were no object, where would you go?

Have clients each take an index card and take turns answering the questions. After a few rounds of doing this, ask clients to take turns sharing one thing they learned about each group member.

Discussion/goals: Socialization, communication and self-awareness.

Weekend planning[1]

Materials: Computer/printer paper (8.5 × 11 inch), markers, pens and pencils.

Procedure: Make a four-page booklet out of the printer paper, copy, staple together and distribute to clients. On the first page of the booklet ask the questions listed below. On the second page ask clients to draw a picture of themselves doing something interesting and fun, on the third page have them draw an illustration of a place they'd like to visit in the future, and on the fourth page suggest they sketch a picture of a place they have visited in the past. Clients may use pencil or marker to create the sketches.

Questions for the first page:

1. What are your plans for the weekend?

2. How will you motivate yourself to be active?

3. Who will you be with this weekend?

4. How will you take care of yourself?

5. What will your self-talk be like?

6. What will you eat?

7. When was the last time you had a really good weekend?

8. What did you do?

9. Who were you with?

10. Make a list of 3–5 weekend activities you might like to do. Examples may include walking/exercising, dining in a restaurant, going to the movies, going to a flea market or museum, journaling, drawing, reading or gardening.

Discussion/goals: Clients explore their attitudes, thoughts and feelings about the weekend. They discuss past experiences in order to review activities they can also do now to improve their lifestyle. Goals include planning, organizing, structuring and examining ways to enhance weekends, holidays and leisure time.

The wall

Materials: Drawing paper, lined writing paper, markers, crayons, pens and pencils.

Procedure: Ask clients to draw a wall. Next ask them to write a description of their drawing. Encourage individuals to ponder the following questions as they write their descriptions:

1. How tall and how strong is the wall?
2. What materials were used to build it?
3. How long has it been up?
4. How long will it stay up?
5. Who built it?
6. Is there a specific reason it was built?
7. Is there any way to take it down?
8. What benefits do you gain by keeping it up?
9. What is harmful about the wall?

Discussion/goals: Goals include exploration of barriers, connections with others, attitude and examination of progress, regression and/or stagnation in therapy.

Diet and nutrition

Materials: Drawing paper, writing paper, pens, pencils and markers.

Procedure: Discuss the importance of good nutrition with clients. Examine how healthy eating habits affect mood and behavior as well as physical health. Explore the benefits of eating fruit and vegetables as well as whole grains, fish and lean meats. Next suggest that clients draw or list the types of food they tend to eat and ask them to describe the effect the food seems to have on their behavior. For example, for some individuals, drinking coffee makes them anxious and causes sleep disturbances.

Discussion/goals: Discussion focuses on the connection between the foods we eat and mood, energy, anxiety, depression and recovery. Goals include education and awareness about the importance of good nutrition for emotional and physical health.

Sleep

Materials: Drawing paper, glue, scissors and markers.

Procedure: Provide the outline of a bed for clients and ask them to glue it on the paper (or the client may draw his own bed). Next ask clients to draw any type of self-representative figure and place it somewhere in relation to the bed. Suggest clients may place themselves in the bed, near it, etc. Direct clients to represent their sleep habits through the positioning of the figure. (If desired, the therapist may provide a figure for clients to fill in and then glue on the paper.)

Discussion/goals: Discuss how lack of sleep can increase anxiety and depression, whereas quality sleep can increase a sense of calm and well-being. Suggest that it's easier to cope with stress when one has a good night's sleep. Ask clients to share how their figure placement relates to their sleep habits. Ask questions such as:

1. How long has your sleep been an issue?

2. Is dreaming a problem?

3. What are your bedtime rituals?

4. Do you eat or exercise close to bedtime?

5. Are you watching the news or stressful shows on television?

6. Is your room quiet or noisy?

7. Do you meditate before trying to fall asleep or are you thinking about your concerns?

8. Is your bed and bedroom comfortable and inviting?

9. What is the temperature of your bedroom?

10. Do you live with someone or alone, and what affect does that have on your quality of sleep?

Goals include identifying sleep problems and sharing credible solutions.

Self-talk

Materials: Drawing paper, colored pencils, pencils and markers.

Procedure: Ask clients to draw two figures (or provide the figures and have clients fill them in). Direct them to draw a circle above each figure showing that the person is speaking (much like they do in cartoons). Next describe this scenario:

It was a beautiful sunny day in April. Two friends chatted as they waited in line for one hour to see an Academy Award-winning movie. It was almost their turn when they were told that the tickets were sold out.

Now ask clients to fill in the first circle over the first figure's head with negative statements about the situation and then fill in the second circle over the second figure's head with positive statements.

Discussion/goals: Compare and contrast the two points of view depicted in the artwork. Explore the importance of self-talk. Share the following quotations and then ask participants for their reactions to them:

- "We can choose to think in a positive or negative manner."

- "We can't determine what happens to us all the time but we can choose how we react to what happens."

Reactions

Materials: Writing paper, drawing paper, pens, pencils and markers.

Procedure: Share the scenarios below with clients and ask them to share their thoughts and responses. The leader may determine if clients should verbally share, write down their answers and/or draw their reactions. After each scenario ask clients:

1. How would you react?
2. What's your feeling?
3. What would you do?

Scenarios:

- You are invited to a party and you accept. Then you are asked to bring a chicken dish. You know you will be busy earlier in the day and you don't feel like cooking.

- You are asked to drive a friend to the doctor. The doctor is an hour a way and the weather is not good.

- You witness a minor accident in the supermarket parking lot. You have a trunk full of groceries and you are in a rush to get home. The police officer asks if you saw what happened.

- You are wearing new white pants and the neighbor's dog jumps on you with muddy paws and gets your pants dirty.

- You have questions for your doctor, but he is obviously in a rush and is gently pushing you out of the office.

- You are in a restaurant and the service is terrible. Do you say something? Do you give the waiter a tip?

- You are on the bus and the person next to you falls asleep and is leaning on your shoulder.

- You are in the supermarket and someone asks you if they can cut in line because they are in a rush and they have to get back to work.

- You are out to dinner with a friend who constantly talks about his problems and nothing else.

- You sent your steak back twice because it was too rare. The waitress brings it to you again and it is *still* rare.

- Your daughter yells at her child and you feel that she was being unfair to your grandchild.

- Your son is spoiling his children.

- You are told you can't drive anymore.

- You are trying to be on a diet; your friend keeps on encouraging you to eat fattening foods.

The therapist may choose to make up new narratives in future groups.

Discussion/goals: Goals include focusing on thoughts, feelings, assertiveness, flexibility, self-talk, choosing one's battles and problem solving.

Traffic light

Materials: Drawing paper, markers, oil pastels and crayons.

Procedure: Provide the outline of a typical traffic light (a vertical rectangle with three circles which will be colored red, yellow and green) or have clients draw their own. Direct group members to fill in the first circle red, the second yellow and the third green. Next ask them to write or illustrate:

- a goal/s next to the green circle.

- methods used to try to obtain the goal/s next to the yellow circle

- obstacles to achieving their goal/s next to the red circle.

Discussion/goals: Examine each client's aspirations and barriers to achieving them. Goals include problem solving and exploration of coping skills.

The turtle

Materials: Drawing paper, pencils, markers, oil pastels and colored pencils.

Procedure: Show clients a few photos of turtles and ask them to draw a turtle. Suggest they choose to depict it inside its shell or with its head and legs outside. If it appears too difficult for clients to draw the turtles, two outlines might be distributed, one with the turtle inside and the other with it displaying its head and legs.

Have group members fill in their outline with color and design. Next ask them to write a brief description connecting their illustration to the way they see themselves—out of their shell or still inside it.

Discussion/goals: Explore the representations of the turtles and examine the safety aspect of the shell. Ask clients: "How can the shell be a help; how is it a hindrance?" Encourage group members to share their own "shells."

Additional questions may include:

1. How strong is your shell?
2. How large is it?
3. When did it begin growing?
4. How often do you hide in it?
5. What would you like to do with it?

Goals include exploration of fear, inhibitions and barriers to change.

Past versus present

Materials: Pencils, markers and oil pastels, typed handout below.

Procedure: Type the following questions; copy and distribute to group members:

1. What types of things did you enjoy doing in the past?
2. What was life like for you years ago?
3. How were music, movies and television different?
4. Did people seem different? How about fashion?
5. Were attitudes dissimilar?
6. Did people appear more relaxed or more tense?

7. Was the world safer or not? Did you feel safer or not?

8. Would you go back in time if you could? If so, what age would you like to be?

9. What do you like about present times?

10. What is life like for you now?

11. What type of music, television and movies do you like?

12. What do you think of people nowadays?

13. Do you feel safe now? Why or why not?

14. Do you think you were born in the right era? If not, which era would you have preferred?

15. How content are you with your life?

Encourage clients to express thoughts about the past versus the present by answering the questions verbally or through written descriptions. Next have them create a quick sketch that represents some of their answers to the questions. For example, a client might choose to draw animals and/or a serene scene to represent growing up on a farm.

Discussion/goals: Discussion involves exploration of conflict, change and acceptance. Goals include reminiscing and increase of self-confidence.

Loneliness/solitude

Materials: Writing paper, drawing paper, pens, pencils, markers and oil pastels.

Procedure: Discuss the differences between feelings of loneliness and solitude. (Loneliness often evokes feelings of sadness, distance, separation, being closed off, lack of support and no company. Solitude evokes serenity, calmness, contentment, relaxation, peace and nurturance.) Have group members write a few lines about a time they felt lonely and a time they experienced solitude. Next suggest they draw one image relating to loneliness and one image relating to solitude.

Discussion/goals: Clients are asked to share their written descriptions and illustrations and to speak about their experiences of loneliness/ solitude. Focus on ways an individual can be by himself and be content. Emphasize that loneliness doesn't always equal being alone.

Coping skills (1)

Materials: Writing paper, drawing paper, pens, pencils, markers and oil pastels.

Procedure: Have clients examine the coping skills list below and select the methods they use most often (they may include additional skills if they like). Next ask them to illustrate one of the coping techniques— for example, a sunset to represent nature/spirituality, someone planting flowers to represent gardening or a cake or cookies to represent baking.

Coping skills:

- confronting the situation calmly
- maintaining control
- being patient
- using relaxation techniques
- learning or developing new skills
- calling a friend
- calling a supportive family member
- trying to get all the facts and not "assume"
- trying to be optimistic
- taking one day at a time
- forgiving others
- maintaining a sense of humor
- doing something creative
- focusing on spirituality (prayer, books, meditation, nature, etc.)
- drawing, painting and/or working with clay
- listening to music
- watching television
- exercising
- writing in a journal
- taking a walk
- working on a hobby
- socializing with others

- helping others—volunteering
- going to therapy
- baking
- deep breathing
- dancing
- watching entertaining movies
- playing with a pet
- gardening
- working on a scrapbook
- learning a new language or subject
- surfing the internet
- doing puzzles
- writing letters to friends and family
- self-processing (thinking things out).

Discussion/goals: Discuss the coping skills and explore the symbolism represented in the illustrations. Clients focus on managing anxiety and stress and work toward developing additional techniques to help deal with symptoms.

Symptoms (2)

Materials: Drawing paper, markers, oil pastels, crayons, pens and pencils.

Procedure: Ask group members to fold their paper in half and illustrate their symptoms on one side of the paper and draw or write coping mechanisms on the other side. Symptoms might include anxiety, stomach ache, headache, fear, lack of sleep. Coping skills may include exercise, mediation, socializing, eating in a healthy manner, going to therapy, deep breathing, taking medications appropriately.

Discussion/goals: The drawings will be examined to better understand the number, severity and impact of each person's symptoms. Goals include self-awareness and exploration of coping mechanisms.

Dreams

Materials: Writing paper, pens, pencils, drawing paper, markers, oil pastels, colored pencils and crayons.

Procedure: Ask clients to draw a dream or part of a dream, recent or in the past, and then have them answer the following questions:

1. What types of dreams do you usually have?
2. Do you usually remember your dreams?
3. Do you remember childhood dreams?
4. Do you have dreams that seem to repeat?
5. Have you ever had a nightmare?
6. Are you ever able to control your dreams?
7. Are you able to do things in your dreams you are not normally able to do?
8. Have you ever had a wonderful dream?
9. Have you ever visited a foreign country or spoken to a famous person in your dream?
10. Do you analyze your dreams?

Discussion/goals: Discussion focuses on the clients' interpretation of the dreams, dream patterns and how dreams affect one's thoughts, mood and quality of sleep. Methods to help control unpleasant dreams, such as journaling and drawing a more positive ending to a frightening dream, may be explored. Clients share wishes, hopes, fears and desires while describing their dreams. Goals include better self-understanding and exploration of unresolved issues.

A 72-year-old woman named Louise described her dream as very dramatic and unnerving. She dreamt she was swimming in the ocean; it was warm and sunny. The sky suddenly darkened and she found herself in the middle of a terrible storm. She stated the waves (as represented by the large black spiked lines forming a zig-zag pattern) were tremendous and very frightening. The thunder was explosive and there was much lightning. She remarked that she was having difficulty breathing; water kept getting into her mouth. The waves kept coming, and her arms and legs were getting tired. She felt she was doomed. She saw a calm area (as depicted by the smooth blue water on either side of the W shape) but she was blocked from reaching it. The smaller squiggles and zig-zag pattern represented her anxiety. She stated she

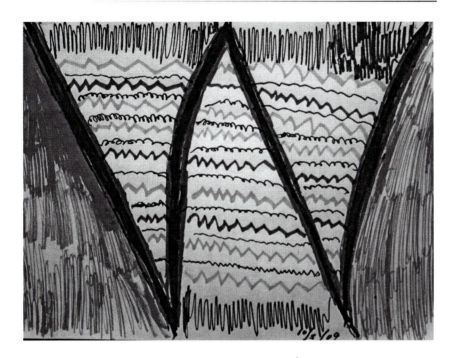

knew she would die, so she closed her eyes and felt herself drowning. Then she woke up with a start.

When asked to associate the dream and the drawing with her life, she remarked that she feels as if she's "drowning in her depression." She did not like the large, black zig-zag spiked shape and felt it was frightening. She connected it to her intense fear of the future. Louise stated she has been on every type of antidepressant and nothing seems to work. She remarked that she's contemplating electroconvulsive therapy, but is fearful of it. She is not only fearful of the procedure, but also fearful that this "is my only hope. If this doesn't work, there is nothing left for me to try." Her fear was explored during this session and in subsequent sessions, and she was supported to take one day at a time and focus on hope instead of defeat.

Bowl of happiness

Materials: Pens, pencils, markers, colored pencils, oil pastels and crayons; pre-drawn bowl on a sheet of paper (or clients may draw their own bowl).

Procedure: Direct clients to fill their bowl in with color according to how much happiness they have in their life. Discuss the amount of happiness in each bowl and explore the following:

1. Is your bowl filled with enough happiness?
2. Will it last?
3. When was the last time the bowl was full?
4. When was the last time, if ever, it was empty?
5. What is "real happiness?"
6. How does attitude affect happiness?
7. How do relationships affect happiness?
8. Are there special habits or rituals that can add to happiness (e.g. praying, planting and taking care of flowers, talking to a family member each day)?
9. How does reaching out and helping others affect happiness?
10. How do you/can you create your own happiness?

Discussion/goals: Discussion focuses on examining ways to increase life satisfaction and acquire a more positive attitude. Goals include increased self-esteem and greater awareness of responsibility for one's own happiness.

Optimism (2)

Materials: Writing paper, pens and pencils.

Procedure: Discuss the saying "When one door closes, another door opens." Ask clients to share a time in their life when one door closed but another opened for them (e.g. getting fired from a job and then finding a better job). Next read the following short story and discuss thoughts and feelings about its meaning:

There is an old Chinese story that tells of a poor farmer who depended on his horse for plowing and getting around. One day the horse left. The neighbors approached him with sadness and talked about how bad it was. The poor farmer said, "Maybe."
The next day the horse returned with two other horses. The neighbors approached him with happiness and talked about how wonderful it was. The poor farmer said, "Maybe." The next day the poor farmer's

son tried to ride one of the horses and it threw him and broke his leg, rendering him unable to work. The neighbors approached him with sadness to talk about how bad it was. The poor farmer said, "Maybe." The next day the army called on the boy to serve. They rejected him because of his broken leg.

Discussion/goals: Discuss the idea of being positive and looking at life with an optimistic attitude. Explore the following questions:

1. Was the farmer an optimist and/or a pragmatist?
2. Did the framer's attitude help him?
3. How did things turn out for the farmer?
4. What are your thoughts about the neighbors and their reactions to the incidents?
5. How important is it to find "the good" in things?
6. How important is your attitude in determining how good or bad a situation is?
7. Have you ever been in a situation where "the bad" turned into "good?"
8. Have you ever worried about something that didn't end up happening?
9. How does our perspective and attitude affect our happiness?
10. What do you think happened next in the story?

Rejecting misery

Materials: Drawing paper, markers, colored pencils, oil pastels and crayons; a large pre-drawn box on a sheet of paper (or have clients draw their own box).

Procedure: Ask participants to draw "misery" in the box. Have them think about the size, shape and color of misery. Next ask them to draw another shape that they consider to be representative of happiness. Have them cut out the happiness shape and place it somewhere in relation to the misery shape. They can place the happiness shape near, on top of or overlapping the misery shape. Next discuss the artwork and its meaning.

Invite group members to answer the following questions:

1. Did you leave the misery shape as it was or did you cover it up or cover part of it?

2. What is the relationship between the two shapes?

3. Which appears stronger?

4. How do you feel when you look at the shapes?

5. What does misery mean for you?

6. How long have you experienced misery (if you presently are experiencing misery in your life)?

7. What can you do to minimize the misery you feel?

8. Is misery a part of life?

Tips to avoid misery:

- don't ignore problems
- try to think in a positive manner
- reach out to others
- volunteer and/or help others
- ask for help when needed
- find your purpose
- make sure to have a hobby
- stay away from people who hurt or upset you
- keep a gratitude journal
- socialize as much as possible
- structure your day
- choose your battles
- meditate
- exercise
- be mindful
- focus on what you have instead of what you don't have
- focus on what is in your control instead of what isn't in your control
- focus on strengths, not weaknesses
- take one day at a time
- accept that life is full of changes, some good and some bad.

Discussion/goals: Goals include awareness of the "victim role," exploration of healthy coping skills and thinking in a more positive manner.

Coping skills (2)

Materials: Drawing paper (12 × 18 inches), markers, oil pastels, crayons, pens and pencils.

Procedure: Distribute the coping skills list below and have clients divide into pairs. Ask them to work together to design a mini poster that includes a variety of the skills listed. Suggest they may also add color and decorations to enhance the poster.

Coping skills:

- take one day at a time
- make time for relaxation
- meditate and/or try yoga
- make sure to have the phone number of a friend, family member, therapist and/or another individual to call when you are stressed
- exercise—relaxed walking is fine
- listen to music
- draw or create
- read
- watch television if that is helpful
- go to a movie or show
- visit a local museum or venture into the city to visit places of interest
- do not make mountains out of molehills
- put things into perspective
- focus on your strengths, not your weaknesses
- look at the bright side; do not dwell on the negative
- do something spiritual: watch a sunset or the full moon and/or enjoy your garden
- garden and/or take care of houseplants; nurture them and watch them grow
- take time to "smell the roses"

- take an inventory of the positive things in your life
- volunteer
- bake something special
- buy yourself flowers
- give yourself a pat on the back for:

    a job well done

    for trying, for doing what you have to do,

    for your accomplishments, no matter how small,

    for just being you

- take yourself out for lunch
- buy yourself a little trinket (even an item from the dollar store can be fun)
- soothe yourself with a warm bath or massage
- enjoy an afternoon treat—a cup of tea, coffee or hot chocolate
- look through photo albums or create your own scrapbook
- write a letter to an old friend
- allow yourself to make mistakes
- don't compare yourself to others.

Discussion/goals: Discussion focuses on each design and the positive suggestions printed on the posters. Have clients share thoughts about working together. Goals include socialization, cooperation, positive feelings and exploration of coping techniques.

What if?

Materials: Drawing paper, markers, crayons, oil pastels, pens and pencils.

Procedure: Distribute sheets divided into three parts with the words "What if?" written on top of them. Ask clients to fill in the first section with all their worries. Have them write the likelihood that their worries will occur in the second section by rating the worries on a 1–10 scale where 1 means the worry will probably not occur and 10 means it will most definitely occur. In the third section, ask clients to create a design using soothing colors such as pale blue and pale yellow to represent calming thoughts that will help minimize worry.

Discussion/goals: Discussion focuses on concerns and fears and the wasted energy exerted while worrying. Erroneous thinking such as catastrophizing and magnification will be examined. Goals include self-awareness and exploration of coping skills such as self-talk, meditation and exercise.

Happiness (2)

Materials: A sheet of paper with a variety of pre-drawn keys on it,[2] scissors, glue, drawing paper, markers, pens, pencils, oil pastels and crayons.

Procedure: Discuss the meaning of the phrase "the key to happiness." Next have group members choose a variety of the keys, cut and color them in, then glue them on the drawing paper. Have group members write what they think is the key to happiness inside the keys or beside them.

Discussion/goals: Discussion focuses on the number of keys chosen and the ideas presented. Goals include problem solving and exploration of coping skills.

Gratitude (2): Treasure chest

Materials: Pre-drawn picture of a treasure chest,[3] pens, pencils and markers.

Procedure: Ask clients to decorate the treasure chest and fill it in with everything they are thankful for in their life (e.g. children, friends, health, rainbows, food, a home).

Discussion/goals: Clients share their treasures and discuss the importance of their positive experiences. Goals include emphasis on optimistic thinking and increased self-esteem.

Feeling descriptions

Materials: Drawing paper, markers, pens and pencils.

Procedure: Have clients write a sentence describing a situation where they experienced each feeling listed below. Then ask them to illustrate two or more of the words using figures, line and/or design.

Feelings:

- accepted
- appreciated

- capable
- comfortable
- confident
- joyful
- excited
- anxious
- sad
- confused.

Discussion/goals: Clients share various experiences and examine how they express their feelings. Goals include self-awareness and a focus on communication skills.

Loss graph

Materials: Drawing paper, markers and pens.

Procedure: Ask clients to draw a straight or wavy line. Have them create small vertical lines on top of the first line and list dates that they experienced a loss in their life. Under the dates have them write their losses, their associated feelings and how the losses affected their mood, attitude, behavior and overall life. They may also draw a symbol to represent their feelings. Allow clients to include minor as well as major losses.

Discussion/goals: Clients share how the losses affected their life and how they came or are coming to terms with them. Goals include exploration of grief, change and coping skills.

Feeling letters

Materials: Lined paper, pens and pencils.

Procedure: Ask clients to write a letter to a feeling. Have them imagine that the feeling is a person. Ask them what they would like to say to it—for instance, they could tell it how it affects them, asks it how it feels, ask it to visit or go away. They may tell it their problems or share positive events.

Discussion/goals: Discussion focuses on what is said and the way the feeling affects the client. Goals include self-awareness and expression of feelings and emotions.

Expressing anger

Materials: Drawing paper, markers, pens and pencils. Clay may be used if it is a clean clay such as Model Magic.

Procedure: Ask clients to design a shape that represents anger. Next have them answer the following questions:

1. What does the shape represent for you?
2. Is it large or small, colorful or not, smooth, sharp or curvy?
3. How do you feel when you examine it?
4. Are you angry about anything now?
5. When was the last time you felt angry?
6. How do you express your anger?
7. What is the difference between acting in a passive, assertive or aggressive manner?
8. What are the problems associated with holding in one's anger?
9. How do your friends and family members express anger?
10. Do you ever escalate to rage?
11. What steps can you take to control and/or dissipate your anger?

Discussion/goals: Discussion focuses on the clients' reactions to the drawn shapes and responses to the related questions. Goals include examining ways to express anger and getting in touch with one's anger and associated issues.

Observation (2)[4]

Materials: Drawing paper, markers, pens and pencils.

Procedure: Divide group members into pairs. Each individual will receive one sheet of paper which he will divide into fourths.

In the first box have clients draw an abstract picture of their partner using line, color and shape. In the second box have clients draw the emotion they believe their partner is presently experiencing, using line, color and shape. Emotions may include happiness, sadness, trust, fear, anger, surprise, anticipation. In the third box clients will write a brief description of their partner. In the fourth box clients will use one or two words from the following list to describe their partner:

- friendly
- well-groomed
- attractive
- sensitive
- practical
- handsome
- charming
- fun
- shy
- creative
- anxious
- angry
- happy
- joyful
- thoughtful
- silly
- good-natured
- thoughtful
- helpful
- humorous
- honest
- sincere
- outgoing
- pleasant
- rigid
- depressed

- wild
- lost
- pessimistic
- negative
- stoic
- fearful
- focused
- unsure
- confident
- helpful
- lazy
- fast
- slow
- hard worker
- kind
- cautious
- intelligent
- talented
- talkative
- social
- loving
- warm
- friendly
- approachable
- pretty
- sweet

- cute
- peaceful
- hesitant
- nervous
- loud
- soft
- caring
- agreeable
- disagreeable
- good listener
- self-focused
- withdrawn
- bossy
- sarcastic
- innocent
- worldly
- wise
- neat
- awkward
- messy
- amusing
- excitable
- belligerent
- peaceful
- interesting
- boring.

Discussion/goals: Discussion focuses on how the clients perceive each other and how they communicate their feelings with one another. Goals include self-awareness and assessing how clients perceive themselves versus how others perceive them.

Reality versus expectation

Materials: Drawing paper, markers, oil pastels, crayons, pens and pencils.

Procedure: Have clients fold their paper in half. On one half ask them to draw hopes for the future, and on the other half have them draw realistic expectations.

Discussion/goals: Clients share fears, wishes, needs, opportunities and desires. Realistic goals and methods of obtaining them are explored. Goals include coming to terms with life as it is and self-awareness.

Thinking positively

Materials: Writing paper, drawing paper, markers, pens and pencils.

Procedure: Discuss what it means to think in a positive manner. Explore the meaning of optimism (hopefulness, brightness, cheerfulness). Ask group members to draw a quick sketch representing hope or optimism. Next have clients write and/or verbally share their answers to the following questions:

1. Are you more of an optimist than a pessimist?
2. When you make a mistake, can you forgive yourself? Are you able to forgive others?
3. What type of things do you do to make yourself happy?
4. When you are in a new situation, how do you feel?
5. Do you socialize with others?
6. Do you look forward to getting up in the morning and starting the day?
7. On a scale of 1–10 where 10 is the most hopeful and 1 is the least hopeful, what number are you in terms of hope for a brighter future?
8. Describe something positive about yourself.

9. What makes you smile?

10. When was the last time you felt joyful?

11. When was the last time you laughed?

12. When was the last time you told someone how special they were?

13. When was the last time someone told you how special you are?

Discussion/goals: Clients explore the symbols represented in their artwork, their approach to life and their responses to the specific questions. Goals include examination of attitude, mood and self-talk.

Spiral of hope

Materials: Drawing paper, pens, pencils, colored pencils and markers.

Procedure: Provide a large spiral (should take up most of the page) with approximately 0.75 inch space in-between the lines that create the spiral. Divide the spiral rings every two inches. Ask clients to fill in the spaces with colors, symbols, words, phrases and affirmations of hope.

Discussion/goals: Discuss the meaning of the symbols, words and phrases that are included in the spirals. Explore how the spiral shape may relate to one's thoughts and feelings. Goals include representation of hope, attitude, mood and direction in life.

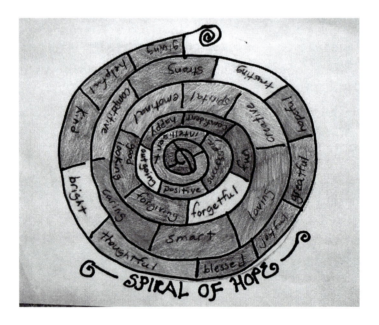

Relationships (2)

Materials: Drawing paper, markers, oil pastels, crayons, pencils and pens.

Procedure: Have clients draw four concentric circles. The first circle will be a small circle and then a larger circle will surround the first, and so on. In the first circle ask clients to use colors, symbols and/or words to represent themselves. In the second circle have them represent the people closest to them. In the third circle have them represent people they know (acquaintances, friends), and in the fourth circle ask them to represent people they would like to know better.

Discussion/goals: Discussion focuses on interactions with friends, family and other people in one's life. Goals include assessing relationships, connections and exploring ways to enhance them.

Self-care (3)

Materials: Drawing paper, markers, pens, pencils, magazines, glue and scissors.

Procedure: Provide an outline of a shopping cart or have clients draw one. Ask participants to fill in the cart with self-care items (e.g. food, shampoo, mouthwash, lotion, books, puzzles, CDs, laundry detergent, vitamins). Magazine photos may be used if desired and pasted into or near the cart.

Discussion/goals: Explore the items placed in the cart and their importance in the clients' lives. Goals include examining various ways to take care of oneself physically and emotionally.

About me

Materials: Drawing paper, pen, pencils, markers, oil pastels and crayons.

Procedure: Instruct clients to read the questions below. Suggest they fold their paper into thirds and illustrate their answers to three of the questions. The remaining questions may be explored later on in the session.

1. What time do you get up in the morning and what time do you go to sleep?

2. What are your favorite movies and/or television shows?

3. What do you like to eat?

4. What type of music do you like?

5. What characteristics do you admire in others?

6. What are your strengths?

7. Do you have pets?

8. What are your future goals?

9. Who comprises your family?

10. Where do you live?

11. Where were your born and where did you grow up?

12. Where/what is your favorite place?

13. Where would you like to go on vacation?

14. What were you like as a child?

15. What games and/or sports have you played in the past?

16. Whom do you like?

17. Whom do you admire?

18. Who puts a smile on your face?

19. If you were on a deserted island, what three items would you bring?

20. What do others tend to say about you?

Discussion/goals: Goals include socialization, sharing and self-awareness.

Shared information

Materials: Writing paper, pens and pencils.

Procedure: Instruct clients to write a brief description of themselves consisting of at least three facts on a sheet of paper. Have them crumple their paper and place it in the center of the table. The group facilitator mixes the papers up and clients choose one of the crumpled papers. Everyone gets a chance to read from the paper they chose while other group members guess who wrote the facts.

Discussion/goals: Goals include sharing, increased communication, unity and learning about others. This is a pleasant game and serves as an effective icebreaker.

Problem solving

Materials: Drawing paper, writing paper, markers, pens and pencils.

Procedure: Clients divide into pairs and review the list of problems below. Each person chooses one or more problems from the list and draws their interpretation of it. Then they give their paper to their partner who writes or draws a possible solution to the problem/s. When everyone is finished, each pair shares their drawings and written responses with all group members.

Problem list includes problems with:

- partner
- spouse
- children
- parents
- friends
- boss and/or co-workers
- job
- money
- worrying too much
- obsessing about too many things
- holidays
- health
- weight
- taking care of oneself emotionally and/or physically
- addictions
- transportation
- law/courts

- memory or concentrating
- finding new hobbies and leisure activities
- home environment
- change
- low self-esteem
- low or no energy
- poor sleep
- poor eating habits
- discomfort in social situations
- loss
- focusing too much on the past
- guilt
- divorce
- loneliness
- relating to others
- feeling like a victim and/or being a victim.

Discussion/goals: Clients share issues and problems and explore possible solutions. Goals include sharing, communication and examination of troubles and matters of importance.

Fear (2)

Materials: Drawing paper, writing paper, pencils and markers.

Procedure: Have clients work together to create a list of fears. Next ask them to draw something/someone they are afraid of now or have been fearful of in the past.

Discussion/goals: Clients share their fear/s and explore the following questions:

1. What is fear? What does it look like and feel like?
2. Is your fear symbol large or small, overpowering or manageable?
3. How does fear affect you?
4. What are the positive and negative aspects of fear?
5. How can your fears be managed?

Clients work together to compile the list. This helps them understand that they are not alone in their worries and concerns; they feel less isolated and less strange. They listen to their peers, view their artwork and analyze their own thoughts and associations. Goals include identifying concerns and developing new coping techniques.

The following is a list of fears a group of clients produced in one session:

- being homeless
- commitment
- growing older
- becoming less attractive
- "losing my hair"
- being physically harmed
- becoming ill
- breast cancer
- crime
- terrorism
- gaining weight
- being judged
- failure
- being alone

- Alzheimer's disease
- diabetes
- heart disease
- arthritis
- losing independence
- getting lost
- moving
- "I won't fit in"
- doctor/dentists visits
- going to the hospital
- insects, "cockroaches"
- pain
- divorce
- being widowed

- traveling
- not seeing grandchildren or children
- accidents
- falling

- no friends
- failing
- "It's too good to last"
- happiness is fleeting.

Communication skills (2)

Materials: Paper, pens and pencils.

Procedure: Ask group members the following questions (the questions may be answered verbally or first written down and then shared):

1. Why are communications skills important?
2. How do you communicate your feelings to others?
3. Are you able to share feelings and opinions with others?
4. How do you let others know you are angry?
5. How do you get your needs met?
6. How do you express happiness, sadness, frustration and satisfaction?
7. When was the last time you let someone know you cared about him or her?
8. How do you feel when you keep your feelings to yourself?
9. Which communication skills do you need to practice?

Next, group members verbally share:

- an accomplishment
- an enjoyable experience
- a difficult time in their life
- a time in their life when they felt confident and strong
- an accomplishment
- an ideal day
- an ideal meal
- a time they felt like laughing
- something they remember about their childhood
- what they do in their leisure time

- where they grew up
- what their lifestyle is like
- what they are working on now to improve their life
- a description of a typical day.

Goals include improving communication with others and exploring how positive communication skills enhance relationships and a sense of inclusion and well-being.

Challenges[5]

Materials: Drawing paper, markers and pencils.

Procedure: Have clients complete the following statement with words and/or pictures:

I have a challenge and that is ....

Examples might include depression, loneliness, anger, bipolar disorder.

Discussion/goals: Clients refocus their issues as challenges, which gives them more power and helps to decrease the likelihood of them falling into the victim role. They identify their challenges and battles and explore coping mechanisms. In addition, clients learn how to separate their problems and illness from themselves; *they are not their illness.* Instead of saying, for instance, "I am a depressed person," one might say, "I'm Mary and I am challenged with depression at this time in my life."

Sorrow

Materials: Drawing paper, markers, crayons, watercolors, brushes, water and oil pastels.

Procedure: Instruct clients to express their sadness by using shapes and colors mixed in with words and phrases. Group members may paint or draw or combine materials.

Discussion/goals: Clients share feelings through their personal images. They reflect on the colors and shapes as well as the overall feel of the illustration. It is easier to share feelings of loss and despair by referring to images rather than words for many of the clients. The colors and shapes encourage communication of thoughts they have hidden and/or have been afraid to express verbally.

"One eye open, one eye closed"

Materials: Drawing paper, markers, oil pastels and crayons.

Procedure: Briefly discuss the meaning of this phrase and then ask clients to draw their association/s with it.

Discussion/goals: Discussion focuses on the drawings and the interpretations. Many clients will probably draw one eye open and one eye closed; they will take the directive literally, so it is the interpretations that will be focused upon.

Interpretations and areas for discussion may include:

- Not seeing the big picture; seeing only part of what is taking place.
- Seeing only what you want to see; closing one eye to what you don't want to see.
- The eyes might represent the present and past or past and future.
- Logic versus emotion may be suggested in the eyes.
- When you look with two eyes, you see in three dimensions. When one eye is closed, things are not so clear.
- The eyes may represent emotions versus logic.

Healthy lifestyle

Materials: Markers, pens, pencils and a sheet of paper divided into nine squares/rectangles with the questions below written inside the squares (at the very top). One question should be placed in each square; there should be room for a small drawing or mini collage.

1. Nutrition: What types of food do you eat?
2. Exercise: How do you stay fit and physically healthy?
3. Socialization: How do you meet people and maintain friendships?
4. Leisure time: What do you do in your spare time? What are your hobbies?
5. Emotional: What are your coping skills? Who do you go to for support?
6. Hygiene: How do you take care of your body, clothes, house, etc.?
7. Enjoyment: What do you do to have fun?
8. Humor: When do you laugh? What do you find humorous?
9. Special occasions: How do you celebrate birthdays, etc.?

Procedure: Have group members respond to each written question by utilizing magazine photos and/or writing or drawing their answers.

Discussions/goals: Clients share various aspects of self-care and examine healthy lifestyle choices. Goals include identifying positive coping skills and improving problematic areas such as lack of exercise or poor nutrition.

Mental health charades[6]

Materials: Construction paper and markers.

Procedure: Part A: Write the following words on 2 × 2 inch slips of red construction paper:

- lack of sleep
- isolation
- off medication
- not expressing
- alcohol
- worry
- limited perspective
- racing thoughts
- dwell on negative past
- feel out of control
- anxiety about the future
- people, places and things
- unhealthy food
- caffeine
- unpleasant people.

Part B: Write the following words on 2 × 2 inch slips of green construction paper:

- therapy
- friends and family
- positive self-talk
- music
- healthy eating
- medication
- humor
- support group
- friends
- hope
- meditation
- exercise
- spirituality
- pet
- massage
- nature
- positive thinking.

Next give group members a quick overview of the way stressors impact our lives and our mental health. Then explain how to play charades and the way body language and facial expression may be used to give clues to words and phrases. A clue giver is chosen and he selects a word from the stressor list category and acts it out while other group members try to guess the word. Go in a circle so everyone gets a turn, choosing words from list A—stressors—and then next time around list B—coping.

Discussion/goals: Discuss the clients' feelings and experiences while playing the game. Explore what they noticed about their level of participation and enthusiasm. Ask clients how learning through positive group interaction can affect their sense of well-being. Goals include cooperation, socialization and exploration of stressors and coping skills.

Notes

1. This project may be broken up into two sessions depending on the length of the session and the focus of the clients.
2. Pictures may be found on Google Images or elsewhere on the internet.
3. Pictures may be found on Google Images.
4. This project may need to be divided into two sessions depending on the energy and level of functioning of the group members.
5. Modified from a suggestion by Evie Sutkowski, NCC, LPC, Princeton House, University Medical Center at Princeton.
6. Larry Schiller, MA, MS, Princeton House, University Medical Center at Princeton
   The therapist may add or change the word list depending on the population he is working with at the time. Charades is a game where words or phrases are represented in pantomime.

CHAPTER 12
REMINISCING

Reminiscing gives us a chance to review what we have experienced over the years. It allows us to ponder our accomplishments as well as our mistakes. It helps us to understand that we are not our illnesses or deficits (as some people think); we are the sum of our experiences, thoughts and feelings over a lifetime. Reminiscing reminds us of who we are; it helps define our identity. It gives us the opportunity to smile and sometimes to frown, to re-experience life as it was long ago. It gives us the chance to focus on the positives we have accomplished and often boosts our self-esteem. Reminiscing is our legacy, an unwritten book of our life.

Reminiscing links the past to the present. It helps seniors identify and recognize their strengths, talents and uniqueness. Clients are supported to embrace special traits they have stopped acknowledging over the years. Reminiscing assists individuals to share achievements and positive experiences. Socialization and connection with others is enhanced. Clients usually enjoy sharing anecdotes about friends, children, grandchildren and other family members. They take pleasure in telling stories related to special events such as surprise parties and exciting vacations. Confidence, communications skills and self-awareness become enhanced while reviewing life events.

Reflections

Materials: Writing paper, pen and pencil.

Procedure: Have clients complete the following and then share their answers with group members.

Describe the last time you:

- laughed heartily . . . .
- felt well . . . .
- had a long talk with a friend or relative . . . .
- baked . . . .
- ate a delicious meal . . . .

- read a good book ....
- saw a movie ....
- took a walk ....
- exercised ....
- socialized ....
- learned something new ....

Discussion/goals: Discussion focuses on remembrances and associated thoughts and feelings. Goals include enhancement of self-awareness, self-care and leisure skills.

Bubble reminiscing[1]

Materials: Plastic bubble containers with a wand, drawing paper, pencils, pens, markers, oil pastels and crayons.

Procedure: Distribute bubbles to clients and ask them to try blowing bubbles of all different sizes. Suggest they think back to when they were a child and engaged in enjoyable activities such as this. Next instruct them to draw a variety of circles on their paper (or distribute pages with circles already outlined). Direct group members to fill in the circles with childhood memories. They may add illustrations near the circles if so desired.

Discussion/goals: Discussion focuses on the clients' reactions to the activity. Some individuals may be reluctant to participate at first but generally join in as they watch others smile and become fully involved. Encourage group members to try remembering the feelings associated with childhood and explore ways to gain some of that childlike enthusiasm and joy now. Suggest clients share their memories and pleasurable times. Explain the importance of acknowledging the inner child in each of us as a way to stay young at heart. Goals include sharing, socializing and recalling fond memories.

Reminiscing/sensations

Materials: Writing paper, pens and pencils.

Procedure: Encourage clients to close their eyes, search for visual imagery and use their senses as they answer a variety of questions about their past.

Questions include:

1. What sounds made you smile as a youngster?
2. What tastes made you smile?
3. What sights pleased you?
4. What textures gave you pleasure?
5. What fragrances and scents made you joyful?
6. Whose touch comforted you?

Discussion/goals: Discussion focuses on past experiences and feelings. Goals include reminiscing and mindfulness.

Drawing of past

Materials: Drawing paper, markers, oil pastels, pens and pencils.

Procedure: Ask clients to draw a scene from any time in their more distant past. When the picture is completed, have them write a brief paragraph describing it.

Discussion/goals: Discussion focuses on who is in the picture, the client's associations with the scene and what is taking place. Goals include evoking memories, sharing and gratification.

Positive and negative

Materials: Drawing paper, markers, pencils and pens.

Procedure: Have clients outline a head and divide it in half. Suggest that facial features may be added if desired. Ask group members to fill in one side with positive thoughts (e.g. I am worthy, I am smart) and the other side with negative thoughts (e.g. I am weak, I will never get well).

Discussion/goals: Encourage clients to explore how their self-talk affects their mood, behavior and recovery. Discuss the idea that we decide much of the course of our life and level of happiness by the way we process our thoughts, the way we choose to think about our ourselves and our circumstances. Goals include self-awareness and re-examination of the messages we are sending and receiving.

Photo frame

Materials: A pre-drawn outline of a simple frame on an 8.5 × 11 inch piece of paper that can be reproduced on a copier; markers, pastels and colored pencils.

Procedure: Ask clients to think of individuals who are or who have been special to them in the past. Suggest they choose one of the individuals and create a picture of that person within the photo frame. For example, the client may create an abstract of colors that symbolize the personality of the individual or draw items that represent his hobbies and/or interests, or perhaps a part of the body that is/was eye-catching such as large blue eyes or curly hair.

Discussion/goals: Discussion centers on the individual depicted and the person's importance to the client. Goals include sharing of relationships and reminiscing about friends and family members. Self-esteem is raised as clients "brag" about their children, grandchildren, nieces and nephews. Self-awareness and strong connections are focused upon.

Memory mini mandala

Materials: Drawing paper, markers, oil pastels, crayons, coffee can or similar size can.

Procedure: Ask clients to outline a circle by tracing the bottom of a coffee can. Suggest they draw their favorite memory within, near or outside of the circle.

Discussion/goals: Discussion focuses on the significance of the memory and the composition of the design. Goals include reminiscing and self-awareness.

Looking backwards

Materials: Drawing paper, markers, oil pastels and crayons.

Procedure: Suggests that clients draw themselves looking backwards. Have them include what they observe.

Discussion/goals: Discussion focuses on the significance of the people, places and/or things that are seen. Goals include reminiscing and exploring how past experiences and relationships affect present feelings and behavior.

Childhood imagery

Materials: Drawing paper, markers, oil pastels and crayons.

Procedure: Suggest clients draw one or more images representing things, people or places that made them feel joyful when they were a child (e.g. an ice-cream cone, a baseball and bat or roller skates).

Discussion/goals: Discussion focuses on relatives, old friends, games played as a youngster and childhood pleasures. Goals include sharing and reminiscing to increase self-esteem and self-awareness.

First house

Materials: Drawing paper, markers, oil pastels and crayons.

Procedure: Have clients draw something they remember about the first house or apartment they lived in as a child. Group members may draw items such as toys, furniture or antiques, pets, people, the entire house, etc.

Discussion/goals: Discussion focuses on sharing personal histories. Goals include making connections between the past and present and reminiscing for enjoyment and introspection.

A client named June drew the outside of her house and added a connection between the house and a tree. A walkway "leading to nowhere" is placed in front of the door. The picture is outlined; only the treetop is filled in with green color. The scene appears barren and lifeless. This client's personality is strikingly similar to the portrayal of her house. She appears stoic and avoids intimacy. She keeps her barriers up by keeping a frown on her face at all times.

June did relate the picture to happier times, when her family lived in the house and enjoyed themselves. She remarked that she had no problems when she was young. She received love and support from family members. June believes that she will never regain the feeling of happiness and stability she had during her teenage years. When asked about the path from the house to the tree, she stated that what looks like a path is really a hammock. June mentioned that she used to enjoy lying on the hammock and relaxing under the warm summer sun. Psychologically, the hammock might represent the umbilical cord and the tree might represent June. She is attached to the family home and can't seem to cut the cord. The top of the tree might represent June's anxiety, chaotic thoughts and indecision about how to proceed with her life. The trunk of the tree is rigid and straight, much like

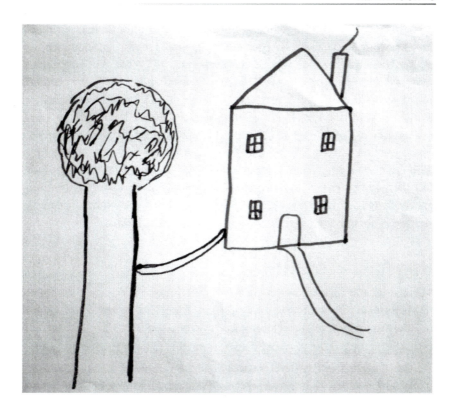

June's stance. June seemed to take comfort in her rendering. She looked longingly at the house. She was asked to explore other ways of feeling needed and secure such as volunteering, joining social clubs and making new friends. Her response was ambiguous.

A client named Matilda drew a cypress clock that was situated on her fireplace mantel. She stated she used to stare at it and thought it looked like a person's face with two arms extended on either side of it. She remarked she would often become anxious if no one else was in the living room. Matilda related her apprehension about the clock to anxiety that would remain with her throughout her life. She remarked that she still becomes nervous if she is alone and hears or sees something a little unusual. She stated that sometimes her eyes play tricks on her, especially in the dark, and she becomes anxious even though she's aware that there is nothing to be afraid of because her home and neighborhood are extremely safe and well protected.

A client named Elizabeth drew her first bedroom. She remarked that this was a place of comfort, beauty and peacefulness. "It was my own enclave; I could invite friends there and we would chat and tell secrets for hours."

She remembered her ruffled bedspread and the tiny pink flowers sprinkled into the design. Elizabeth stated she had the most comfortable comforter of all her friends: "everyone wanted to sit on my bed." What she remembered most were the paintings she had designed, taped to her wall. "I would fall off to sleep staring at my artwork; it felt so good." She focused on the snowman painting, which she worked on for quite a long time. "I asked my mother to hang it up so I could look at it any time I pleased, and she put it up immediately." Elizabeth remarked that her self-esteem was high when she was a youngster. She was asked what she could do to raise it now, but she hadn't a clue. It was suggested that perhaps she could begin doing artwork again. Elizabeth looked unsure but remarked she would consider it; she was enjoying art therapy and other related crafts groups.

Reminiscing to music

Materials: CD player, music of the 1940s and 1950s such as Benny Goodman, Frank Sinatra, Dean Martin, Bing Crosby and Perry Como; drawing paper, markers, pastels and crayons.

Procedure: Play the music and encourage clients to dance, sway and/or move to the music. After a while reduce the volume of the music and ask group members to draw memories associated with the songs they heard.

Discussion/goals: Discussion focuses on memories such as first dates, dances, parties, friends, fun times, weddings and birth of children. Goals include encouraging positive feelings by reflecting on past experiences and increasing self-awareness (viewing oneself as a sum of one's experiences and not labeling oneself solely by one's present situation).

Reminiscing (1)

Materials: Writing paper, pens and pencils.

Procedure: Ask clients to think about memories that might appear mundane to the average person—for example, eating dinner each night with the family, going to church on Sundays, Sunday morning breakfast with relatives, visiting grandparents, brushing your teeth, doing daily chores, washing dishes, cooking, doing homework and walking to and home from school. Direct clients to write about some of these memories and add how they felt while engaging in the activities listed—for example, walking to school (feeling weary, anxious) or doing chores (feeling restless, in a hurry to finish).

Discussion/goals: Discussion focuses on the significance of the memories. Group members explore how ordinary activities may have/had an important impact on their life. Encourage participants to examine how they feel nowadays when they engage in routine activities. Do they see a relationship between the past and present? Goals include reminiscing and focusing on what is meaningful in life.

Reminiscing (2)

Materials: Writing paper, pens and pencils.

Procedure: Share and discuss the following description about reminiscing and then encourage clients to choose one or more of the suggestions below and write and/or draw their responses.

Reminiscing gives us a chance to review what we have experienced over the years. It allows us to ponder our accomplishments as well as our mistakes. It helps us to understand that we are not our illnesses or deficits (as some people think); we are the sum of our experiences, thoughts, and feelings over a lifetime. Reminiscing reminds us of who we are; it helps define our identity. It gives us the opportunity to smile and sometimes to frown, to re-experience life as it was long ago. It gives us the chance to focus on the positives we have accomplished and often boosts our self-esteem. Reminiscing is our legacy, an unwritten book of our life.

- Share one of your most pleasant experiences.
- Share an exiting adventure and/or vacation experience.
- Share a challenge you have experienced in your life.
- Share your thoughts and feelings when your children, nieces, nephews and/or friend's children were born.
- What period in your life was the easiest?
- What period in your life was most difficult?
- Describe your childhood (include your parents, siblings, friends, etc.).
- If you could go back in time, what period in your life would you like to experience again?
- What childhood games do you remember playing?
- Did you have a pet as a child?

- What type of town did you live in when you were growing up?
- What do you remember about World War II?
- What do you remember about the Depression?
- Who were your favorite stars/favorite movies?
- What type of jobs did you have over the years?
- Do you remember your first date?
- Describe your special friends.
- What classes/teachers did you like/dislike in school?
- Did you have favorite foods/restaurants growing up?
- Describe how you looked in the past. For instance, what type of clothes did you wear?
- Was your hairstyle the same as or different from the way you wear it now?
- Share a time in your life when you were brave.
- Share how you coped when your children left home.
- Share some of your life lessons.
- If you could change something about your life, what would you change?
- What would you say now to someone you knew in the past if given the opportunity?
- What was your first apartment or house like?
- Where did you grow up? Describe your neighborhood.
- What was the best and worst thing about being a youngster?
- Write about your mother and/or father.
- Write about your siblings.
- What were your first memories? Describe childhood pets.
- Describe the process of aging.
- Write about hurdles and heartbreaks.
- Write about regrets.

Discussion/goals: Encourage clients to share their verbal responses, written work and artwork. Assist clients to draw strength from reviewing past achievements and experiences. Goals include self-awareness, increase of self-esteem, release of feelings, sharing/socialization and enjoyment.

A widow in her 70s wrote:

> If I could go back in time, it would be when my husband was still alive. My husband and I spent wonderful times together with our children. We went on vacations to places that were very enjoyable. We went to Disney World several times, and each time was equally special. My children loved Disney World, especially the rides and the amusing characters. I will always remember how lovely life was while my children were growing up.

Mary, an 89-year-old woman, wrote:

> First Grade—Ranchito School
> I think my mother was not happy about it, but for me first grade was a lovely time. We were in a rural part of Southern California and most of my classmates were children of farm workers. Since I was blonde I stuck out. On Valentine's Day everyone brought me a card.
> Learning to read was a great thrill and so I rehearsed for my mother while she cooked. I remember reading to her and asking, "Now does this word sound the way it looks, or is this an exception?"
> When my birthday came around, I invited the whole class to my house for a party. The problem was that I didn't tell my mother about this inspiration. I can't remember how it turned out, so I assume that she rose to the occasion.

As this client was reading her story she had a wide smile on her face. Group members giggled. Mary thought she was so "cheeky" to invite the whole class without telling her mother. She stated she wanted to include everyone. Group members supported her for this thoughtful behavior.

Marc, a 90-year-old widower, wrote:

> After World War II my biggest experience was seeing victorious US soldiers in Bavaria Germany. At that time I encountered the loss of my entire family (eight members) and I fell into a depression. I was treated with ECT (electroconvulsive therapy). I recuperated quickly.
> In 1948 I stepped my feet on Israeli soil that was just proclaimed as a Jewish state. I was mobilized into the newly founded army.

Marc was in a deep depression because he had recently lost his wife of many years. Before attending the outpatient program, he had wanted to commit suicide. His family members, especially his children, urged him to get help, and so he began attending the Senior Link program. Group members heard his story and knew of his experience in the Holocaust. They declared him a survivor, which he was able to acknowledge with a slight nod.

A lonely and depressed woman in her early 70s named Dora wrote:

I grew up in a tight-knit family. Our home was a pleasant, comfortable one, a place we could invite our friends to visit. I was the oldest of four children. We all went to the same elementary school and many of us had the same teachers. We enjoyed sharing our experiences with these teachers who were kind and interested in us. I had many friends throughout high school and college. I shared something special with each friend.

Teaching was my first work experience. I also had the responsibility of mentoring the debate club. This took up much of my free time. It was exciting watching the young students mature into responsible debaters. I finished up my work career as a school social worker, working with children from pre-school age to high school. It was a challenge working with such a diverse age group.

My world began to fall apart when we started losing members of our family. Now I am the one left behind with my nieces and nephews. This is my big challenge—I need to start my life all over again.

Memories

Materials: Writing paper, pens and pencils; soothing background music.

Procedure: Have clients relax and ponder the following questions for a few minutes. Suggest they write down their answers and then share with group members.

1. Name a few things you remember about your childhood.
2. What do you remember about your teenage years?
3. What occurred in your 20s and 30s?
4. What was life like in your 50s and 60s?
5. How is life different now from 10 or 20 years ago?
6. What period of time would you like to return to if you could turn back the hands of time?

Discussion/goals: Discussion focuses on memories and associated thoughts and feelings. Goals include socialization, sharing and expressing feelings about significant events, pleasant experiences and possible regrets.

"The good old days"

Materials: Writing paper, pens, pencils, markers and oil pastels.

Procedure: Ask clients to write and/or draw their reactions to the phrase "The good old days."

Discussion/goals: Explore memories, events and notable moments from the past. Goals include reminiscing to increase self-awareness and self-esteem.

An 81-year-old widow named Anita drew her marriage ceremony. She spoke about her beautiful wedding, the gorgeous wedding dress her mother made for her, and her dear friends and family who attended. She shared positive qualities about her husband whom she adored. Anita remarked, "It was love at first sight." She shared that her wedding day was the best day of her life.

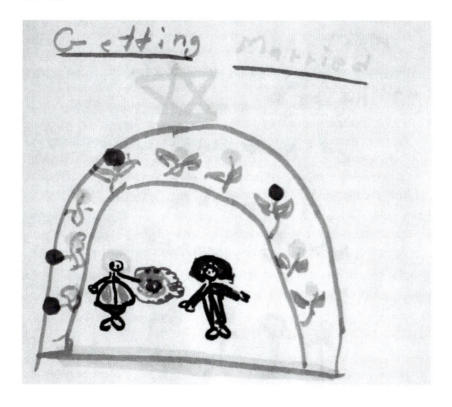

Significant other

Materials: Drawing paper, markers, oil pastels and crayons.

Procedure: Clients are asked to draw the circumstances that led up to meeting their life partner. Have them think about where they were at the time, how they felt, what they were doing (e.g. working, riding a bicycle).

Discussion/goals: Goals include reminiscing and sharing special qualities of important people in one's life. Group members often feel less stressed as they share past relationships. Their mood lightens and much lighthearted discussion usually occurs.

The seashore[2]

Materials: A variety of seashells, sand and beach items; a CD with sounds of the seashore (waves, seagulls, etc.) and CD player.

Procedure: Provide items typically used for the beach (sunglasses, suntan lotion, beach towel, etc.) and place on a table. Play a CD of beach sounds, which will probably include a breeze blowing, seagulls, waves breaking at the shoreline, etc. Instruct clients to close their eyes and imagine themselves at the shore. Have them think of the sounds, sights, smells, tastes and textures of the beach. If possible, provide shells and a bit of sand in a shallow bowl for them to feel and manipulate. Allow them to stay in this meditative state for 5–10 minutes or longer. The length of time will depend on the clients' ability to focus, their functioning and their desire to engage in this type of exercise. Next have participants open their eyes and draw their reactions to this experience and/or draw from the theme "A day at the beach."

Discussion/goals: Clients share their reaction to the mindfulness exercise and their artwork and reminisce about enjoyable visits and vacations at the shore. Goals include sharing and recapturing positive experiences.

This directive helps unify group members and facilitates communication and bonding. Almost everyone can relate to the theme of the seashore.

Notes

1. This exercise is best suited for clients who have experienced a "normal" childhood. In addition, clients will blow bubbles for a short period of time; they will be seated. The bubbles will most likely land on the table, so the floor will probably not get wet, but the group leader must be aware to clean up any spill or moisture from the floor so clients do not slip.
2. Modified from a directive by Tracy Addario of Genesis Eldercare.

CHAPTER 13
DIVERSE DIRECTIVES

This chapter includes an assortment of ideas that help clients expand their awareness, knowledge and experiences. The directives often combine materials that aim to enhance creative expression, problem solving and abstract thinking. A few creative games are introduced. They aid in memory enhancement, socialization, attentiveness and communication.

The exercises introduce clients to various ways of expressing issues, thoughts and emotions. Several of the tasks are more crafts-oriented and would likely be presented in an open art studio group. Clients focus on following directions, manipulating media and discovering new ways of enhancing their creativity. They work independently, concentrating on their own style and manner of creating art. Several of the exercises help increase self-esteem and a sense of mastery. Clients are able to work on many of the projects from start to finish, which enables them to take home a completed piece of artwork. They have something tangible to admire and treasure.

Some of the themes presented include growth, communication and serenity. While engaging in the exercises, clients become aware of techniques that they could use daily to enrich, entertain and relax themselves. They learn to expand their cognitive skills while problem solving and analyzing their unique work.

Bread tag: Jazzy jewelry[1]

Materials: Aleene's® Super Thick Tacky Glue™, white paper scrap, 33 plastic tabs from bread bags in assorted sizes, acrylic paint—black, paintbrush, Tulip® 3D fashion paint: silver, gold, bronze, needlenose pliers, 44 gold finish jump rings, 28 size-10 brass snap swivels, 2 size-7 brass snap swivels (available wherever fishing tackle is sold) and 1 pair fishhook earrings.

Procedure: The therapist will introduce the project and method to group members. The directive will be broken down into steps and clients will be assisted and supported while they work.

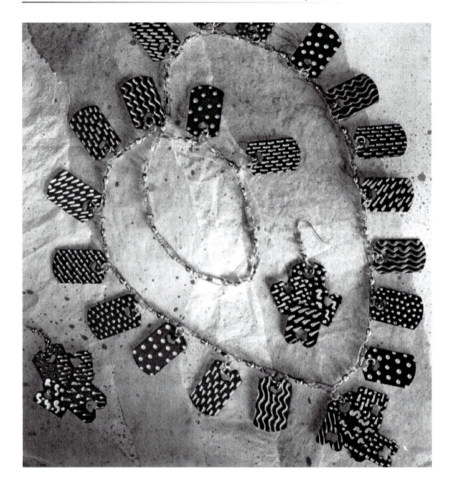

1. Cut two tiny strips of paper for each of 23 plastic tabs. Glue one strip to each side of one tab to cover slit only. Allow to dry. Repeat for each of 22 more tabs. (This step will help to keep the jump rings from pulling through the slit in the tabs.)

2. Paint both sides of each tab black. Allow to dry. For necklace charm, glue five tabs together, using one tab with paper strips at top of charm (see photo). Allow to dry. In the same manner, glue four tabs together for each earring. Paint one side of each tab, necklace charm and earring design with metallic dimensional paint. Allow to dry. For the necklace charm, glue five tabs together, using one tab with paper strips at the top of the charm, Allow to dry. In the same

manner glue four tabs together for each earring. Paint one side of each tab, necklace charm and earring design.

3. Using needlenose pliers, attach one jump ring to each of 20 tabs. Attach one jump ring to necklace charm. Attach a second jump ring to each jump ring. To assemble necklace, link together all size-10 snap swivels. Attach jump rings to necklace. For each earring, remove snap from each size-7 snap swivel. Using needlenose pliers, attach one jump ring to each earring design. Attach jump ring to one end of one size-7 swivel. Attach fishhook earring to other end of swivel. Repeat for other earring.

Heidi's designer tip: For added strength, be sure to add a dab of dimensional paint over the area where you glued the strip of paper. This will give added strength to this area where the jump rings are attached.

Discussion/goals: Clients share their unique designs and thoughts about creating wearable items that are made from recycled materials. The group leader assists clients in learning a novel skill and possible new hobby to pursue in the future. Goals include problem solving, following directions and the increased self-esteem that occurs when an individual learns something new and completes a project that is attractive and functional.

Growth

Materials: Small clay flowerpots or papier-mâché pots, acrylic paints, permanent markers, magazines, scissors, glue, brushes, sealant, planting soil and seeds.

Procedure: Have clients decorate the pots by painting them or using permanent markers to decorate them. The markers may be used to outline a design, which makes it easier for clients; they can just paint within the lines. If the clients do not wish to paint or use the markers, they may cut small magazine pictures and glue them on the pot. The leader would later paint a sealant on the pot so that it would be waterproof. Next have clients fill the pots with a little soil, put in the seeds, add more soil and a little bit of water. This next step may be completed the following day if there is not enough time or if the leader thinks the clients will become confused by too many steps.

Discussion/goals: Discussion focuses on the decorative pots and on the process of planting the seeds.

Questions for clients to ponder include:

1. How can the seed relate to where you are in therapy?

2. What does growth mean to you?

3. You will need to be patient while the seed is forming roots and beginning to develop. How can you relate that type of patience to the patience needed while waiting for medication to take effect and while working towards recovery from depression and/or anxiety?

4. What do you think will happen to this plant as it grows? What changes do you see happening to you as you continue to grow and develop?

Goals include introspection and relaxation. Gardening and planting helps clients relax and are positive and therapeutic leisure activities. Encourage clients to plant/garden at home for stress reduction and enjoyment.

Personal calendar

Materials: Collage materials, magazines, glue markers, scissors, pens, calendar pages and stapler.

Procedure: Each client is given a 12-month calendar, which can be obtained from a variety of sites on the internet including www.printable-calendar. net. Ideally the calendar should have a blank space where a small collage or drawing can be inserted. Have clients spend time thinking about each month and penciling in special dates such as birthdays, holidays and anniversaries. Ask them to create a design at the top of the page (or wherever there is room) that represents their feelings about that month or their feelings in general. For example, they may find photos of babies or children having fun to represent the month their own child was born. When each month has been filled in and completed, clients staple the pages together to create their own calendar.

Discussion/goals: Clients share the artwork that represents each particular month as well as holidays, significant days and events. Goals include organization and detailed review of the upcoming year. The beginning of the year would be the best time for this directive, but it can be worked on at any time throughout the year.

Most clients derive much satisfaction from this enjoyable, structured directive. They like having a visual aid that they can utilize and refer back to periodically.

Emma, a woman in her early 80s, filled the months in with many of her memories in addition to special dates. For the month of June, the month she was married, she glued pictures of a boat, a sun and people laughing and swimming to represent her honeymoon in Florida. Emma stated that it was one of the best times in her life. She described carefree days in the sun and sand and evenings dining in "glorious restaurants." Emma laughed as she recounted the time her husband sat in the sun too long and was "red as a beet." He had difficulty walking because "he even burned the bottoms of his feet." Emma remarked that his attitude was so positive that he still went fishing and boating, although she noticed a wince now and then. She poignantly shared that he was "the most caring person in the world."

Another client named Ralph included all of his children's, grandchildren's and great-grandchildren's birthdays. This added up to about 20 birthdays altogether. He admitted it becomes difficult for him to keep track of so many dates and that the calendar would be a great benefit to him. He also focused on holidays like July 4th because that is when "the family gets together for a big picnic." He spoke about the importance of family togetherness and solidarity. Ralph also sadly mentioned the anniversary dates of the deaths of some family members. He remarked that he has "never gotten over such tragic losses and never will." He was trying to function effectively, although he stated he has remained in mourning for a very prolonged period of time.

Stone mosaic

Materials: Small colorful rocks and stones, strong glue or glue gun, thin wood frame (approximately 4.5 × 8 inches) or flat wooden wall hanging.

Procedure: Instruct clients to set up a design with the stones and glue them onto the wood until they are satisfied with the piece. Suggest they pay attention to color, size and shape.

Discussion/goals: Discussion focuses on the colors, shine, texture and placement of the stones and the client's reaction to the finished product. Goals include increased self-esteem, problem solving and stress reduction.

Patients enjoyed this project very much. Many individuals said it promoted relaxation, was enjoyable and allowed them to focus and work slowly.

"Picking up and examining the beautiful stones was a lot of fun." This directive usually guarantees success because the stones are brilliant and simple to manipulate. Almost every design is attractive and unique.

Masks

Materials: Paint, brushes, magazines, scissors, glue, Mod Podge,[2] tissue paper, collage materials such as buttons, feathers, sequins, glitter and cut paper. Pre-made papier-mâché masks may be purchased through Nasco Arts and Crafts, or clients may create a mask with balloons and papier-mâché paste. The latter might be too messy for seniors.

Procedure: Provide clients with masks and suggest they decorate them in a series of steps. The first step would be to decide what type of mask they would like to create. Clients may sketch pictures of designs they find appealing. Next have them paint the masks and then add collage materials, if desired. Clients may also create collage masks, using small pieces of magazine photos or tissue paper glued onto the masks and then painted with Mod Podge or varnish.

Discussion/goals: Group members share ways in which the masks reflect various aspects of their personality. Goals include decision making, self-expression and exploration of self-image.

Gloria, a widow in her 80s, used small shiny smiling faces to design her mask. She added red hair and outlined the eyes with black paint. Gloria was able to relate her design to the lifting of her depression and her more jovial mood. She stated she would use it to motivate her to smile more often; she planned to hang it on her kitchen wall.

Free-spirited painting: Computer-generated art

Procedure: Provide a computer for use and go to the site http://makeeverydayaholiday.com/to-do-make-your-own-jackson-pollock-art/. Allow clients to have fun creating designs and shapes, then make copies and distribute.

Clients may add color or paint to the artwork if it is printed in black and white. In addition, they may try to find images they recognize in the designs, outline the images and fill them in with color. Encourage group members to think of a title for their artwork.

Discussion/goals: Clients share their experience and analyze their "painting." Goals include desensitizing clients to computer activities, creative expression, freedom to create as one pleases, loosening of boundaries and barriers, and enjoyment.

Learning about art and artists

Materials: Posters and descriptions of a variety of artists such as van Gogh, Picasso, O'Keefe, Seurat, Manet and Monet.

Procedure: Introduce the artists by showing samples of their artwork and reading brief biographies and descriptions of their paintings. Explore color, shape, design and specific themes. Encourage group members to make free associations with the paintings. Next support clients to draw a picture in the same style as the artist they most admire. For instance, if they choose Picasso, they may use abstract shapes and create a distorted face; if they choose van Gogh, they may utilize wavy lines or create a large sunflower; if they choose Seurat, they may try pointillism. Clients may also choose to draw a symbol in the painting, such as a bird, flower, religious symbol or animal.

Discussion/goals: Learning about art and artists helps to broaden one's horizons and can be used as an enjoyable and enlightening leisure skill. Benefits of learning about the artists:

- Increased knowledge enhances self-esteem and self-awareness.
- Clients improve memory and thinking skills.
- Art stimulates both sides of the brain.
- Art stimulates perception.
- Individuals learn to think abstractly and improve problem-solving skills.
- Art nourishes the human soul.
- Art bridges racial stereotypes, barriers and prejudices.
- Art enhances creative thinking and open-mindedness.
- Learning about artists encourages clients to develop their own unique artistic skills.

Brag book

Materials: Construction paper, drawing paper, manilla folders, markers, crayons and oil pastels, collage materials such as glitter, buttons and sequins, scissors, glue and magazines.

Procedure: The manilla folder will contain the book. Place three or four pieces of construction or drawing paper within the folder. Punch holes in the folder and papers with a three-hole punch. Have clients create a cover for their book (outside of the folder) using markers and the collage materials. They may label it "Brag Book" or anything else they desire. Next have them create a decorative frame around the remaining pages using marker, pastels and collage materials. The pages will be attached using ribbon or wool and tied in knots or bows. Have clients fill in the brag book with words, reminiscences, photos and illustrations of family members, friends and themselves.

Discussion/goals: Have clients share positive thoughts, relationships and experiences. Goals include increased self-esteem and focus on gratitude and positive aspects of one's life.

Affirmation cups

Materials: Wooden candle cups (⅞ inch)[3], paint, markers, tiny sequins, stickers, glitter, paper and pens.

Procedure: Direct group members to decorate the cups using paint, markers, sequins, glitter, etc. Then have them write one or two affirmations on a small piece of paper that will fit into the cup. Suggest they keep the cup in an obvious place, such as on their nightstand, a dresser or on an end table in their living room next to their favorite chair. Suggest that the affirmations be changed frequently.

Discussion/goals: Clients share their cups, the designs and the affirmations. Goals include increased self-esteem and a focus on gratitude and positive thoughts. Having a small reminder of their attributes will help reinforce healthy thinking and optimism.

Communication skills: Color game

Materials: Index cards, 8.5 × 11 inches copier/computer paper, markers or crayons, pens and pencils.

Procedure: Everyone draws a large circle consisting of one color on a piece of paper. Group members receive one index card and redraw the circle on the front of the card using the same color. On the back of the card, clients write three general questions aimed at knowing other group members better. Questions may include goals, feelings, hobbies, likes and dislikes, characteristics, friends and family, favorite vacations, favorite movies, habits and descriptions of one's home life. The facilitator collects the index cards. The participants exchange their circles with one another so that everyone has a circle other than his original.

The facilitator shuffles the index cards and reads one of the questions on each card. The individual who holds the same color circle as the one on the index card answers the question. This goes on until everyone has the opportunity to answer at least one question. It may be repeated up to three times.

Discussion/goals: Clients learn about each other's thoughts, feelings and characteristics in an enjoyable manner. Goals include communication, socialization and a focus on connections with others.

Bottle cap jewelry

Materials: Tops from water bottles, permanent markers that won't smudge on plastic, sharp small scissors or tiny sharp screwdriver, long straight pins, string, cord, wool or thin ribbon.

Procedure: Everyone collects bottle caps until there is one for each group member. The group facilitator pokes holes through the top and bottom of the caps with small sharp scissors or any other sharp instrument (the cap will be in an upright position when this is done). Clients are instructed to decorate the cap in any way they please. A small bead should be put through a long straight pin in order create a more stable and attractive base for the focal point (the cap). The straight pin should have a small metal base so that the bead is able to stay on it and not slip through the pin. The top of the pin will stick out of the bottle cap. It is bent and a loop will be created with the remainder of it.[4] String, yarn or ribbon is threaded through the loop and a personal necklace is created.

Discussion/goals: Discussion focuses on the necklace designs and the clients' reactions to their creative work. Explore whether or not the artwork is self-representative. Goals include focusing, problem solving, following step-by-step directions, increase in self-esteem that comes about by working on a project from start to finish and then having a finished product to wear, share or give to someone special.

Bottle cap game: Communication skills

Materials: Bottle caps from water bottles, index cards (approximately 3–4 per group member), small white stickers and markers.

Procedure:

1. Number the tops of the caps with permanent marker or place small white stickers on the caps and number the stickers. The number of caps should match the number of participants. For example, if there are 12 people in the group, the caps should number 1–12.

2. The caps do not have to be given out in numerical order.

3. For each cap have a corresponding index card with the same number on it. Questions about the clients' lives should be written on each index card.

Possible questions include:

- Where is your favorite place to go on holiday?
- Whom do you admire?
- What makes you feel joyful?
- How do you handle stress?
- When was the last time you laughed?
- What type of movies do you like?
- What was your childhood like?
- If you could go back in time, what age would you like to be? Why?
- What are your hobbies and interests?
- How do you like to spend the weekend?

4. Put all the caps in a shoebox or coffee can and have each client choose a cap.
5. The group facilitator picks up an index card from a pile placed in front of him.
6. Clients sit around a table and take turns according to the order in which they are sitting. The first client chosen by the therapist takes his turn. If his cap number matches the index card number in the therapist's hand, the client answers the question and receives one point.
7. He puts his cap back in the box.
8. If the bottle cap number is not the same as the index card number, the client has the option of answering the question and not receiving a point or skipping his turn. The therapist emphasizes the importance of good sportsmanship and answering the question whether or not a point is received.
9. This continues until the therapist or participants deem the game over.[5] The person with the most points is the winner and may receive a round of applause or, if allowed, a small prize.

Discussion/goals: Clients share some of their past history, their present living conditions, thoughts and feelings, likes and dislikes, and family issues. Goals include communication, problem solving, sharing, focusing and enjoyment.

Cartooning

Materials: Markers, pens, copies of cartoons taken from www.incredibleart. org. Go to the site and click "Art Activities and Games." Then click "Make Belief Comics." The therapist can create comics that the clients can complete in any way they please. Clients can add dialogue in the dialogue boxes, add decorations and describe how the characters feel. The comics can be printed and copied for distribution. In addition, if a computer is available to clients, they can create their own comics from scratch on the site.

Discussion/goals: Discussion focuses on what the characters say to each other and their mood and attitude. The client gains control by deciding how the characters will respond to each other based on the scenarios set by the group facilitator. For instance, are the characters facing away from each other? Do they appear angry or joyful? Are they giving each other presents or playing an instrument? Goals include exploration of communication skills and examination of relationships.

Life box[6]

Materials: A tissue or cigar box (or similar type of cardboard box), magazines, construction paper, collage materials such as buttons, felt, sequins and glitter, glue and scissors, marker, pens and small pieces of white paper.

Procedure: Have clients decorate the outside of the box so that it represents them in some way. They may use the magazine photos and/or the collage materials. Have them find pictures that are self-representative and place them in the box. They may use their own photos if desired. They may also write about themselves and family members and place those descriptions inside the box. When the boxes are completed, clients will share the boxes and photos with group members.

Discussion/goals: Clients share their history, experiences, relationships, interactions with family members and facts about themselves. Goals include self-expression, life review, sharing, increased communication with others and increased self-esteem.

People in my life

Materials: Drawing paper, figure outlines, markers, oil pastels, crayons, scissors and glue.

Procedure: The leader draws and/or finds various figure outlines from Google Images (all shapes and sizes). Clients are given one or two sheets filled with outlines of men, women and children. Next, clients cut out as many of the figures as they please, glue them onto the drawing paper and create an environment around them. Direct group members to consider whom the figures would represent, what they might be doing and where they would be located. For instance, are the figures their friends, parents, children, etc. and are they in a park, at home, at the shore, etc?

Discussion/goals: Clients are given the opportunity to manipulate the figures and place them in an environment. They choose facial expressions, colors and style of dress. Participants decide who is placed next to whom and the significance of the placement. Relationships, the quality of those relationships and the effect they have on one's mood, behavior and goals are explored.

Clients enjoy this directive because it is structured, but still allows them to make many decisions. Participants are given the figures but determine how to create the overall design.

Lila, aged 68, decided to draw freehand instead of cutting out figures because her arthritis was bothering her. She represented her daughter and grandchildren. The daughter has red hair, an orange shirt and an orange and brown patterned skirt. Her eyebrows are pointed downwards and her expression appears angry. The youngest grandchild (right side of page) seems pleased and is depicted as being overweight. Lila stated he tends to be large and sloppy and needs to improve his grades in high school. "He usually does as he pleases, and eats too much junk food. I don't think my daughter sets limits at all. He hardly calls or writes." There is a tall, freckled man who is smiling. "He is my pride and joy." Lila stated, "Dennis is going to medical school and wants to be a surgeon." A figure on the left of the page represented 12-year-old Matthew. Lila stated, "He's a good kid and makes me happy when I see him." There is a figure sitting in the background; "He is my ex-husband," explained Lila. "He was always aloof and isolated from all of us. I don't even know why I put him in the picture." Lila smiled as she stared at the picture and sighed, "My life is my family."

In reality, Lila gets along very poorly with her "loved ones," and during a family meeting the 12-year-old complained, "Grandma is selfish." Other family members called her narcissistic. Her daughter stated that she always puts herself first. Lila needs to continue to work on her relationships and accept her role in the families' problems.

Collage bottle vase

Materials: Water bottles, colored masking tape, scissors, Mod Podge and brushes.

Procedure: Each participant receives a 16.9 oz (500 ml) water bottle. Clients are asked to tear or cut the masking tape into pieces of varying sizes. If clients want the bottle to look like a mosaic, they may use small squares of tape placed next to each other. Next they begin adhering the tape onto the bottle, using a variety of colors. Group members continue doing this until the bottle is completely covered. Some clients may find that larger pieces of tape are easier to manipulate. When the bottles are completed, they may use ModPodge to brush over the bottle in order to help preserve it and create a glossy finish. Tissue paper flowers or real flowers may be placed in it.

Discussion/goals: Clients share their decorative vases and discuss whether they will keep them or give them to someone special. Goals include focusing, stress reduction and decision making. The project is easy and almost always guarantees a successful outcome. Clients are usually amazed how attractive the bottles turn out and feel proud of their work. Many individuals report feeling relaxed while working on this project. In addition, they are recycling and helping the environment.

Mosaic mural[7]

Materials: Large sheet of poster board, spray adhesive, glue, Mod Podge, square pieces of different colored poster board or cardboard (approximately 3 × 3 inches).

Procedure: Clients decide the placement of the square cards as they lay them out on the poster board. Once the cards are placed in the desired position, clients or the group leader sprays an adhesive on the cardboard. The adhesive takes the place of using a glue stick. Next, group members take turns placing the squares where the cardboard has been sprayed. This may be done line by line if desired. Allow the adhesive to dry and then apply a few coats of Mod Podge. The finished project is then ready to hang up as an attractive wall decoration.

Discussion/goals: Clients share their contributions to the mural, their thoughts and feelings about being part of the group and their assessment of the completed work. Goals include communication, socialization, problem solving and abstract thinking.

Flowerpot drip[8]

Materials: Water-based paint, small cups, brushes and papier-mâché flowerpots.

Procedure: Clients paint their flowerpots whatever color/s they please and let them dry. Next they mix additional paint colors in small cups, adding water until a thin consistency is formed. They place their flowerpots upside down and then slowly drip the paint on the pots, starting from the base of the pots, and slowly turning them until all sides are covered. Various colors may be used if desired. The effect will be dramatic; long drips of color will cover the pots. If clients feel like experimenting further, they may use brushes to drip or splatter the paint.

Discussion/goals: Clients discuss their experience; they may find it thought-provoking to compare traditional painting to working abstractly. Participants share thoughts regarding what type of flower they would like to plant in the pot. Goals include experimentation, decision making and thinking outside of the box. Self-esteem is increased as group members admire the attractive pot that is ready to bring home and utilize.

"Serenity Poem" decoration[9]

Materials: "Serenity Poem" (see below) or other self-help poetry (provide at least one or two additional poems), paper, markers, oil pastels, crayons, glue and scissors.

Procedure: Distribute the poem to clients on 8.5 × 11 inch paper and have them glue it on a sheet of 12 × 18 inch paper. Suggest clients create a design/environment surrounding the poem that reflects its meaning. Clients may use another poem if they don't choose to use the "Serenity Poem". In addition, they may change it by omitting the word "God" and beginning the prayer with "Grant."

Discussion/goals: Group members share symbols and colors in their artwork that represent their thoughts and feelings about the poem. Goals include exploration of coping skills, self-awareness and mindfulness.

"Serenity Poem"
God, grant me the serenity
to accept the things I cannot change,
the courage to change the things I can,
and the wisdom to know the difference.
(Reinhold Niebuhr)

"Look Well to This Day"
Look well to this day,
For it and it alone is life.
In its brief course
Lie all the essence of your existence:
The glory of growth
The satisfaction of achievement
The splendor of beauty
For yesterday is but a dream,
And tomorrow is but a vision.
But today well lived makes every yesterday a dream of happiness,

And every tomorrow a vision of hope.
(Anonymous, 50 BC)

"That I a Better Person May Be"
Light that lies deep inside of me
Come forth in all thy majesty.
Show me thy gaze,
Teach me thy ways,
That I a better person may be.

Darkness that lies deep inside of me
Come forth in all thy mystery.
Show me thy gaze,
Teach me thy ways,
That I a better person may be.

Love that lies deep inside of me
Come forth in all thy unity.
Let me be thy gaze,
Let me teach thy ways,
That I a better person may be.
(Author unknown)

Art therapy bingo

I have included this game once again because it continues to be extremely popular at Princeton House, especially for older adults. It is very common for clients to request that it be played. They find it pleasurable and relaxing, as well as challenging.

Materials: (See "Procedure".)

Procedure: Take a 9 × 12 inch sheet of drawing paper and divide it into 12 boxes. Outline the boxes with black marker. At the bottom of each box write the name of something that is easy to draw (e.g. a tree, a sun). On the top of each box make a small circle. Make as many copies of this as there are clients in the group. Next write a number (1–40) on 3 × 5 inch index cards (one number for each card). The therapist then distributes the paper, and group members are asked to write numbers in the circles on the top of the page (any number 1–40 in any order). The therapist shuffles the index cards and calls out the numbers. Every time a number is called, the client looks to see if he has written that number in one of the circles on his page. If he has the number that is called, he has to draw what is written (house, person, etc.) in that square to the best of his ability. The first person to fill up his boxes across or down wins (a variation of the game is the first person to fill all of his boxes wins). The winner has to show everyone all of his pictures and describe them. If the therapist desires, a small prize may be given to the winner.

Discussion/goals: This is a game clients usually enjoy very much. It is especially popular with the higher-functioning schizophrenic patient and older clientele. It is a very non-threatening way to encourage participants to draw and learn how to sketch basic symbols. Goals include socialization and problem solving.

Personal mandala

Materials: Markers, oil pastels, crayons, collage materials such as buttons, felt, foam, tissue paper and sequins, scissors, glue, paper plates, various types of paper and cardboard.

Procedure: Direct clients to outline a circle from the cardboard, paper or plate. Ask them to decide what type of materials they'd like to work with and suggest they create a mandala that has significance for them. It might represent their mood, attitude, thoughts and/or personality. They will be instructed to glue the materials and/or draw within the circle.

Discussion/goals: Clients share personality characteristics symbolized in the mandala. Goals include focusing, healing, socialization and experiencing inner peace.

A 74-year-old woman named Edith designed this well-balanced mandala. She was surprised that group members were so impressed with her design because she had little artistic experience. She related the mandala to feeling less depressed and more willing to share with others. Edith had been living at her daughter's home in New Jersey because she was too frightened and depressed to live alone. She stated she felt ready to be more independent and resume her life in New York City. Her colors were subdued; she remarked that working on the project made her feel calm and at ease.

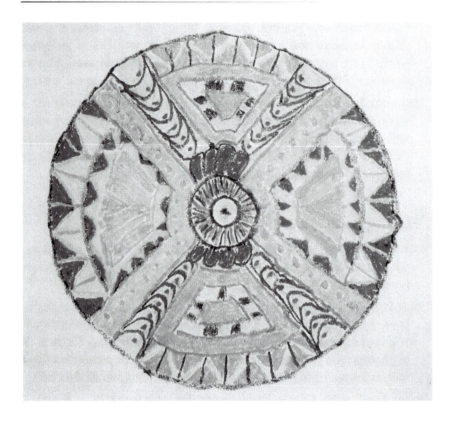

Goodbye beading

When a client leaves a program or therapy group, it is beneficial if there is some sort of goodbye ceremony. In this way, everyone has the opportunity to wish the individual good luck and best wishes for the future. Ceremonies may include a stone ceremony (where everyone bestows his best wishes on an attractive rock or stone, which is passed from one group member to another), cards, a farewell mural, send-off collages or a personal beaded necklace.

Materials: Assortment of colorful beads with large holes, stretchy string.

Procedure: To design the jewelry, direct clients to take turns placing one bead at a time on a long stretchy string until the necklace is completed. Each time a client places a bead on the string, encourage him to say one supportive word or phrase to the person who is leaving. When it has been designed, the "graduate" has a necklace filled with positive thoughts created by all group members. It becomes a lovely keepsake and memory of supportive peers and friends.

Discussion/goals: The client leaves the program or group with something that can be worn and treasured. Having an item such as this helps an individual transition from the group and gives him a tangible object of love, hope and support.

Notes

1. Idea by author and designer Heidi Borchers (www.heidiborchers.com).
2. Mod Podge is a glue that can also be used like a varnish to protect artwork.
3. Candle cups can be bought on www.larascrafts.com and/or in many craft stores, including Michael's (www.michaels.com).
4. Go to www.youtube.com to see various tutorials on how to create a loop. A variety of necklaces can be made, including affirmation necklaces, good-luck necklaces or abstract designs.
5. Three or four rounds of this game is optimum; it will enable clients time to become accustomed to the game, to earn points and share thoughts and information about themselves. During each round clients will choose different bottle caps and a new grouping of questions will be asked.
6. Modified from an idea by the Kennedy Center Arts Edge, "A Character Life Box." See http://artsedge.kennedy-center.org/educators/lessons/grade-6-8/Character_Life_Box.aspx. This project may take two or three sessions.
7. Idea modified from "Jennifer" of favecraft's (www.favecrafts.com). The base may also be a plywood or pine panel; however, you would first paint the wood piece. These cards can be found in various stores, such as Home Depot. Most paint supply stores allow you to take the free colored paint cards. This can be done as an individual or group project.
8. Modified from a suggestion by Tracylynn Navarro, MA, ATR-BC, Princeton House, University Medical Center at Princeton.
9. Modified from a directive by Tracylynn Navarro, ATR-BC Princeton House, University Medical Center at Princeton.

REFERENCES

Buchalter, S. (2009) *Art Therapy Techniques and Applications*. London: Jessica Kingsley Publishers.

Buchalter, S. (2004) *A Practical Art Therapy*. London: Jessica Kingsley Publishers.

Buchalter, S. (1989) "Barrier Drawings for Depressed Patients." In H. Wadeson, J. Durkin and D. Perach (eds) *Advances in Art Therapy*. New York, NY: John Wiley & Sons Inc.

Buck, J.N. (1978) *The House-Tree-Person Techniques*. Los Angeles, CA: Western Psychological Services.

Frost, R. (1916) "The Road Not Taken," *Mountain Interval*. New York, NY: Henry Holt & Co.

Fox, J. (1997) *Poetic Medicine: The Healing Art of Poem-Making*. New York, NY: Penguin Putnam Inc.

Fox, J. (1995) *Finding What You Didn't Lose: Expressing your Truth and Creativity Through Poem-Making* (Inner Workbook). New York, NY: Penguin Putnam, Inc.

Gleick, J. (1988) *Chaos: Making a New Science*. New York, NY: Penguin Books.

Jung, C.G. (1972) *Mandala Symbolism*. New Jersey, NJ: Princeton University Press.

Landgarten, H. (1981) *Clinical Art Therapy: A Comprehensive Guide*. New York, NY: Brunner/ Mazel Publishers.

Nimmer, D. (2008) *Art from Intuition: Overcoming Your Fears and Obstacles to Making Art*. New York, NY: Watson-Guptill Publications.

Piper, W. (1930) *The Little Engine That Could*. New York, NY: Platt and Monk Publishers.

Rolfs, A.M. (2003) *Opening Again to Music*. Columbus, OH: Pudding House Publications.

Woolston, C. (2000) "Writing for Therapy Helps Erase Effects of Trauma." 16 March CNN, Communication.

INDEX

CPSIA information can be obtained at www.ICGtesting.com
Printed in the USA
BVOW04s1659100514

353141BV00009B/189/P

9 781849 058308